Fodor's

SECOND NEW EDITION

Nova Scotia, New Brunswick, Prince Edward Island

Reprinted from *Fodor's Canada*

Fodor's Travel Publications, Inc.
New York • Toronto • London • Sydney • Auckland

**Copyright © 1994
by Fodor's Travel Publications, Inc.**

ISBN 0–679–02582–0

The introduction by Bob Levin was originally published as "A Sense of Country" in *Maclean's* magazine. Reprinted by permission from *Maclean's*. July 25, 1990.

Fodor's Nova Scotia

Editor: Alison Hoffman
Contributors: Bob Blake, Hannah Borgeson, David Brown, Marian Bruce, Silver Don Cameron, Peter Gard, Margaret M. Kearney, Laura M. Kidder, Bob Levin, Caroline Liou, Alice Oshins, Melanie Roth, Linda K. Schmidt, Mary Ellen Schultz, Colleen Whitney Thompson, Ana Watts
Art Director: Fabrizio La Rocca
Cartographer: David Lindroth
Illustrator: Karl Tanner
Cover Photograph: Bob Krist

Design: Vignelli Associates

Special Sales

MANUFACTURED IN THE UNITED STATES OF AMERICA
10 9 8 7 6 5 4 3 2 1

Contents

Maps and Plans

Foreword

We wish to express our gratitude to those who helped prepare this guide: the Canadian Consulate General office in New York, particularly Lois Gerber and Barbara Cartwright; the Government of Newfoundland and Labrador Department of Development, especially Kay Coxworthy; Helen-Jean Newman of the New Brunswick Department of Tourism; the Nova Scotia Department of Tourism, especially Pat Lynch; and Lynda Hanscombe of the PEI Department of Tourism and Parks.

While every care has been taken to ensure the accuracy of the information in this guide, the passage of time will always bring change, and consequently, the publisher cannot accept responsibility for errors that may occur.

All prices and opening times are based on information supplied to us at press time. Hours and admission fees may change, however, and the prudent traveler will avoid inconvenience by calling ahead.

Fodor's wants to hear about your travel experiences, both pleasant and unpleasant. When a hotel or restaurant fails to live up to its billing, let us know and we will investigate the complaint and revise our entries where the facts warrant it. Send your letters to the editors of Fodor's Travel Publications, 201 E. 50th Street, New York, NY 10022.

Highlights
and
Fodor's Choice

Highlights

In 1993 then-Prime Minister Brian Mulroney retired, and Kim Cambell was voted in by the Progressive Conservatives, to complete the term. Cambell is the first female prime minister and is expected to run for re-election in 1994.

The 7% **Goods and Services Tax** that went into effect in 1991 imposed on virtually all goods and services, including restaurant meals, fast-food, hotel rooms, car rentals, and admission fees. In some provinces, the nationwide GST tax replaces former provincial taxes, but in others it is levied in addition to provincial taxes. It is refundable however, to tourists from other countries, provided they keep original receipts and apply for the refund. The refund system is complicated, so you may want to obtain information before you travel, by calling 613/991–3346 (outside Canada) or, from within Canada, 800/66–VISIT. You can also write to Revenue Canada, Customs and Excise Visitor's Rebate Program, Ottawa, Canada K1A 1J5, or pick up refund application forms and an explanatory booklet at airports, shops, hotels, and border crossing stations.

Nova Scotia The province's most recently opened national park, **Kekimkujik Seaside Adjunct,** a formerly private preserve, is still wild and remote, though hiking trails make it accessible to the public. To attract convention business, the province has been opening **meeting facilities** in places besides Halifax, which is still the major convention center. Inverary Lodge, in Baddeck, and White Point Beach Lodge, in Liverpool, now offer facilities for groups of 100 to 150.

Prince Edward Island A government announcement of a **causeway** to be built linking New Brunswick and Prince Edward Island has caused mixed reaction on the island. Although improved accessibility may increase tourism revenues and lower the cost of many goods currently shipped to the island, residents also fear disruption of their peaceful, unspoiled lifestyle, which is in itself a tourist draw. No construction date has been set—it may in fact be years away.

New Brunswick A 223-room Sheraton hotel opened in late spring 1992 in **Fredericton,** adding significantly to that city's supply of hotel rooms, although Saint John still offers more beds. About 11 miles west of Fredericton, the **Kings Clear Hotel and Resort** has opened—a new modern hotel, with an interesting history. It is operated by the Malicete Indian Band at Mactaquac, who received government help in building and running the motel as compensation for their voluntary surrender of their traditional net-fishing activity, which was endangering the Atlantic salmon.

The section of the **Trans-Canada Highway** that runs through New Brunswick is being upgraded, with the notable addition of signposts alerting travelers to the existence of special "scenic trails," off-the-beaten-track roads that motorists might otherwise miss.

Newfoundland and Labrador In 1993 the province began gearing up for the festivities to come in 1997, celebrating John Cabot's landing in North America.

Maine **Commercial train service** will again become a reality in Maine. By 1994, Amtrak is expected to begin service from Boston to Wells, Biddeford-Saco, Old Orchard Beach (in season), and Portland.

Professional baseball is scheduled to begin in April 1994, when the **Sea Dogs**, a minor-league farm team, will man the bases at Hadlock Field in Portland.

The marine creatures of the Gulf of Maine will be the stars of a new **aquarium** at McKown Point in West Boothbay. The facility will open in summer 1994.

Fodor's Choice

No two people will agree on what makes a perfect vacation, but it's fun and helpful to know what others think. We hope you'll have a chance to experience some of Fodor's Choices yourself in Canada. For detailed information about each entry, refer to the appropriate chapter.

Nova Scotia

Sights The Citadel, Halifax

Fortress Louisbourg, Cape Breton Island

Mabou Harbour, Cape Breton

Peggy's Cove

Restaurants Amherst Shore Country Inn, Amherst (*Expensive*)

Clipper Cay, Halifax (*Expensive*)

Old Man Morias, Halifax (*Moderate*)

Hotels Amherst Shore Country Inn, Lorneville (*Expensive*)

Prince Edward Island

Attractions Annual musical *Anne of Green Gables* at Confederation Center of the Arts, Charlottetown

Fort Amherst Port LaJoie National Historic Site, Rocky Point

Green Gables, Cavendish

Province House, Charlottetown

Restaurants The Griffon Room, Charlottetown (*Moderate–Expensive*)

Claddagh Room Restaurant, Charlottetown (*Moderate–Expensive*)

Hope River (*Moderate*)

Hotels Dalvay-by-the-Sea, Grand Tracadie (*Very Expensive*)

Prince Edward Hotel and Convention Centre, Charlottetown (*Very Expensive*)

Shaw's Hotel and Cottages, Brackley Beach (*Very Expensive*)

New Brunswick

Attractions Acadian Village, Grande Anse, near Caraquet

Kings Landing Historical Settlement, Prince William, near Fredericton

Shopping Craft and antiques shops of St. Andrews and Gagetown

Mulhouse Country Classics, Fredericton

Restaurants La Belle Vie, Saint John (*Expensive*)

Cy's, Moncton (*Moderate*)

Hotels Hotel Beausejour, Moncton (*Expensive*)

Marshlands Inn, Sackville (*Moderate–Expensive*)

Shadow Lawn Country Inn, Saint John (*Moderate–Expensive*)

Chez Françoise, Shediac (*Inexpensive–Moderate*)

Newfoundland and Labrador

Attractions L'Anse aux Meadows, northern tip of Newfoundland
Signal Hill, St. John's

Gros Morne Mountain, Gros Morne National Park

Shopping NONIA, St. John's, for crafts

Restaurants The Cellar, Baird's Cove (*Expensive*)

Stone House, Kenna's Hill (*Expensive*)

Hotels Hotel Newfoundland, St. John's (*Expensive*)

Compton House Bed & Breakfast, St. John's (*Moderate*)

Prescott House Bed & Breakfast, St. John's (*Moderate*)

Maine

Attractions Boothbay Railway Village, Boothbay

Children's Museum of Maine, Portland

Maine Maritime Museum, Bath

Portland Museum of Art, Portland

Restaurants The Back Bay Grill, Portland (*Expensive–Very Expensive*)

Cafe Always, Portland (*Moderate–Expensive*)

Street & Co., Portland (*Inexpensive–Moderate*)

Lodgings Portland Regency Inn, Portland (*Expensive*)

Canada

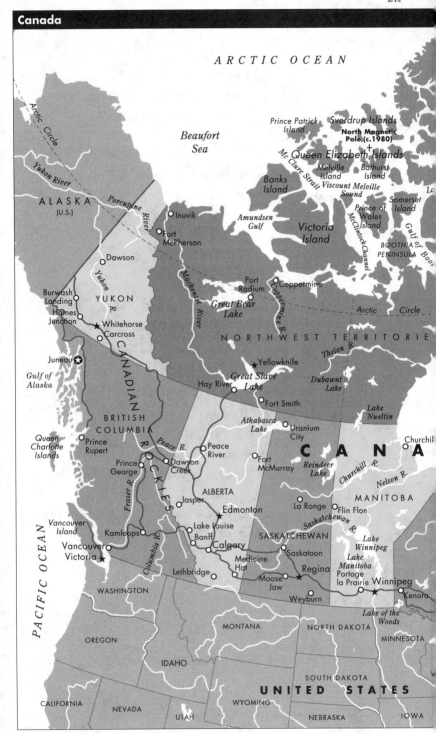

ARCTIC OCEAN

Arctic Circle

Prince Patrick Island

Sverdrup Islands

North Magnetic Pole (c.1980)

Beaufort Sea

Mc Clure Strait

Queen Elizabeth Islands

Melville Island

Bathurst Island

Banks Island

Viscount Melville Sound

Somerset Island

Amundsen Gulf

Victoria Island

Prince of Wales Island

McClintock Channel

Gulf of Boo.

Yukon River

Porcupine

River

BOOTHIA PENINSULA

ALASKA (U.S.)

Inuvik

Fort McPherson

Port Radium

Coppermine

Arctic   Circle

Dawson

Yukon R.

YUKON

Mackenzie River

Great Bear Lake

Coppermine R.

NORTHWEST TERRITORIE

Burwash Landing

Haines Junction

Whitehorse

Carcross

Thelon R.

Juneau

CANADIAN

Yellowknife

Great Slave Lake

Dubawnt Lake

Lake Nueltin

Gulf of Alaska

Hay River

Fort Smith

BRITISH COLUMBIA

Athabasca Lake

Uranium City

C A N A

Churchil

Queen Charlotte Islands

Prince Rupert

Peace R.

Peace River

Fort McMurray

Reindeer Lake

Churchill R.

Nelson R.

Prince George

Dawson Creek

ROCKIES

Fraser R.

La Ronge

Flin Flon

MANITOBA

Jasper

ALBERTA

Edmonton

Saskatchewan R.

Vancouver Island

Kamloops

Lake Louise

Banff

Calgary

Columbia R.

SASKATCHEWAN

Saskatoon

Lake Winnipeg

Lake Manitoba

PACIFIC OCEAN

Vancouver

Victoria

Medicine Hat

Regina

Portage la Prairie

Winnipeg

Lethbridge

Moose Jaw

Kenora

WASHINGTON

Weyburn

Lake of the Woods

OREGON

MONTANA

NORTH DAKOTA

MINNESOTA

IDAHO

SOUTH DAKOTA

UNITED   STATES

CALIFORNIA

NEVADA

UTAH

WYOMING

NEBRASKA

IOWA

ICELAND

GREENLAND
(Denmark)

Denmark Strait

*Baffin
Bay*

Ellesmere Island

Devon
Island

Lancaster Sound

Baffin Island

*Davis
Strait*

othia

Prince
Charles
Island

*Foxe
Basin*

Lake Amadjuak

Iqaluit

*Southampton
Island*

Lake Harbour

Hudson   Strait

Cape Chidley

*Labrador
Sea*

Coats
Island   Mansel
Island

Ivujivik

*Ungava
Bay*

Nain

N E W F O U N D L A N D

*Hudson
Bay*

hill

D   A

*Belcher
Islands*

LABRADOR

Battle Harbour

Fort Severn

Schefferville

Goose Bay

Gander

Severn R.

Fort George

Q U E B E C

Labrador City

St. John's

*James
Bay*

*Lake
Mistassini*

Sept-Iles

Anticosti Island

*Gulf of
St. Lawrence*

Newfoundland

Moosonee

River

GASPÉ
PENINSULA

ST. PIERRE AND
MIQUELON
(France)

O N T A R I O

Rimouski

PRINCE
EDWARD
ISLAND

Sydney

*Lake
Nipigon*

Cochrane

Chicoutimi

NEW
BRUNSWICK

Charlottetown

Thunder
Bay

Timmins

Ste. Agathe-
Des-Monts

Québec
City

Fredericton

NOVA
SCOTIA

Lake Superior

Sudbury

North
Bay

Trois-
Rivières

Saint John

Halifax

Sault
Ste. Marie

Montréal

MAINE

*Bay of
Fundy*

N

*Lake
Huron*

Ottawa

St. Lawrence

VT.

*ATLANTIC
OCEAN*

WISCONSIN

Toronto

*Lake
Ontario*

N.H.

Lake Michigan

Niagara
Falls

NEW YORK

MASSACHUSETTS

0   400 miles

MICHIGAN

Lake Erie

CONN.   R.I.

0   600 km

ILLINOIS

INDIANA

OHIO

PENNSYLVANIA

N.J.

World Time Zones

Numbers below vertical bands relate each zone to Greenwich Mean Time (0 hrs.).
Local times frequently differ from these general indications,
as indicated by light-face numbers on map.

Algiers, **29**
Anchorage, **3**
Athens, **41**
Auckland, **1**
Baghdad, **46**
Bangkok, **50**
Beijing, **54**

Berlin, **34**
Bogotá, **19**
Budapest, **37**
Buenos Aires, **24**
Caracas, **22**
Copenhagen, **33**
Dallas, **10**

Delhi, **48**
Denver, **8**
Djakarta, **53**
Dublin, **26**
Edmonton, **7**
Hong Kong, **56**
Honolulu, **2**

Istanbul, **40**
Jerusalem, **42**
Johannesburg, **44**
Lima, **20**
Lisbon, **28**
London (Greenwich), **27**
Los Angeles, **6**
Madrid, **38**
Manila, **57**

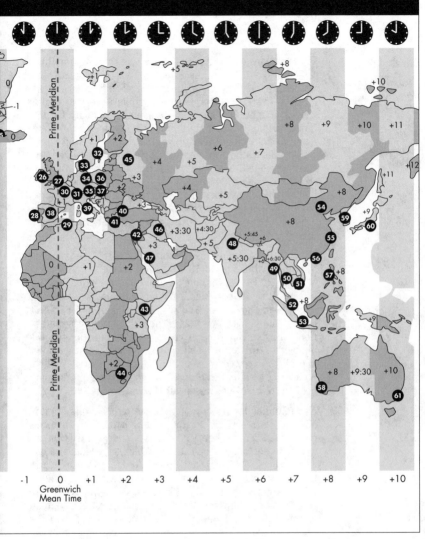

Introduction

by Bob Levin

Originally from Philadelphia, Pennsylvania, Maclean's *Foreign Editor Bob Levin moved to Toronto in October 1985.*

It has been on trips outside Toronto, to the more far-flung sectors of this most resolutely regional of nations, that I have found Canada at its most extreme, independent, quirky—even romantic, as un-Canadian a word as that is supposed to be. One snow-swept morning in Pouch Cove, a fishing-village-turned-suburb north of St. John's, Newfoundland, I visited William Noseworthy in his white clapboard house high on Noseworthy's Hill. Blue-eyed and ruddy-cheeked, Noseworthy sat in the kitchen by a wood stove, distractedly smoking a cigarette. He was 66 and had just retired the year before after four decades of fishing, but he still stared out the window at the North Atlantic. "There's something that draws you to it," he said in the rich accent of "the Rock."

His son, 31-year-old Barry, sipping a Labatt's beer, recalled that once, when he was 13, his father caught him whistling in a boat. "He was going to throw me overboard," said Barry. "It's just bad luck." William explained: "You don't whistle on the water. You wouldn't dare. You wouldn't launch your boat on Friday either. They're just superstitions, maybe. But several years ago, someone launched a big fishing trawler on a Friday, and she was lost on a Friday, and all the crew members, too." A minute later, William pulled out a shiny red accordion and played a jig, tapping his foot, but his eyes never left the water.

Newfoundland was also a place to sample Canadian regionalism at its most craggy and entrenched. The province's inshore fishermen claim that their very way of life is endangered by declining code catches, which they blame on offshore trawling, often by foreigners. And they blame Ottawa for not looking out for their interests—even 40 years after joining Confederation, the old refrain still comes quickly to some residents' lips: "A Newfoundlander first, a Canadian second." But in a Pouch Cove twine store, where four diehard fishermen repaired their cod traps while country music drawled from a tape player, Frank Noseworthy, a slim, mustachioed cousin of Barry, said that he rejected the Newfoundlanders-first sentiment—and would far rather be Canadian than American. "In the States," he said, "them that's got it, gets more; them that don't, gets less. The Canadian government's more generous toward people that don't have."

In general, Canadians strike me as more outward-looking than Americans. They did not, after all, grow up being told that they already live in the greatest country on earth. "Americans are like TV evangelists," maintained Roger Bill, an Indiana native who is now the Newfoundland-based Atlantic field producer for CBC Radio's *Sunday Morning* show. "They really believe theirs is the best way and every-one else should follow. Canadians aren't nearly so arro-gant." They do, however, take a palpable pride in place, with a decided prejudice toward the small, friendly, and relaxed. "I wouldn't live in the States, or in Toronto or Montréal," said Richard Harvey, a high-school principal from Upper Gullies, Newfoundland. "You couldn't pay me enough."

1 Essential Information

Before You Go

Government Tourist Offices

In the United States Contact the tourism department of the province or territory you plan to visit: **Tourism New Brunswick** (Box 12345, Fredericton, NB E3B 5C3, tel. 800/561–0123), **Nova Scotia Dept. of Tourism and Culture** (Box 130, Halifax, NS B3J 2M7, tel. 800/341–6096). **Prince Edward Island Dept. of Tourism and Parks** (Visitor Services Division, Box 940, Charlottetown, PEI C1A 7M5, tel. 800/565–0267) and the **Newfoundland and Labrador Dept. of Development** (Tourism Branch, Box 8730, Saint John's, NF A1B 4K2, tel. 800/563–6353).

The U.S. Department of State's **Citizens Emergency Center** issues Consular Information Sheets, which cover crime, security, and health risks as well as embassy locations, entry requirements, currency regulations, and other routine matters. For the latest information, stop in at any passport office, consulate, or embassy; call the interactive hotline (tel. 202/647–5225); or, with your PC's modem, tap into the Bureau of Consular Affairs' computer bulletin board (tel. 202/647–9225).

In the United Kingdom Contact the **Canadian High Commission Department of Tourism,** Canada House, Trafalgar Square, London W1, tel. 071/930–8540.

Tours and Packages

Should you buy your travel arrangements to Canada packaged or do it yourself? There are advantages either way. Buying packaged arrangements saves you money, particularly if you can find a program that includes exactly the features you want. You also get a pretty good idea of what your trip will cost from the outset. Generally, you have two options: fully escorted tours and independent packages.

Escorted tours are most often via motorcoach, with a tour director in charge. They're ideal if you don't mind having limited free time and traveling with strangers. Your baggage is handled, your time rigorously scheduled, and most meals planned. Escorted tours are therefore the most hassle-free way to see a destination, as well as generally the least expensive. Independent packages allow plenty of flexibility. They generally include airline travel and hotels, with certain options available, such as sightseeing, car rental, and excursions. Independent packages are usually more expensive than escorted tours, but your time is your own.

Travel agents are your best source of recommendations for both tours and packages. They will have the largest selection, and the cost to you is the same as buying direct. Whatever program you ultimately choose, be sure to find out exactly what is included: taxes, tips, transfers, meals, baggage handling, ground transportation, entertainment, excursions, sports or recreation (and rental equipment if necessary). Ask about the level of hotel used, its location, the size of its rooms, the kind of beds, and its amenities, such as pool, room service, or programs for children, if they're important to you. Find out the operator's cancellation penalties. Nearly everyone charges them, and the only way to avoid them is to buy trip-cancellation insurance (*see* Trip Insurance, *below*). Also ask about the single supplement, a surcharge assessed to solo travelers. Some operators do not make you pay it if you agree to be matched up with a roommate of the same sex, even if one is not found by departure time. Remember that a program that has features you won't use, whether for rental sporting equipment or discounted museum admissions, may not be the most cost-wise choice for you.

Fully Escorted Tours Escorted tours are usually sold in three categories: deluxe, first-class, and tourist or budget class. The most important differences are the price, of course, and the level of accommodations. Some operators specialize in one category, while others offer a range. You'll find that stays in individual provinces are often part of larger tours.

Top operators include **Maupintour** (Box 807, Lawrence, KS 66044, tel. 913/843–1211 or 800/255–4266) and **Tauck Tours** (11 Wilton Rd., Westport, CT 06881, tel. 203/226–6911 or 800/468–2825) in the deluxe category; **Brendan Tours** (15137 Califa St., Van Nuys, CA 91411, tel. 818/985–9696 or 800/421–8446), **Domenico Tours** (751 Broadway, Bayonne, NJ 07002, tel. 201/823–8687 or 800/554–8687), **Gadabout Tours** (700 E. Tahquitz Way, Palm Springs, CA 92262, tel. 619/325–5556 or 800/952–5068), **Globus** (95-25 Queens Blvd., Rego Park, NY 11374, tel. 800/221–0090), and **Princess Tours** (2815 Second Ave., Suite 400, Seattle, WA 98121, tel. 206/728–4215 or 800/426–0442) in the first-class category. In the budget category try **Cosmos,** a sister company of Globus (*see above*).

Most itineraries are jam-packed with sightseeing, so you see a lot in a short amount of time (usually one place per day). To judge just how fast-paced the tour is, review the itinerary carefully. If you are in a different hotel each night, you will be getting up early each day to head out, travel to your next destination, do some sightseeing, have dinner, and go to bed, then you'll start all over again. If you want some free time, make sure it's mentioned in the tour brochure; if you want to be escorted to every meal, confirm that any tour you consider does that. Also, when comparing programs, be sure to find out if the motorcoach is air-conditioned and has a rest room on board. Make your selection based on price and stops on the itinerary.

Independent Packages Independent packages are offered by airlines, tour operators who may also do escorted programs, and any number of other companies from large, established firms to small, new entrepreneurs. Contact **Air Canada** (tel. 800/776–3000), **American Airlines Fly AAway Vacations** (tel. 800/321–2121), **Delta Dream Vacations** (tel. 800/872–7786), and **Supercities** (Box 1789, Minneapolis, MN 55440, tel. 800/333–1234).

Their programs come in a wide range of prices based on levels of luxury and options—in addition to hotel and airfare, sightseeing, car rental, transfers, admission to local attractions, and other extras. Note that when pricing different packages, it sometimes pays to purchase the same arrangements separately, as when a rock-bottom promotional airfare is being offered, for example. Again, base your choice on what's available at your budget for the destinations you want to visit.

Special-Interest Travel Special-interest programs may be fully escorted or independent. Some require a certain amount of expertise, but most are for the average traveler with an interest and are usually hosted by experts in the subject matter. When the program is escorted, it enjoys the advantages and disadvantages of all escorted programs; because your fellow travelers are apt to be passionate or knowledgeable about the subject, they can prove as enjoyable a part of your travel experience as the destination itself. The price range is wide, but the cost is usually higher—sometimes a lot higher—then for ordinary escorted tours and packages because of the expert guiding and special activities.

Cruises **Commodore Cruise Line** (800 Douglas Rd., Suite 600, Coral Gables, FL 33134, tel. 305/529–3000 or 800/237–5361) explores coastal Nova Scotia and Prince Edward Island and the St. Lawrence. **Royal Viking Line** (95 Merrick Way, Coral Gables, FL 33134, tel. 305/447–9660 or 800/442–8000) calls at Charlottetown (Prince Edward Island), Halifax (Nova Scotia), St. John (New Brunswick), and Montréal.

Fall Foliage Contact **Domenico Tours** (*see* Fully Escorted Tours, *above*) and **Parker Tours** (218–14 Northern Blvd., Bayside, NY 11361, tel. 718/428–7800 or 800/833–9600).

Skiing **AirCanada** (*see above*) has skiing programs to both eastern and Rockies resort areas.

When to Go

When to go will depend on your itinerary and your interests. In the maritime provinces of **Nova Scotia, New Brunswick,** and **Prince Edward Island,** the weather is relatively mild, though snow can remain on the ground well into spring and fog is common year-round. In **Newfoundland** and **Labrador** temperatures vary widely; winter days can be about 32 degrees Fahrenheit (0°C) in St. John's—and as low as –50°F (–45°C) in Labrador and on the west coast.

Climate The following are average daily maximum and minimum temperatures for Halifax in Nova Scotia.

Jan.	33F	1C	May	58F	14C	Sept.	67F	19C
	20	–7		41	5		53	12
Feb.	33F	1C	June	67F	19C	Oct.	58F	14C
	19	–7		50	10		44	7
Mar.	39F	4C	July	73F	23C	Nov.	48F	9C
	26	–3		57	14		36	2
Apr.	48F	9C	Aug.	73F	24C	Dec.	37F	3C
	33	1		58	13		25	–4

Information Sources For current weather conditions for cities in the United States and abroad, plus the local time and helpful travel tips, call the **Weather Channel Connection** (tel. 900/932–8437; 95¢ per minute) from a touch-tone phone.

Government Holidays

Though banks, schools, and government offices close for national holidays, many stores remain open. As in the United States, the move has been to observe certain holidays on the Monday nearest the actual date, making for a long weekend.

National Holidays National holidays for 1994 are: New Year's Day (January 1), Good Friday (April 1), Easter Monday (April 4), Victoria Day (May 23), Canada Day (July 1), Labor Day (September 5), Thanksgiving (October 10), Remembrance Day (November 11), Christmas (December 25), and Boxing Day (December 26).

Provincial Holidays **New Brunswick:** New Brunswick Day (August 1). **Nova Scotia:** Civic Holiday (August 1). **Newfoundland** and **Labrador:** St. Patrick's Day (March 17), St. George's Day (April 26), Discovery Day (June 21), Orangeman's Day (July 12).

Festivals and Seasonal Events

Contact the tourist boards to see what's in the offing for the time you'll be visiting, and inquire about any advance tickets you may need. The following are some of the top events.

New Brunswick **June:** Covered Bridge Spud and Spoke Days, in Hartland, features truck-tractor rodeos, beauty pageants, and sporting events.

July: Loyalist Days, in Saint John, celebrates the town's founding with parades, dancing, and sidewalk festivities; the Shediac Lobster Festival takes place in the town that calls itself the Lobster Capital of the World; there's an Irish festival in Chatham; St. Andrews Summer Arts Festival runs throughout July and August.

August: Mirimachi Folk Song Festival, in Newcastle, features fiddling competitions, casinos, beer gardens, and a parade; Foire Brayonne, in Edmundston, is the largest French festival outside of Québec; Festival By the Sea, in Saint John, attracts more than 200 entertainers from across Canada and includes cultural and ethnic performances; Acadian Festival, at Caraquet, celebrates the region's Acadian heritage with folk singing and indigenous food; the Chocolate Festival in St. Stephen includes suppers, displays, and children's events.

Newfoundland **June:** Opening of rainbow trout and salmon fishing seasons; St.
and Labrador John's Day celebrations in St. John's.

July: Codroy Valley Strawberry Jamboree; Stephenville Festival of the Arts; the Hangashore Folk Festival in Corner Brook; The Exploits Valley Salmon Festival in the Grand Falls area; The Fish, Fun and Folk Festival in Twillingate; the Conception Bay Folk Festival in Carbonear; Signal Hill Tattoo in St. John's through August.

August: The Festival of Flight in Gander; Une Longue Veillée in Cape St. George; The St. John's Regatta, St. John's; The Newfoundland and Labrador Folk Festival in St. John's; The Labrador Straits Bakeapple Folk Festival in southern Labrador.

September: Humber Valley Agricultural Home and Handicraft Exhibition in Deer Lake.

December: First Night is a nonalcoholic New Year's Eve celebration featuring dozens of activities and concerts in St. John's.

Nova Scotia **May:** Apple Blossom Festival, in Annapolis Valley, includes dancing, parades, and entertainment.

July: Antigonish Highland Games; Nova Scotia International Tattoo in Halifax has entertainment and competitions; Nova Scotia Bluegrass and Oldtime Music Festival at Ardoise.

August: Mahone Bay Wooden Boat Festival; Nova Scotia Fisheries Exhibition and Fishermen's Reunion in Lunenburg; Lunenburg Folk Harbour Festival; the Nova Scotia Gaelic Mod in St. Anns is a festival of Scottish culture; Scallop Days in Digby.

September: Shearwater International Air Show.

Prince Edward Island **June:** Irish Moss Festival in Tignish; Charlottetown Festival Theatre (through September) offers a series of concerts and musicals.

July: Rollo Bay Fiddle Festival; Summerside Lobster Carnival, in Summerside, is a week-long feast of lobster.

August: Highland Games, in Belfast, is a gathering of Scotsmen for games and celebrations; Annual Community Harvest Festival in Kensington; Old Home Week in Charlottetown; Festival Acadien de la Region Evangeline, Wellington Station.

What to Pack

Clothing How you pack will depend on when you go and what you plan to do. Layering is the best defense against Canada's cold winters; a hat, scarf, and gloves are essential. For summer travel, loose-fitting natural-fiber clothes are best; bring a wool sweater and light jacket. If you're planning to spend time in large cities, pack both casual clothes for day touring and more formal wear for evenings out. If your visit includes a stay at a large city hotel, bring a bathing suit in any season to take advantage of the indoor pool.

Miscellaneous Bring an extra pair of eyeglasses or contact lenses. If you have a health problem that may require you to purchase a prescription drug, pack enough to last the duration of the trip, or have your doctor write a prescription using the drug's generic name, since brand names vary from country to country. And don't forget to pack a list of the addresses of offices that supply refunds for lost or stolen traveler's checks.

Luggage Regulations Free baggage allowances on an airline depend on the airline, the route, and the class of your ticket. In general, on domestic flights and on international flights between the United States and foreign destinations, you are entitled to check two bags—neither exceeding 62 inches, or 158 centimeters (length + width + height), or weighing more than 70 pounds (32 kilograms). A third piece may be brought aboard as a carryon; its total dimensions are generally limited to less than 45 inches (114 centimeters), so it will fit easily under the seat in front of you or in the overhead compartment. There are variations, so ask in advance. The single rule, a Federal Aviation Administration safety regulation that pertains to carry-on baggage on U.S. airlines, requires only that carryons be properly stowed and allows the airline to limit allowances and tailor them to different aircraft and operational conditions. Charges for excess, oversize, or overweight pieces vary, so inquire before you pack.

Safeguarding Your Luggage Before leaving home, itemize your bags' contents and their worth; this list will help you estimate the extent of your loss if your bags go astray. To minimize that risk, tag them inside and out with your name, address, and phone number. (If you use your home address, cover it so that potential thieves can't see it.) At check-in, make sure that the tag attached by baggage handlers bears the correct three-letter code for your destination. If your bags do not arrive with you, or if you detect damage, do not leave the airport until you've filed a written report with the airline.

Money Matters

American money is readily accepted in much of Canada (especially in communities near the border), and traveler's checks and major U.S. credit cards are accepted in larger cities and resorts.

Traveler's Checks Although you will want plenty of cash when visiting small cities or rural areas, traveler's checks are usually preferable. The most widely recognized are **American Express, Thomas Cook, Visa,** and those issued by major commercial banks such as **Citibank** and **Bank of America.** American Express also issues *Traveler's Cheques for Two,* which can be counter-signed and used by you or your traveling companion. Some checks are free; usually the issuing company or the bank at which you make your purchase charges 1% of the checks' face value as a fee. Be sure to buy a few checks in small denominations to cash toward the end of your trip, when you don't want to be left with more foreign currency than you can spend. Always record the numbers of checks as you spend them, and keep this list separate from the checks.

Currency Exchange Banks and bank-operated exchange booths at airports and railroad stations are usually the best places to change money. Hotels, stores, and privately run exchange firms typically offer less favorable rates.

Before your trip, pay attention to how the dollar is doing vis-à-vis Canadian currency. If the dollar is losing strength, try to pay as many travel bills as possible in advance, especially the big ones. If it is getting stronger, pay for costly items abroad, and use your credit card whenever possible—you'll come out ahead, whether the exchange rate at which your purchase is calculated is the one in effect the day the vendor's bank abroad processes the charge, or the one prevailing on the day the charge company's service center processes it at home.

Getting Money from Home

Cash Machines Automated-teller machines (ATMs) are proliferating; many are tied to international networks such as **Cirrus** and **Plus.** You can use your bank card at ATMs away from home to withdraw money from an account and get cash advances on a credit-card account (providing your card has been programmed with a personal identification number, or PIN). Check in advance on limits on withdrawals and cash advances within specified periods. Ask whether your bank-card or credit-card PIN number will need to be reprogrammed for use in the area you'll be visiting—a possibility if the number has more than four digits. Remember that on cash advances you are charged interest from the day you get the money from ATMs as well as from tellers. And note that, although transaction fees for ATM withdrawals abroad will probably be higher than fees for withdrawals at home, Cirrus and Plus exchange rates tend to be good.

For specific Cirrus locations in the United States and Canada, call 800/424–7787 and press the area code and first three digits of the number you're calling from (or the calling area where you want an ATM).

American Express The company's **Express Cash** system lets you withdraw cash
Cardholder and/or traveler's checks from a worldwide network of 57,000
Services American Express dispensers and participating bank ATMs.
You must *enroll first* (call 800/227–4669 for a form and allow
two weeks for processing). Withdrawals are charged not to
your card but to a designated bank account. You can withdraw
up to $1,000 per seven-day period on the basic card, more if
your card is gold or platinum. There is a 2% fee (minimum
US$2.50, maximum US$10) for each cash transaction, and a 1%
fee for traveler's checks (except for the platinum card), which
are available only from American Express dispensers.

At AmEx offices, cardholders can also cash personal checks for
up to $1,000 in any seven-day period (21 days abroad); of this
$200 can be in cash, more if available, with the balance paid in
traveler's checks, for which all but platinum cardholders pay a
1% fee. Higher limits apply to the gold and platinum cards.

Wiring Money You don't have to be a cardholder to send or receive an **American Express MoneyGram** for up to US$10,000. To send one, go
to an American Express MoneyGram agent, pay up to
US$1,000 with a credit card and anything over that in cash, and
phone a transaction reference number to your intended recipi-
ent, who needs only present identification and the reference
number to the nearest MoneyGram agent to pick up the cash.
There are MoneyGram agents in more than 60 countries (call
800/543–4080 for locations). Fees range from 5% to 10%, depending on the amount and how you pay. You can't use American Express, which is really a convenience card—only
Discover, MasterCard, and Visa credit cards.

You can also use **Western Union.** To wire money, take either
cash or a check to the nearest office. (Or you can call and use a
credit card.) Fees are roughly 5%–10%. Money sent from the
United States or Canada will be available for pickup at agent
locations in Canada within minutes. (Note that once the money
is in the system it can be picked up at *any* location. You don't
have to miss your train waiting for it to arrive in City A, because
if there's an agent in City B, where you're headed, you can pick
it up there, too.) There are approximately 20,000 agents worldwide (call 800/325–6000 for locations).

Canadian Currency

The units of currency in Canada are the Canadian dollar (C$)
and the cent, in almost the same denominations as U.S. currency—the $1 bill is no longer used; instead it has been re-
placed by a $1 coin ($2, $5, $10, $20, 1¢, 5¢, 10¢, 25¢, etc.). The
use of $2 paper currency is common here although rare in the
United States. At press time (September 1993), the exchange
rate was C$1.30 to US$1 and C$1.37 to £1. The Canadian dollar
has decreased significantly in value relative to the U.S. dollar
in recent months.

What It Will Cost

Throughout this guide, unless otherwise stated, prices are
quoted in Canadian dollars.

With some exceptions, most food prices are higher in Canada
than in the United States, but lower than in much of Western
Europe. The biggest expense of the trip will be accommoda-

tions, but a range of choices, from economy to deluxe, is available in metropolitan areas, the country, and in resort areas.

Sample Prices The following prices are for most major cities: Dinner at an Expensive restaurant, without tax, tip, or drinks, will cost $30–$40; Moderate, $20–$30; Inexpensive, under $20. A double room at an Expensive hotel costs $130–$200 or more; Moderate, $90–$130; Inexpensive, $65–$90, with suburban motels being cheaper. (Prices in other cities and regions are often lower.) A soda (pop) costs about 95¢; a glass of beer, $3–$5; a sandwich, $2.75; a taxi, as soon as the meter is turned on, $1.50; a movie, about $8. (*See* Staying in Nova Scotia, GST and Sales Tax, *below*).

Passports and Visas

U.S. Citizens Because of the volume of border traffic between Canada and the United States, entry requirements are fairly simple. Citizens and legal residents of the United States do not need a passport or a visa to enter Canada, but proof of citizenship (a birth certificate, valid passport, or voter registration card) and proof of identity may be requested. U.S. residents entering Canada from a third country must have a valid passport, naturalization certificate, or "green card." For more information, contact the **Canadian Embassy** (501 Pennsylvania Ave. NW, Washington, DC 20001, tel. 202/682–1740).

U.K. Citizens Citizens of the United Kingdom need a valid passport to enter Canada for stays of up to six months; all visitors must have a return ticket out of Canada. Applications for new and renewal passports are available from main post offices as well as at the six passport offices, located in Belfast, Glasgow, Liverpool, London, Newport, and Peterborough. You may apply in person at all passport offices, or by mail to all except the London office. Children under 16 may travel on a parent's passport when accompanying them. All passports are valid for 10 years. Allow a month for processing.

Customs and Duties

On Arrival American and British visitors may bring in the following items duty-free: 200 cigarettes, 50 cigars, and two pounds of tobacco; 1 bottle (1.14 litres or 40 imperial oz.) of liquor, or 24 355 ml. (12 oz.) bottles or cans of beer for personal consumption; gifts up to the value of $40 per gift. A deposit is sometimes required for trailers (refunded upon return). Cats and dogs must have a certificate issued by a licensed veterinarian that clearly identifies the animal and certifies that it has been vaccinated against rabies during the preceding 36 months. Plant material must be declared and inspected.

Returning Home Provided you've been out of the country for at least 48 hours
U.S. Customs and haven't already used the exemption, or any part of it, in the past 30 days, you may bring home US$400 worth of foreign goods duty-free. So can each member of your family, regardless of age; and your exemptions may be pooled, so one of you can bring in more if another brings in less. A flat 10% duty applies to the next US$1,000 of goods; above US$1,400, the rate varies with the merchandise. (If the 48-hour or 30-day limits apply, your duty-free allowance drops to US$25, which may not be

pooled.) Please note that these are the *general* rules, applicable to most countries, including Canada.

Travelers 21 or older may bring back 1 liter of alcohol duty-free, provided the beverage laws of the state through which they reenter the United States allow it. In addition, 100 non-Cuban cigars and 200 cigarettes are allowed, regardless of your age. Antiques and works of art more than 100 years old are duty-free.

Gifts valued at less than US$50 may be mailed duty-free to stateside friends and relatives, with a limit of one package per day per addressee (do not send alcohol or tobacco products, nor perfume valued at more than US$5). These gifts do not count as part of your exemption, unless you bring them home with you. Mark the package "Unsolicited Gift" and include the nature of the gift and its retail value.

For a copy of "Know Before You Go," a free brochure detailing what you may and may not bring back to the United States, rates of duty, and other pointers, contact the **U.S. Customs Service** (Box 7407, Washington, DC 20044, tel. 202/927–6724).

U.K. Customs From countries outside the EC such as Canada, you may import duty-free 200 cigarettes, 100 cigarillos, 50 cigars or 250 grams of tobacco; 1 liter of spirits or 2 liters of fortified or sparkling wine; 2 liters of still table wine; 60 millileters of perfume; 250 millileters of toilet water; plus £36 worth of other goods, including gifts and souvenirs.

For further information or a copy of "A Guide for Travellers," which details standard customs procedures as well as what you may bring into the United Kingdom from abroad, contact **HM Customs and Excise** (New King's Beam House, 22 Upper Ground, London SE1 9PJ, tel. 071/620–1313).

Traveling with Cameras, Camcorders, and Laptops

Film and Cameras If your camera is new or if you haven't used it for a while, shoot and develop a few rolls of film before leaving home. Pack some lens tissue and an extra battery for your built-in light meter, and invest in an inexpensive skylight filter, to both protect your lens and provide some definition in hazy shots. Store film in a cool, dry place—never in the car's glove compartment or on the shelf under the rear window.

Films above ISO 400 are more sensitive to damage from airport security X-rays than others; very high-speed films, ISO 1000 and above, are exceedingly vulnerable. To protect your film, don't put it in checked luggage; carry it with you in a plastic bag and ask for a hand inspection. Such requests are honored at American airports, up to the inspector abroad. Don't depend on a lead-lined bag to protect film in checked luggage—the airline may very well turn up the dosage of radiation to see what you've got in there. Airport metal detectors do not harm film, although you'll set off the alarm if you walk through one with a roll in your pocket. Call the Kodak Information Center (tel. 800/242–2424) for details.

Camcorders Before your trip, put new or long-unused camcorders through their paces, and practice panning and zooming. Invest in a skylight filter to protect the lens, and check the lithium battery that lights up the LCD (liquid crystal display) modes. As for the rechargeable nickel-cadmium batteries that are the camera's power source, take along an extra pair, so while you're using your camcorder you'll have one battery ready and another recharging.

Videotape Unlike still-camera film, videotape is not damaged by X-rays. However, it may well be harmed by the magnetic field of a walk-through metal detector. Airport security personnel may want you to turn the camcorder on to prove that that's what it is, so make sure the battery is charged when you get to the airport.

Laptops Security X-rays do not harm hard-disk or floppy-disk storage. Most airlines allow you to use your laptop aloft but request that you turn it off during takeoff and landing so as not to interfere with navigation equipment. Make sure the battery is charged when you arrive at the airport, because you may be asked to turn on the computer at security checkpoints to prove that it is what it appears to be. If you're a heavy computer user, consider traveling with a backup battery. For international travel, register your laptop with U.S. Customs as you leave the country, providing it's manufactured abroad (U.S.-origin items cannot be registered at U.S. Customs); when you do so, you'll get a certificate, good for as long as you own the item, containing your name and address, a description of the laptop, and its serial number, that will quash any questions that may arise on your return. If your laptop is U.S.-made, call the consulate of the country you'll be visiting to find out whether it should be registered with customs in that country upon arrival. Some travelers do this as a matter of course and ask customs officers to sign a document that specifies the total configuration of the system, computer and peripherals, and its value. In addition, before leaving home, find out about repair facilities at your destination.

Language

Canada's two official languages are English and French. Though English is widely spoken, it is useful to learn a few French phrases when you travel to the French Canadian communities in the maritime provinces of Nova Scotia, New Brunswick, and Prince Edward Island. Canadian French, known as Québecois or *joual*, is a colorful language often quite different from that spoken in Paris.

Insurance

For U.S. Residents Most tour operators, travel agents, and insurance agents sell specialized health-and-accident, flight, trip-cancellation, and luggage insurance as well as comprehensive policies with some or all of these features. But before you make any purchase, review your existing health and homeowner policies to find out whether they cover expenses incurred while traveling.

Health-and- Supplemental health-and-accident insurance for travelers is
Accident Insurance usually a part of comprehensive policies. Specific policy provisions vary, but they tend to address three general areas, beginning with reimbursement for medical expenses caused by illness or an accident during a trip. Such policies may reimburse anywhere from US$1,000 to US$150,000 worth of medical expenses; dental benefits may also be included. A second common feature is the personal-accident, or death-and-dis-

memberment, provision, which pays a lump sum to your bene-
ficiaries if you die or to you if you lose one or both limbs or your
eyesight. This is similar to the flight insurance described below,
although it is not necessarily limited to accidents involving airplanes or even other "common carriers" (buses, trains, and
ships) and can be in effect 24 hours a day. The lump sum
awarded can range from US$15,000 to US$500,000. A third
area generally addressed by these policies is medical assistance (referrals, evacuation, or repatriation and other services). Some policies reimburse travelers for the cost of such
services; others may automatically enroll you as a member of
a particular medical-assistance company.

Flight Insurance This insurance, often bought as a last-minute impulse at the
airport, pays a lump sum to a beneficiary when a plane crashes
and the insured dies (and sometimes to a surviving passenger
who loses eyesight or a limb); thus it supplements the airlines'
own coverage as described in the limits-of-liability paragraphs
on your ticket (up to US$75,000 on international flights,
US$20,000 on domestic ones—and that is generally subject to
litigation). Charging an airline ticket to a major credit card
often automatically signs you up for flight insurance; in this
case, the coverage may also embrace travel by bus, train, and
ship.

Baggage Insurance In the event of loss, damage, or theft on international flights,
airlines limit their liability to US$20 per kilogram for checked
baggage (roughly about US$640 per 70-pound bag) and
US$400 per passenger for unchecked baggage. On domestic
flights, the ceiling is US$1,250 per passenger. Excess-valuation
insurance can be bought directly from the airline at check-in
but leaves your bags vulnerable on the ground.

Trip Insurance There are two sides to this coin. **Trip-cancellation-and-inter-
ruption insurance** protects you in the event you are unable to
undertake or finish your trip. **Default** or **bankruptcy insurance**
protects you against a supplier's failure to deliver. Consider
the former if your airline ticket, cruise, or package tour does
not allow changes or cancellations. The amount of coverage to
buy should equal the cost of your trip should you, a traveling
companion, or a family member get sick, forcing you to stay
home, plus the nondiscounted one-way airline ticket you would
need to buy if you had to return home early. Read the fine print
carefully; pay attention to sections defining "family member"
and "preexisting medical conditions." A characteristic quirk of
default policies is that they often do not cover default by travel
agencies or default by a tour operator, airline, or cruise line if
you bought your tour and the coverage directly from the firm
in question. To reduce your need for default insurance, give
preference to tours packaged by members of the United States
Tour Operators Association (USTOA), which maintains a fund
to reimburse clients in the event of member defaults. Even better, pay for travel arrangements with a major credit card, so
that you can refuse to pay the bill if services have not been
rendered—and let the card company fight your battles.

Comprehensive Companies supplying comprehensive policies with some or all
Policies of the above features include **Access America, Inc.,** underwritten by BCS Insurance Company (Box 11188, Richmond, VA
23230, tel. 800/284–8300); **Carefree Travel Insurance,** underwritten by The Hartford (Box 310, 120 Mineola Blvd., Mineola,
NY 11501, tel. 516/294–0220 or 800/323–3149); **Tele-Trip** (Mu-

tual of Omaha Plaza, Box 31762, Omaha, NE 68131, tel. 800/228–9792), a subsidiary of Mutual of Omaha; **The Travelers Companies** (1 Tower Sq., Hartford, CT 06183, tel. 203/277–0111 or 800/243–3174); **Travel Guard International,** underwritten by Transamerica Occidental Life Companies (1145 Clark St., Stevens Point, WI 54481, tel. 715/345–0505 or 800/782–5151); and **Wallach and Company, Inc.** (107 W. Federal St., Box 480, Middleburg, VA 22117, tel. 703/687–3166 or 800/237–6615), underwritten by Lloyds, London. These companies may also offer the above types of insurance separately.

U.K. Residents Most tour operators, travel agents, and insurance agents sell specialized policies covering accident, medical expenses, personal liability, trip cancellation, and loss or theft of personal property. Some policies include coverage for delayed departure and legal expenses, winter sports, accidents, or motoring abroad. You can also purchase an annual travel-insurance policy valid for every trip you make during the year in which it's purchased (usually only trips of less than 90 days). Before you leave, make sure you will be covered if you have a preexisting medical condition or are pregnant; your insurers may not pay for routine or continuing treatment, or may require a note from your doctor certifying your fitness to travel.

For advice by phone or a free booklet, "Holiday Insurance," that sets out what to expect from a holiday-insurance policy and gives price guidelines, contact the **Association of British Insurers** (51 Gresham St., London EC2V 7HQ, tel. 071/600–3333; 30 Gordon St., Glasgow G1 3PU, tel. 041/226–3905; Scottish Provincial Bldg., Donegall Sq. W, Belfast BT1 6JE, tel. 0232/249176; call for other locations).

Car Rentals

All major car-rental companies are represented in eastern Canada, including **Avis** (tel. 800/331–1212, 800/879–2847 in Canada); **Budget** (tel. 800/527–0700); **Hertz** (tel. 800/654–3001, 800/263–0600 in Canada); **National** (tel. 800/227–7368), affiliated with **Tilden Rent-a-Car** (tel. 514/842–9445). In cities, rates range from about $50 per day for an economy car to $70 for a large car; weekly rates range from $190 to $350. Unlimited mileage rentals are available only in limited areas. This does not include the 7% GST tax.

Requirements Any valid state or national driver's license is acceptable. If you have rented in the United States, be sure to keep the rental contract with you to indicate that use in Canada is authorized by the rental agency.

Extra Charges Picking up the car in one city or country and leaving it in another may entail drop-off charges or one-way service fees, which can be substantial. The cost of a collision or loss-damage waiver (*see below*) can be high, also. Automatic transmissions and air-conditioning are not universally available abroad; ask for them when you book if you want them, and check the cost before you commit yourself to the rental.

Cutting Costs If you know you will want a car for more than a day or two, you can save by planning ahead. Major international companies have programs that discount their standard rates by 15%–30% if you make the reservation before departure (anywhere from two to 14 days), rent for a minimum number of days (typically three or four), and prepay the rental. Ask about these advance-purchase schemes when you call for information. More economical rentals are those that come as part of fly/drive or other packages, even those as bare-bones as the rental plus an airline ticket (*see* Tours and Packages, *above*).

Other sources of savings are the several companies that operate as wholesalers—companies that do not own their own fleets but rent in bulk from those that do and offer advantageous rates to their customers. Rentals through such companies must be arranged and paid for before you leave the United States. Among them is **Auto Europe** (Box 1097, Camden, ME 04843, tel. 207/236–8235, 800/223–5555, in Canada, 800/458–9503). You won't see these wholesalers' deals advertised; they're even better in summer, when business travel is down. Always ask whether the prices are guaranteed in U.S. dollars or foreign currency and if unlimited mileage is available. Find out about any required deposits, cancellation penalties, and drop-off charges, and confirm the cost of the CDW.

One last tip: Remember to fill the tank when you turn in the vehicle, to avoid being charged for refueling at what you'll swear is the most expensive pump in town.

Insurance and Collision Damage Waiver The standard rental contract includes liability coverage (for damage to public property, injury to pedestrians, etc.) and coverage for the car against fire, theft (not included in certain countries), and collision damage with a deductible—most commonly US$2,000–US$3,000, occasionally more. In the case of an accident, you are responsible for the deductible amount unless you've purchased the collision damage waiver (CDW), which costs an average $12 a day, although this varies depending on what you've rented, where, and from whom.

Because this adds up quickly, you may be inclined to say "no thanks"—and that's certainly your option, although the rental agent may not tell you so. Note before you decline that deductibles are occasionally high enough that totaling a car would make you responsible for its full value. Planning ahead will help you make the right decision. By all means, find out if your own insurance covers damage to a rental car while traveling (not simply a car to drive when yours is in for repairs). And check whether charging car rentals to any of your credit cards will get you a CDW at no charge.

Rail Passes

Although **VIA Rail,** Canada's major passenger carrier, has made considerable cuts in its services, it is still possible to travel coast to coast on its trains. The **Canrailpass** allows 12 days of coach-class travel within a 30 day period; sleeping cars are available, but they sell out very early and must be reserved at least a month in advance during the high season. During the high season (June 7–Sept. 30) the pass is US$419.63 for adults age 25–60, US$376.72 for travelers under 25 or over 60. Low season rates (Oct. 1–Dec. 14 and Jan. 6–June 6) are US$282.33 for adults and US$256.58 for youth and seniors. The pass is not valid during the Christmas period (Dec. 15–Jan. 5). The Canrailpass must be purchased prior to arrival in Canada; for more information and reservations, contact VIA Rail (tel. 800/665–0200 in the United States) or Compass Travel (Box 113, Peterborough, PE1 1LE, tel. 0733/51780, in the United Kingdom).

Student and Youth Travel

Travel Agencies The foremost U.S. student travel agency is **Council Travel,** a subsidiary of the nonprofit Council on International Educational Exchange. It specializes in low-cost travel arrangements, is the exclusive U.S. agent for several discount cards, and, with its sister CIEE subsidiary, **Council Charter,** is a source of airfare bargains. The Council Charter brochure and CIEE's twice-yearly *Student Travels* magazine, which details its programs, are available at the Council Travel office at CIEE headquarters (205 E. 42nd Street, New York, NY 10017, tel. 212/661–1450) and at 37 branches in college towns nationwide (free in person, US$1 by mail). The **Educational Travel Center** (ETC, 438 N. Francis St., Madison, WI 53703, tel. 608/256–5551) also offers low-cost rail passes, domestic and international airline tickets (mostly for flights departing from Chicago), and other budgetwise travel arrangements. Other travel agencies catering to students include **Travel Management International** (TMI, 18 Prescott St., Suite 4, Cambridge, MA 02138, tel. 617/661–8187) and **Travel Cuts** (187 College St., Toronto, Ont. M5T 1P7, tel. 416/979–2406).

Discount Cards For discounts on transportation and on museum and attractions admissions, buy the **International Student Identity Card** (ISIC) if you're a bona fide student, or the **International Youth Card** (IYC) if you're under 26. In the United States the ISIC and IYC cards cost US$15 each and include basic travel accident and sickness coverage. Apply to **CIEE** (*see* address *above*, tel. 212/661–1414; the application is in *Student Travels*). In Canada the cards are available for US$15 each from **Travel Cuts** (*see above*). In the United Kingdom they cost £5 and £4 respectively at student unions and student travel companies, including Council Travel's London office (28A Poland St., London W1V 3DB, tel. 071/437–7767).

Hosteling An **International Youth Hostel Federation** (IYHF) membership card is the key to more than 5,300 hostel locations in 59 countries; the sex-segregated, dormitory-style sleeping quarters, including some for families, go for US$7–US$20 a night per person. Membership is available in the United States through **American Youth Hostels** (AYH, 733 15th St. NW, Washington, DC 20005, tel. 202/783–6161), the American link in the worldwide chain, and costs US$25 for adults 18–54, US$10 for those under 18, US$15 for those 55 and over, and US$35 for families. Volume 2 of the two-volume *Guide to Budget Accommodation* lists hostels in Asia and Australasia as well as in Canada and the United States (US$13.95 including postage). IYHF membership is available in Canada through the **Canadian Hostelling Association** (CHA, 1600 James Naismith Dr., Suite 608, Gloucester, Ont. K1B 5N4, tel. 613/748–5638) for $26.75, and in the United Kingdom through the **Youth Hostel Association of England and Wales** (Trevelyan House, 8 St. Stephen's Hill, St. Albans, Herts. AL1 2DY, tel. 0727/55215) for £9.

Traveling with Children

Publications *Family Travel Times,* published 10 times a year by Travel With
Newsletter Your Children (TWYCH, 45 W. 18th St., 7th Floor Tower, New

York, NY 10011, tel. 212/206–0688; annual subscription $55), covers destinations, types of vacations, and modes of travel.

Books *Traveling with Children—And Enjoying It*, by Arlene K. Butler (US$11.95 plus US$3 shipping per book; Globe Pequot Press, Box 833, Old Saybrook, CT 06475, tel. 800/243–0495, in CT, 800/962–0973), helps plan your trip with children, from toddlers to teens. Also from Globe Pequot is *Recommended Family Resorts in the United States, Canada, and the Caribbean*, by Jane Wilford with Janet Tice (US$12.95).

Getting There On international flights, the fare for infants under 2 not occu-
Air Fares pying a seat is generally 10% of the accompanying adult's fare; children ages 2–11 usually pay half to two-thirds of the adult fare. On domestic flights, children under 2 not occupying a seat travel free, and older children currently travel on the "lowest applicable" adult fare.

Baggage In general, infants paying 10% of the adult fare are allowed one carry-on bag, not to exceed 70 pounds or 45 inches (length + width + height). The adult baggage allowance applies for children paying half or more of the adult fare. Check with the airline for particulars, especially regarding flights between two foreign destinations, where allowances for infants may be less generous than those above.

Safety Seats The FAA recommends the use of safety seats aloft and details approved models in the free leaflet "Child/Infant Safety Seats Recommended for Use in Aircraft" (available from the Federal Aviation Administration, APA–200, 800 Independence Ave. SW, Washington, DC 20591, tel. 202/267–3479). Airline policy varies. U.S. carriers must allow FAA-approved models, but because these seats are strapped into a regular passenger seat, they may require that parents buy a ticket even for an infant under 2 who would otherwise ride free. Foreign carriers may not allow infant seats, may charge the child's rather than the infant's fare for their use, or may require you to hold your baby during takeoff and landing, thus defeating the seat's purpose.

Facilities Aloft Airlines do provide other facilities and services for children, such as children's meals and freestanding bassinets (to those sitting in seats on the bulkhead, where there's enough legroom to accommodate them). Make your request when reserving. The annual February/March issue of *Family Travel Times* gives details of the children's services of dozens of airlines (US$10; *see above*). "Kids and Teens in Flight" (free from the U.S. Department of Transportation, tel. 202/366–2220) offers tips for children flying alone.

Lodging Although most major hotels in Canada welcome children, the policies and programs they offer are usually limited to a free stay for children under a certain age when sharing a room with their parents. For example, the Sheraton Hotels worldwide offer a free stay to children under the age of 17. At Best Westerns, the age limit ranges from 12 to 16, depending on the hotel. Baby-sitting services can often be arranged at the front desk of most hotels. In addition, priority for connecting rooms is often given to families. Inquire about programs and discounts when you make your reservation.

Hints for Travelers with Disabilities

Organizations
In Canada

Canadian Paraplegic Association National Office (520 Sutherland Dr., Toronto, Ont., M4G 3U9, tel. 416/422–5640) provides information about touring in Canada.

In the United States

Several organizations provide travel information for people with disabilities, usually for a membership fee, and some publish newsletters and bulletins. Among them are the **Information Center for Individuals with Disabilities** (Fort Point Pl., in MA, 27–43 Wormwood St., Boston, MA 02210, tel. 617/727–5540 or, in MA, 800/462–5015 between 11 and 4, or leave message; TDD/TTY tel. 617/345–9743); **Mobility International USA** (Box 3551, Eugene, OR 97403, voice and TDD tel. 503/343–1284), the U.S. branch of an international organization based in Britain (*see below*) and present in 30 countries; **Moss-Rehab Hospital Travel Information Service** (1200 W. Tabor Rd., Philadelphia, PA 19141, tel. 215/456–9603, TDD tel. 215/456–9602); the **Society for the Advancement of Travel for the Handicapped** (SATH, 347 5th Ave., Suite 610, New York, NY 10016, tel. 212/447–7284, fax 212/725–8253); the **Travel Industry and Disabled Exchange** (TIDE, 5435 Donna Ave., Tarzana, CA 91356, tel. 818/368–5648); and **Travelin' Talk** (Box 3534, Clarksville, TN 37043, tel. 615/552–6670).

In the United Kingdom

Main information sources include the **Royal Association for Disability and Rehabilitation** (RADAR, 25 Mortimer St., London W1N 8AB, tel. 071/637–5400), which publishes travel information for the disabled in Britain, and **Mobility International** (228 Borough High St., London SE1 1JX, tel. 071/403–5688), the headquarters of an international membership organization that serves as a clearinghouse of travel information for people with disabilities.

Travel Agencies and Tour Operators

Directions Unlimited (720 N. Bedford Rd., Bedford Hills, NY 10507, tel. 914/241–1700), a travel agency, has expertise in tours and cruises for the disabled. **Evergreen Travel Service** (4114 198th St. SW, Suite 13, Lynnwood, WA 98036, tel. 206/776–1184 or 800/435–2288) operates Wings on Wheels Tours for those in wheelchairs, White Cane Tours for the blind, and tours for the deaf and makes group and independent arrangements for travelers with any disability. **Flying Wheels Travel** (143 W. Bridge St., Box 382, Owatonna, MN 55060, tel. 800/535–6790, in MN, 800/722–9351), a tour operator and travel agency, arranges international tours, cruises, and independent travel itineraries for people with mobility disabilities. **Nautilus,** at the same address as TIDE (*see above*), packages tours for the disabled internationally.

Publications

In addition to the fact sheets, newsletters, and books mentioned above are several free publications available from the Consumer Information Center (Pueblo, CO 81009): "New Horizons for the Air Traveler with a Disability," a U.S. Department of Transportation booklet describing changes resulting from the 1986 Air Carrier Access Act and those still to come from the 1990 Americans with Disabilities Act (include Department 608Y in the address), and the Airport Operators Council's *Access Travel: Airports* (Dept. 5804), which describes facilities and services for the disabled at more than 500 airports worldwide.

Twin Peaks Press (Box 129, Vancouver, WA 98666, tel. 206/694–2462 or 800/637–2256) publishes the *Directory of Travel Agencies for the Disabled* (US$19.95), listing more than 370 agencies worldwide; *Travel for the Disabled* (US$19.95), listing some 500 access guides and accessible places worldwide; the *Directory of Accessible Van Rentals* (US$9.95) for campers and RV travelers worldwide; and *Wheelchair Vagabond* (US$14.95), a collection of personal travel tips. Add US$2 per book for shipping.

Hints for Older Travelers

Organizations The **American Association of Retired Persons** (AARP, 601 E St. NW, Washington, DC 20049, tel. 202/434–2277) provides independent travelers the Purchase Privilege Program, which offers discounts on hotels, car rentals, and sightseeing, and the AARP Motoring Plan, provided by Amoco, which furnishes domestic trip-routing information and emergency road-service aid for an annual fee of US$39.95 per person or couple (US$59.95 for a premium version). AARP also arranges group tours, cruises, and apartment living through AARP Travel Experience from American Express (400 Pinnacle Way, Suite 450, Norcross, GA 30071, tel. 800/927–0111); these can be booked through travel agents, except for the cruises, which must be booked directly (tel. 800/745–4567). AARP membership is open to those 50 and over; annual dues are US$8 per person or couple.

Two other membership organizations offer discounts on lodgings, car rentals, and other travel products, along with such nontravel perks as magazines and newsletters. The **National Council of Senior Citizens** (1331 F St. NW, Washington, DC 20004, tel. 202/347–8800) is a nonprofit advocacy group with some 5,000 local clubs across the United States; membership costs US$12 per person or couple annually. **Mature Outlook** (6001 N. Clark St., Chicago, IL 60660, tel. 800/336–6330), a Sears Roebuck & Co. subsidiary with 800,000 members, charges US$9.95 for an annual membership.

Note: When using any senior-citizen identification card for reduced hotel rates, mention it when booking, not when checking out. At restaurants, show your card before you're seated; discounts may be limited to certain menus, days, or hours. If you are renting a car, ask about promotional rates that might improve on your senior-citizen discount.

Educational Travel **Elderhostel** (75 Federal St., 3rd floor, Boston, MA 02110, tel. 617/426–7788) is a nonprofit organization that has offered inexpensive study programs for people 60 and older since 1975. Programs take place at more than 1,800 educational institutions in the United States, Canada, and 45 countries; courses cover everything from marine science to Greek myths and cowboy poetry. Participants generally attend lectures in the morning and spend the afternoon sightseeing or on field trips; they live in dorms on the host campuses. Fees for programs in the United States and Canada, which usually last one week, run about US$300, not including transportation.

Tour Operators **Saga International Holidays** (222 Berkeley St., Boston, MA 02116, tel. 800/343–0273), which specializes in group travel for people over 60, offers a selection of variously priced tours and cruises covering five continents.

Discounts **VIA Rail Canada** (tel. 800/665–0200) offers those 60 and over a 10% discount on basic transportation for travel any time and with no advance-purchase requirement. This 10% discount can also apply to off-peak reduced fares that have advance-purchase requirements.

Further Reading

Andrew Malcolm gives a cultural and historical overview of the country in *The Canadians*. Stephen Brook's *The Maple Leaf Rag* is a collection of idiosyncratic travel essays. *My Country*, by Pierre Burton, is one of many of Burton's books about Canada worth reading for a personal look at Canada. *Short History of Canada*, by Desmond Morton, is a recent historical account of the country.

Arriving and Departing

From North America by Plane

Flights are either nonstop, direct, or connecting. A **nonstop** flight requires no change of plane and makes no stops. A **direct** flight stops at least once and can involve a change of plane, although the flight number remains the same; if the first leg is late, the second waits. This is not the case with a **connecting** flight, which involves a different plane and a different flight number.

Airports and Airlines You can fly nonstop to Canada from most major U.S. cities; every major U.S. airline has nonstop service. The major international hubs are Montréal, Toronto, and Vancouver, but international flights also fly into Halifax, Calgary, and Edmonton.

Flying Time **To Halifax:** 2 hours from New York, 5³/₄ hours from Chicago, 7 hours from Los Angeles. **To Sydney:** 3¹/₂ hours from New York, 7 hours from Chicago, 9 hours from Los Angeles. **To St. John's:** 4¹/₂ hours from New York, 6¹/₂ hours from St. John's, 10 hours from Los Angeles.

Cutting Flight Costs The Sunday travel section of most newspapers is a good source of deals. When booking, particularly through an unfamiliar company, call the Better Business Bureau to find out whether any complaints have been registered against the company, pay with a credit card if you can, and consider trip-cancellation and default insurance (*see* Insurance, *above*).

Promotional Airfares All the less expensive fares, called promotional or discount fares, are round-trip and involve restrictions. The exact nature of the restrictions depends on the airline, the route, and the season and on whether travel is domestic or international, but you must usually buy the ticket—commonly called an **APEX** (advance purchase excursion) when it's for international travel—in advance (seven, 14, or 21 days are usual). You must also respect certain minimum- and maximum-stay requirements (for instance, over a Saturday night or at least seven and no more than 30, 45, or 90 days), and you must be willing to pay penalties for changes. Airlines generally allow some changes for a fee. But the cheaper the fare, the more likely the ticket is nonrefundable; it would take a death in the family for the airline to give you any of your money back if you had to cancel. The cheapest fares are also subject to availability; because only a certain percentage of the plane's total seats will be sold at that price, they may go quickly.

Consolidators Consolidators or bulk-fare operators—also known as bucket shops—buy blocks of seats on scheduled flights that airlines anticipate they won't be able to sell. They pay wholesale prices, add a markup, and resell the seats to travel agents or directly to the public at prices that still undercut the airline's promotional or discount fares. You pay more than on a charter but ordinarily less than for an APEX ticket, and, even when there is not much of a price difference, the ticket usually comes without the advance-purchase restriction. Moreover, although tickets are marked nonrefundable so you can't turn them in to the airline for a full-fare refund, some consolidators sometimes give you your money back. Carefully read the fine print detailing penalties for changes and cancellations. If you doubt the reliability of a company, call the airline once you've made your booking and confirm that you do, indeed, have a reservation on the flight.

The biggest U.S. consolidator, C.L. Thomson Express, sells only to travel agents. Well-established consolidators selling to the public include **UniTravel** (Box 12485, St. Louis, MO 63132, tel. 314/569–0900 or 800/325–2222); **Council Charter** (205 E. 42nd St., New York, NY 10017, tel. 212/661–0311 or 800/800–8222), a division of the Council on International Educational Exchange and a longtime charter operator now functioning more as a consolidator; and **Travac** (989 6th Ave., New York, NY 10018, tel. 212/563–3303 or 800/872–8800), also a former charterer.

Charter Flights Charters usually have the lowest fares and the most restrictions. Departures are limited and seldom on time, and you can lose all or most of your money if you cancel. (Generally, the closer to departure you cancel, the more you lose, although sometimes you will be charged only a small fee if you supply a substitute passenger.) The charterer, on the other hand, may legally cancel the flight for any reason up to 10 days before departure; within 10 days of departure, the flight may be canceled only if it becomes physically impossible to operate. The charterer may also revise the itinerary or increase the price after you have bought the ticket, but if the new arrangement constitutes a "major change," you have the right to a refund. Before buying a charter ticket, read the fine print for the company's refund policy and details on major changes. Money for charter flights is usually paid into a bank escrow account, the name of which should be on the contract. If you don't pay by credit card, make your check payable to the escrow account (unless you're dealing with a travel agent, in which case, his or her check should be payable to the escrow account). The Department of Transportation's Consumer Affairs Office (I–25, Washington, DC 20590, tel. 202/366–2220) can answer questions on charters and send you its "Plane Talk: Public Charter Flights" information sheet.

Charter operators may offer flights alone or with ground arrangements that constitute a charter package. Well-established charter operators include **Council Charter** (205 E. 42nd St., New York, NY 10017, tel. 212/661–0311 or 800/800–8222), now largely a consolidator, despite its name, and **Travel Charter** (1120 E. Long Lake Rd., Troy, MI 48098, tel. 313/528–3570 or 800/521–5267), with Midwestern departures. **DER Tours** (Box

1606, Des Plains, IL 60017, tel. 800/782–2424), a charterer and consolidator, sells through travel agents.

Discount Travel Clubs Travel clubs offer their members unsold space on airplanes, cruise ships, and package tours at nearly the last minute and at well below the original cost. Suppliers thus receive some revenue for their "leftovers," and members get a bargain. Membership generally includes a regular bulletin or access to a toll-free telephone hot line giving details of available trips departing anywhere from three or four days to several months in the future. Packages tend to be more common than flights alone, so if airfares are your only interest, read the literature before joining. Reductions on hotels are also available. Clubs include **Discount Travel International** (114 Forrest Ave., Suite 203, Narberth, PA 19072, tel. 215/668–7184; US$45 annually, single or family), **Moment's Notice** (425 Madison Ave., New York, NY 10017, tel. 212/486–0503; US$45 annually, single or family), **Travelers Advantage** (CUC Travel Service, 49 Music Sq. W, Nashville, TN 37203, tel. 800/548–1116; US$49 annually, single or family), and **Worldwide Discount Travel Club** (1674 Meridian Ave., Miami Beach, FL 33139, tel. 305/534–2082; US$50 annually for family, US$40 single).

Enjoying the Flight Fly at night if you're able to sleep on a plane. Because the air aloft is dry, drink plenty of beverages while on board; remember that drinking alcohol contributes to jet lag, as do heavy meals. Sleepers usually prefer window seats to curl up against; restless passengers ask to be on the aisle. Bulkhead seats, in the front row of each cabin, have more legroom, but since there's no seat ahead, trays attach awkwardly to the arms of your seat, and you must stow all possessions overhead. Bulkhead seats are usually reserved for the disabled, the elderly, and people traveling with babies.

Smoking Smoking is now banned on all domestic flights of less than six hours duration in the United States, and on all Canadian flights, including flights to and from Europe and the Far East. The U.S. ban also applies to domestic segments of international flights aboard U.S. and foreign carriers. On U.S. carriers flying to other destinations abroad, a seat in a no-smoking section must be provided for every passenger who requests one, and the section must be enlarged to accommodate such passengers if necessary as long as they have complied with the airline's deadline for check-in and seat assignment. If smoking bothers you, request a seat far from the smoking section.

From the U.S. by Car

Drivers must have proper owner registration and proof of insurance coverage, which is compulsory in Canada. The Canadian Non-Resident Inter-Provincial Motor Vehicle Liability Insurance Card, available from any U.S. insurance company, is accepted as evidence of financial responsibility anywhere in Canada. Minimum insurance requirement in Canada is $200,000, except in Québec where the minimum is $50,000. For more information, contact the Insurance Bureau of Canada (181 University Ave., Toronto, Ontario, M5H 3M7, tel. 416/362–2301). If you are driving a car that is not registered in your name, carry a letter from the owner that authorizes your use of the vehicle. (*See also* Getting around by Car, *below.*) The U.S.

Interstate Highway System leads directly into eastern Canada: I–95 goes from Maine to New Brunswick.

From the U.S. by Train, Bus, and Ship

By Train **Amtrak** (tel. 800/872–7245) has service from New York to Montréal and Toronto, and from Chicago to Toronto. Amtrak's *Montrealer* departs from New York's Pennsylvania Station at 8:25 PM and arrives in Montréal the next day at about 10:45 AM. Sleepers are highly recommended for the overnight trip but must be booked well in advance. The *Montrealer* is the only Amtrak train to Canada that requires reservations.

A second Amtrak train to Montréal leaves New York from Pennsylvania Station in the morning and takes 10½ hours; the trip from New York to Toronto (passing through Buffalo) takes 11 hours and 45 minutes; travel from Chicago to Toronto takes 12 hours. In addition to these direct routes, there are connections from many major cities. On the west coast, Amtrak offers frequent service to Seattle. From there, buses are available to Vancouver and other Canadian destinations.

By Bus **Greyhound** has the most widespread bus service to Canada, and you can get from almost any point in the United States to any point in Canada on its extensive network.

By Ship You can take a car ferry between Maine and Nova Scotia (*see* Essential Information in individual chapters). Many Canadian cities are also accessible by water on private yachts and boats. Local marine authorities can advise you about the necessary documentation and procedure.

From the U.K. by Plane

Airlines The major carriers between Great Britain and Canada are **Air Canada** (tel. 081/759–2331 in the London area, or 0800/181313 elsewhere), **British Airways** (tel. 081/897–4000), and **Canadian Airlines International** (tel. 071/930–3501). Air Canada has the most flights and serves the most cities, with at least one flight a day to Toronto, Vancouver, and Montréal from Heathrow, and considerably more at peak periods. Air Canada also flies to Calgary, Edmonton, Halifax, and St. John's from Heathrow; to Toronto from Birmingham and Manchester; and to Calgary, Halifax, Toronto, and Vancouver from Prestwick (Glasgow). British Airways has as many as 23 flights a week to Canada from Heathrow, serving Montréal, Toronto, and Vancouver. Canadian Airlines International serves Calgary, Edmonton, Ottawa, and Vancouver from London Gatwick, has at least one flight a day to Toronto, and has service from Manchester to Toronto.

Staying in Nova Scotia

Getting Around

By Plane **Air Canada** (tel. 800/776–3000) operates in every province. The other major domestic carrier is **Canadian Airlines International** (tel. 800/426–7000). Regularly scheduled flights to every major city and to most smaller cities are available on Air Canada or Canadian Airlines International or the domestic carriers associated with them: **Air Nova** and **Air Atlantic** are the principal airlines in the Atlantic region. These airlines can be contacted at local numbers within each of the many cities they serve. Check with the territorial tourist agencies for charter companies and with the District Controller of Air Services in the territorial (and provincial) capitals for the locations of air bases that allow private flights and for regulations.

By Train   Transcontinental rail service is provided by **VIA Rail Canada** (tel. 800/665–0200). If you're planning on traveling to several major cities in Canada, the train may be your best bet. Routes run across the country as well as within individual provinces, with the exception of the Northwest Territories and the Yukon, Newfoundland and Prince Edward Island.

You can choose either sleeping-car or coach accommodations on most trains. Both classes allow access to dining cars. Sleeping-car passengers can enjoy comfortable parlor cars, drawing rooms, bedrooms, and roomettes. First-class seats, sleeping-car accommodations, and Dayniter seats between Ontario, Québec, and the maritime provinces require reservations. VIA has a new "Silver and Blue" service on its transcontinental trains that provides first-class "cruise" comfort and amenities including exclusive use of their dome car. In the United Kingdom, **Compass Travel** (Box 113, Peterborough, PE1 1LE, tel. 0733/51780) represents VIA Rail.

By Bus   The bus is an essential form of transportation in Canada, especially if you want to visit out-of-the-way towns that do not have airports or rail lines. Two major bus companies, **Greyhound** (222 1st Ave. SW, Calgary, Alb. T2P 0A6, tel. 403/265–9111) and **Voyageur** (505 E Boulevard Maisonneuve H2L 1Y4, Montréal, tel. 514/843–4231), offer interprovincial service. In the United Kingdom, contact **Greyhound World Travel Ltd.,** Sussex House, London Road, East Grinstead, West Surrey, RHI9 1LD (tel. 0342/317317).

By Car   Canada's highway system is excellent. It includes the Trans-Canada Highway, the longest highway in the world, which runs about 5,000 miles from Victoria, British Columbia, to St. John's, Newfoundland, using ferries to bridge coastal waters at each end. The second-largest Canadian highway, the Yellowhead Highway, follows the old Indian route from the Pacific Coast and over the Rockies to the prairie. North of the population centers, roads become fewer and less developed.

You are required to wear seat belts and use infant seats. Some provinces have a statutory requirement to drive with vehicle headlights on for extended periods after dawn and before sunset.

Speed limits vary from province to province, but they are usually within the 90–100 kph (50–60 mph) range outside the cities. The price of gasoline varies more than the speed limit, from 40¢ to 72¢ a liter. (There are 3.8 liters in a U.S. gallon, 4.5 liters in a Canadian Imperial gallon.) Distances are now always shown in kilometers, and gasoline is always sold in liters. The Imperial gallon is seldom used.

Foreign driver's licenses are valid in Canada. Members of the Automobile Association of America (AAA) can contact the **Canadian Automobile Association** (1775 Courtwood Crescent, Ottawa, Ont. K2C 3J2, tel. 613/226–7631; emergency road service, tel. 800/336–4357). Members of the Automobile Association of Great Britain, the Royal Automobile Club, the Royal Scottish Automobile Club, the Royal Irish Automobile Club and the automobile clubs of the Alliance Internationale de Tourisme (AIT) and Fédération Internationale de l'Automobile (FIA) are entitled to all the services of the CAA on presentation of a membership card.

By Ferry Car ferries provide essential transportation on the east coast of Canada. **Marine Atlantic** (Box 250, North Sydney, NS B2A 3M3, tel. 902/794–5700 or 800/341–7981) operates ferries between Nova Scotia and Newfoundland; New Brunswick and Prince Edward Island; New Brunswick and Nova Scotia; and also between Portland, Maine, and Nova Scotia.

Telephones

Phones work as they do in the United States. Drop 25¢ in the slot and dial; pay phones eagerly accept American coins, unlike U.S. phones, which spit out Canadian money. There are no problems dialing direct to the United States; U.S. telephone credit cards are accepted. For directory assistance, dial 1, the area code, and 555–1212. To place calls outside Canada and the United States, dial "0" and ask for the overseas operator.

Mail

Postal Rates In Canada you can buy stamps at the post office or from automatic vending machines in most hotel lobbies, railway stations, airports, bus terminals, many retail outlets, and some newsstands. Within Canada, postcards and letters up to 30 grams cost 46¢; between 30 grams and a kilogram, the cost is $3.75. Letters and postcards to the United States cost 52¢ for up to 30 grams, and $3.40 for up to 250 grams. Prices include GST.

International mail and postcards run 92¢ for up to 30 grams, and $2.10 for up to 100 grams.

Telepost is a fast "next day or sooner" service that combines the CN/CP Telecommunications network with letter-carrier delivery service. Messages may be telephoned to the nearest CN/CP Public Message Centre for delivery anywhere in Canada or the United States. Telepost service is available 24 hours a day, seven days a week, and billing arrangements may be made at the time the message is called in. **Intelpost** allows you to send documents or photographs via satellite to many Canadian, American, and European destinations. This service is available at main postal facilities in Canada, and is paid for in cash.

Visitors may have mail sent to them c/o General Delivery in the town they are visiting, for pickup in person within 15 days, after which it will be returned to the sender.

Tipping

Tips and service charges are not usually added to a bill in Canada. In general, tip 15% of the total bill. This goes for waiters, waitresses, barbers and hairdressers, taxi drivers, etc. Porters and doormen should get about 50¢–$1 a bag ($1 or more in a luxury hotel). For maid service, $1 a day is sufficient ($2 in luxury hotels).

Opening and Closing Times

Stores, shops, and supermarkets are usually open Monday through Saturday from 9 to 6—although in major cities, supermarkets are often open from 7:30 AM until 9 PM. Blue laws are in effect in much of Canada, but a growing number of provinces have stores with limited Sunday hours (usually from noon to 5). Retail stores are generally open on Thursday and Friday evenings, most shopping malls until 9 PM. Most banks in Canada are open Monday through Thursday from 10 to 3, and from 10 to 5 or 6 on Friday. Some banks are open longer hours and are also open on Saturday morning. All banks are closed on national holidays. Drugstores in major cities are often open until 11 PM, and convenience stores are often open 24 hours a day, seven days a week.

GST and Sales Tax

A countrywide goods and services tax of 7% (GST) applies on virtually every transaction in Canada except for the purchase of basic groceries. Nonresidents can get a full GST refund on any purchase taken out of the country and on short-term accommodations (but not on food, drink, tobacco, car or motorhome rentals, or transportation); rebate forms, which must be submitted within 60 days of leaving Canada, may be obtained from certain retailers, duty-free shops, customs officials, or Revenue Canada (Visitor's Rebate Program, Ottawa, Ont. K1A 1J5). Instant rebates are provided by some duty-free shops when leaving Canada, and most provinces do not tax goods that are shipped directly by the vendor to the purchaser's home. You'll need your sales slips.

In addition to the GST, all provinces except Alberta, the Northwest Territories, and the Yukon levy a sales tax from 4% to 12% on most items purchased in shops, on restaurant meals, and sometimes on hotel rooms. New Brunswick charges an 11% tax on hotel rooms. Nova Scotia and Newfoundland offer a sales-tax rebate system similar to the federal one; call the provincial toll-free information lines for details (*see* Government Tourist Offices, *above*).

Shopping

The current favorable exchange rate can mean savings for Americans, even considering the sales tax and GST.

Arts and Crafts Sweaters, silver objects, pottery, and Acadian crafts can be found in abundance in New Brunswick. For pewter, head for Fredericton. For woven items, visit the village of St. Andrews. In Québec, check out the wood carvings. The Mennonite communities of Ontario sell their handmade quilts each May at the Mennonite Relief sale. Prices can run to $2,000 for a large quilt.

Maple Syrup Eastern Canada is famous for its sugar maples. The trees are tapped in early spring, and the sap is collected in buckets to be boiled down into maple syrup. This natural confection is sold all year. Avoid the tourist shops and department stores; for the best prices and information, stop at farm stands and markets in the provinces of Québec, Ontario, and New Brunswick. A small can of syrup costs about $6–$9.

Sports and Outdoor Activities

Biking   Eastern Canada offers some of the best bicycling in the country, from the flats of Prince Edward Island to the varied terrain of New Brunswick and Nova Scotia. Write to the provincial tourist boards for road maps (which are more detailed than the maps available at gas stations) and information on local cycling associations.

Boating   Boating is extremely popular throughout Canada. Boat rentals are widely available, and provincial tourism departments can provide lists of companies.

Camping   Canada's 2,000-plus campgrounds range from simple roadside turnoffs with sweeping mountain vistas to fully equipped facilities with groomed sites, trailer hookups, recreational facilities, and vacation village atmosphere. Many of the best sites are in Canada's national and provincial parks, with nominal overnight fees. Commercial campgrounds offer more amenities, such as electrical and water hookups, showers, and even game rooms and grocery stores. They cost more and are—some think—antithetical to the point of camping: getting a little closer to nature. Contact tourist offices for listings.

Canoeing and Kayaking   Your degree of expertise and experience will dictate where you will canoe. Beginners will look for waterways in more settled areas; the pros will head north to the streams and rivers that flow into the Arctic Ocean. Provincial tourist offices and the federal Department of Northern Development and Indian Affairs (Ottawa, Ont. K1A OH4, tel. 819/997–0002) can be of assistance, especially in locating an outfitter to suit your needs. You can also contact the **Canadian Recreational Canoeing Association** (5–1029 Hyde Park Rd., London, Ont. N0M 1Z0, tel. 519/473–2109).

Fishing   Anglers can find their catch in virtually any region of the country, though restrictions, seasons, license requirements, and bag limits vary from province to province. In addition, a special fishing permit is required to fish in all national parks; it can be obtained at any national park site, for a nominal fee. **Newfoundland** offers cod, mackerel, salmon, and sea trout in the Atlantic and speckled trout and rainbow trout in its other waters. The waters surrounding **Prince Edward Island** have some of the best deep-sea tuna fishing. **Nova Scotia** has some of the most stringent freshwater restrictions in Canada, but the availability of Atlantic salmon, speckled trout, and striped bass makes the effort worthwhile. Salmon, trout, and black bass are abundant in the waters of **New Brunswick,** and although many salmon pools in the streams and rivers are leased to private freeholders, either individuals or clubs, fly fishing is still readily available for visitors.

Hiking   Miles and miles of trails weave through all of Canada's national and provincial parks. Write to the individual provincial tourist offices (*see* Essential Information in individual chapters) or the Inquiry Center for the National Parks Department (Environment Canada, Ottawa, Ontario K1A 0H3, tel. 819/997–2800).

Scuba Diving   More than 3,000 shipwrecks lie off the coast of Nova Scotia, making it particularly attractive to divers. The provincial Department of Tourism can provide details on the location of wrecks and where to buy or rent equipment.

Skiing Skiing is probably the most popular winter sport in Canada, with downhill and cross-country skiing available in every province.

Whale Watching On the Atlantic coast, the waters around Newfoundland offer excellent whale watching, and giant humpback, right whales, finback and minke whales can be seen in the Bay of Fundy. Boat trips are available from New Brunswick and Nova Scotia.

Winter Sports Canadians flourish in winter, as the range of winter sports attests. In addition to the sports already mentioned, at the first drop of a snowflake Canadians will head outside to ice-skate, toboggan, snowmobile, dogsled, snowshoe, and ice-fish.

Dining

The earliest European settlers of Canada—the British and the French—bequeathed a rather bland diet of meat and potatoes. But though there are few really distinct national dishes here, the strong ethnic presence in Canada makes it difficult not to have a good meal. This is especially true in the larger cities, where Greek, Italian, Chinese, Indian, and other immigrants operate restaurants. In addition, each province is well known for various specialties. **Newfoundland, Nova Scotia, New Brunswick,** and **Prince Edward Island** are known for their seafood. Fiddleheads, curled young fern fronds picked in the spring, often accompany dishes in the restaurants of the maritime provinces.

Lodging

Canada's range of accommodations more closely resembles that of the United States than Europe. In the cities you'll have a choice of luxury hotels, moderately priced modern properties, and smaller older hotels with perhaps fewer conveniences but a bit more charm. Options in smaller towns and in the country include large full-service resorts; small, privately owned hotels; roadside motels; and bed-and-breakfast establishments. Canada's answer to the small European family-run hotel is the mom-and-pop motel, but even though Canada is as attuned to automobile travel as the United States, you won't find these motels as frequently. Even here you'll need to make reservations at least on the day on which you're planning to pull into town.

Chain Hotels There are two advantages to staying at a chain hotel. The first is that you'll be assured of standard accommodations, your own bathroom, and a range of services at the front desk. The second is the ease with which you can get information and make or change reservations, since most chains have toll-free booking numbers.

The major hotel chains in Canada include **Best Western International** (tel. 800/528–1234, in the U.K., 081/541–0033), **CP (Canadian Pacific) Hotels & Resorts** (tel. 800/828–7447, in the U.K., 071/798–9866), **Delta Hotels** (tel. 800/877–1133, in the U.K., 071/937–8033), **Holiday Inns** (tel. 800/465–4329, in the U.K., 071/722–7755), 081/688–1640), **Radisson Hotels** (tel. 800/333–3333, in the U.K., 0992/441517), **Ramada** (tel. 800/228–2828, in the U.K., 071/235–5264), and **Sheraton** (tel. 800/325–3535, in the U.K., 0800/353535).

Room Rates Expect accommodations to cost more in summer, peak tourist season, than in the off-season. But don't be afraid to ask about special deals and packages when reserving. Big city hotels that cater to business travelers often offer weekend packages, and many city hotels offer rooms at up to 50% off in winter. If you're planning to visit a major city or resort area during the high season, book well in advance. Also be aware of any special events or festivals that may coincide with your visit and block every room for miles around. For resorts and lodges, consider the winter ski-season high as well and plan accordingly (*See* GST and Sales Tax, *above*).

Bed-and-Breakfasts and Country Inns One way to save on lodging and spend some time with a native Canadian is to stay at a bed-and-breakfast establishment. They are gaining in popularity and are located in both the country and the cities. Every provincial tourist board either has a listing of B&Bs or can refer you to an association that will help you secure reservations. Rates range from $20 to $70 a night and include a Continental or a full breakfast. Because most bed-and-breakfasts are in private homes, you might not have your own bathroom. And some B&B hosts lock up early. Be sure to ask about your host's policies. Room quality varies from home to home as well, so don't be bashful about asking to see a room before making a choice. **Fodor's** guide *Canada's Great Country Inns* lists wonderful places to stay from coast to coast—from unpretentious houses with something special to the elegant Relais & Châteaux (*see below*). You can buy it in most bookstores or ask to have it ordered.

Credit Cards

The following credit card abbreviations are used throughout this guide: AE, American Express; D, Discover; DC, Diners Club; MC, MasterCard; V, Visa. It's a good idea to call ahead to check current credit-card policies.

2 Nova Scotia

*By Silver Donald
Cameron*

*Novelist, playwright,
and sailor, Silver
Donald Cameron is
one of Canada's most
versatile authors. His
recent books* Wind,
Whales and Whisky,
A Cape Breton
Voyage *and* Sniffing
the Coast: An
Acadian Voyage
*record cruises in
Nova Scotia and
Prince Edward
Island with his wife
and son in*
Silversark, *a 27-foot
cruising sailboat,
which they built
themselves.*

"Infinite riches in a little room," said Elizabethan playwright
Christopher Marlowe. Was he speaking of Nova Scotia, Canada's second-smallest province that packs an impossible variety of cultures and landscapes into a mass that's half the size
of Ohio?

Nova Scotia's landscapes echo every region of Canada. Mountain clefts in Cape Breton Island could pass for crannies in British Columbia. Stretches of the Tantramar Marshes are as
board-flat as the prairies. The glaciated interior, spruce-
swathed and peppered with lakes, looks just like the Canadian
Shield in northern Manitoba. The apple blossoms in the Annapolis Valley are as glorious as those in Niagara, and parts of
Halifax could masquerade as downtown Toronto. A massive
Catholic church in a tiny French village recalls Québec. The
warm salt water and long sandy beaches of Prince Edward Island are also found on the mainland side of Northumberland
Strait, and the brick-red mudflats of the Bay of Fundy echo
their counterparts in New Brunswick. Neil's Harbour looks
just like a Newfoundland outport—and sounds like one, too,
since many of its people are Newfoundlanders by origin.

As with the land, so with the people. The Micmac Indians have
been here for 10,000 years. The French came to the Annapolis
Basin in 1605. In the 1750s, the English settled cockneys and
Irish in Halifax and "Foreign Protestants"—chiefly Ger-
mans—in Lunenburg. By then Yankees from New England
were putting down roots in Liverpool, Cape Sable Island, and
the Annapolis Valley. In the 1780s they were joined by thousands of "Loyalists"—many of them black—displaced by the
American Revolution. Soon after, the Scots poured into northern Nova Scotia and Cape Breton, evicted from the Highlands
by their landlords' preference for sheep. The last wave of immigrants, in the 1890s, became steelworkers and coal miners
in Cape Breton. They came from Wales, the West Indies, Poland, the Ukraine, and the Middle East. They're all Nova Scotians, and they're all still here, eating their own foods,
worshipping in their own churches, speaking in their rich, full-
flavored voices.

Infinite riches: Gaelic street signs in Pugwash and Mabou.
French masses in Cheticamp and Point de l'Eglise. Black gos-
pel choirs in Halifax and Micmac handcrafts in Eskasoni.
Onion-dome churches in Sydney, sauerkraut in Lunenburg,
and Yankee Puritanism in Clark's Harbour.

This is a little buried nation, compact and distinctive, with a
capital city the same size as Marlowe's London. Before Canada
was formed in 1867, Nova Scotians were prosperous ship-
wrights and merchants, trading with the world. Who created
Cunard Lines? A Haligonian, Samuel Cunard. Those spacious
days brought democracy to the British colonies, left Victorian
mansions in all the salty little ports that dot the coastline, and
created a uniquely Nova Scotian outlook: worldly, approach-
able, sturdily independent.

"Infinite riches in a little room." Kit Marlowe would love it here.

Essential Information

Important Addresses and Numbers

Tourist Information The **Nova Scotia Department of Tourism and Culture** (Box 456, Halifax, NS B3J 2R5, tel. 902/424–5000) publishes a range of literature, including an exhaustive annual travel guide to sights, accommodations, and transportation.

Halifax The **Nova Scotia Tourism Information Centre** (Old Red Store at Historic Properties, tel. 902/424–4247), and **Tourism Halifax** (City Hall, Duke and Barrington Sts., tel. 902/421–8736) are open mid-June–Labor Day, daily 9–6, and sometimes later; Labor Day–mid-June, weekdays 9–4:30.

Emergencies Dial "0" for operator in emergencies; check the front of the local phone book for specific medical services.

Hospital **Victoria General** (tel. 902/428–2110) is Halifax's major hospital.

Arriving and Departing

By Plane The **Halifax International Airport** is 40 kilometers (25 miles) northeast of downtown Halifax. **Sidney Airport** is 13 kilometers (8 miles) east of Sidney.

Air Canada (tel. 902/429–7111 or 800/776–3000) provides regular, daily service to Halifax and Sydney, Nova Scotia, from New York, Boston, Toronto, Montréal, and St. John's, Newfoundland. **Canadian Airlines International** (tel. 800/527–8499) has service to Halifax via Toronto and Montréal. **Air Nova** (tel. 902/429–7111 or 800/776–3000) and **Air Atlantic** (tel. 800/426–7000 or 800/665–1177 in Canada) provide regional service to both airports with flights to Toronto, Montréal, and Boston.

Between Airport and City Center Airport bus service to most of Halifax's downtown hotels costs $18 round-trip, $11 one-way. Normal taxi fare is $33 each way, but if you book in advance with **Aero Cab** (tel. 902/445–3393) the fare is $24.60 cash, slightly more by credit card (MC or V). The trip takes 30–40 minutes.

By Car The Trans-Canada Highway reaches Nova Scotia through New Brunswick. Entering the province at Amherst, it becomes Highway 104. To reach Halifax, pick up Highway 102 at Truro. To reach Cape Breton, continue on Highway 104.

Highways throughout Nova Scotia, numbered from 100 to 199, are all-weather, limited-access roads, with 100 kilometers-per-hour (62.5 miles-per-hour) speed limits. The last two digits usually match the number of an older trunk highway along the same route, numbered from 1 to 99. Thus, Highway 102, between Halifax and Truro, matches the older Route 2, between the same towns. Roads numbered from 200 to 399 are secondary roads that usually link villages. Unless otherwise posted, the speed limit is 80 kilometers per hour (50 miles per hour) except on the 100-series highways.

Most highways in the province lead to Halifax-Dartmouth. Highways 3/103, 7, 2/102, and 1/101 terminate in the twin cities.

Rental Cars Halifax is the most convenient place from which to begin your driving tour of the province. The following list details city and airport venues of rental-car agencies: **Avis** (5600 Sackville St., tel. 902/423–6303; airport, tel. 902/873–3523); **Budget** (1558 Hollis St., tel. 902/421–1242; airport, tel. 902/873–3509); **Hertz** (Halifax Sheraton, tel. 902/421–1763; airport, tel. 902/873–3700); **Thrifty** (6930 Lady Hammond, tel. 902/422–4455; airport, tel. 902/873–3527); **Tilden** (1130 Hollis St., tel. 902/422–4433; airport, tel. 902/873–3505).

By Ferry Three car ferries connect Nova Scotia with Maine and New Brunswick. **Marine Atlantic** (tel. 800/341–7981) sails from Bar Harbor, Maine, and **Prince of Fundy Cruises** (tel. 800/341–7540) from Portland; both arrive in Yarmouth. From Saint John, New Brunswick, to Digby, Nova Scotia, ferry service is provided by **Marine Atlantic** (tel. 800/565–9470 in New Brunswick).

Marine Atlantic also operates ferries between New Brunswick and Prince Edward Island, and between Cape Breton and Newfoundland. In Nova Scotia, call 902/794–5700; in Newfoundland, 709/772–7701.

Between May and December, **Northumberland Ferries** (tel. 902/485–6580; in Nova Scotia, 800/565–0201) operate between Caribou, Nova Scotia, and Wood Islands, Prince Edward Island.

By Train **Via Rail** (tel. 800/561–3949) provides service from Montréal to Halifax via Moncton and Saint John, in New Brunswick; and Amherst and Truro, in Nova Scotia.

Amtrak (tel. 800/USA–RAIL) from New York City makes connections in Montréal.

By Bus **Greyhound** (800/231–2222) from New York, and **Voyageur Inc.** (tel. 613/238–5900) from Montréal, connect with **Scotia Motor Tours** or **SMT** (tel. 506/458–6000) through New Brunswick, which links (rather inconveniently) with **Acadian Lines Limited** (tel. 902/454–8279), which provides inter-urban services within Nova Scotia.

Getting Around

Halifax Walking and biking are excellent ways to get around and see the city, especially on weekdays when parking in the downtown area can be a problem. A pleasant alternative, however, is to take one of the rickshaws, available downtown during summer.

By Taxi Rates begin at about $2.40 and increase based on mileage and time. A crosstown trip should cost $4–$5, depending on traffic. Hailing a taxi can be difficult, but there are taxi stands at major hotels and shopping malls. Most Haligonians simply phone for a taxi service. Call **Aero Cab** (tel. 902/445–3393).

By Bus The **Metropolitan Transit Commission** (tel. 902/421–6600) bus system covers the entire Halifax-Dartmouth area. The base fare is $1.15 adults, 65¢ children 5–15; exact change only.

By Ferry The **Dartmouth Ferry Commission** (tel. 902/464–2336) runs two-passenger ferries from the George Street terminal in Halifax to the Portland Street and Woodbine terminals in Dartmouth, from 6 AM to midnight on an hourly and half-hourly schedule. The fare for a single crossing is 65¢, which is well worth it considering you get an up-close view of both waterfronts.

Elsewhere in Nova Scotia You will need a car to explore the province beyond Halifax. For rental car information, *see* Rental Cars in Arriving and Departing by Car, *above.*

As you explore Nova Scotia, be on the lookout for the 10 designated "Scenic Trails" that appear throughout the province and are easily identified by roadside signs with icons that correspond with trail names. These routes, as well as tourist literature (maps and the provincial *Tour Guide*) that has been published in accordance with this scheme, have been developed by the Nova Scotia Department of Tourism and Culture.

Guided Tours

Boat Tours **Halifax Water Tours** (tel. 902/420–1015) operates an excellent two-hour, narrated cruise of Halifax Harbor and the Northwest Arm, from mid-June through October. Tours depart from Privateer's Wharf up to four times a day in mid-season, and cost $13.50 for adults, $12.50 for senior citizens, $10 for youths 13–18, $8 children 5–12, $29.50 families.

Bluenose II (tel. 902/422–2678 or 902/424–5000) is an exact replica of Nova Scotia's 143-foot fishing schooner *Bluenose*, the ship that was the undefeated champion in international schooner racing for nearly 20 years and is featured on the Canadian dime. *Bluenose II* departs from Privateer's Wharf three times daily on a two-hour harbor sail in summer. Fares are $14 for adults, $7 for senior citizens and children, but are subject to change.

Bus Tours Both **Gray Line Sightseeing** (tel. 902/454–8279) and **Cabana Tours** (tel. 902/423–6066) run coach tours through Halifax-Dartmouth and Peggy's Cove. **Halifax Double Decker Tours** (tel. 902/420–1155) offers two-hour tours on double-decker buses that leave daily from Historic Properties. You can also charter a bus from the **Metropolitan Transit Commission** (tel. 902/421–6600) for a narrated tour.

Exploring Nova Scotia

Highlights for First-time Visitors

Cape Breton Highlands National Park, Tour 4: Cape Breton Island
Fortress Louisbourg National Historic Park, Tour 4: Cape Breton Island
Halifax Citadel National Historic Park, Tour 1: Halifax and Dartmouth
Historic Annapolis Royal, Tour 2: The South Shore and Annapolis Valley
Historic Properties and *Bluenose II*, Tour 1: Halifax and Dartmouth
Lunenburg's Nautical Heritage, Tour 2: The South Shore and Annapolis Valley
Pictou's Scottish Heritage, Tour 3: Northern Nova Scotia
Sherbrooke Village, Tour 3: Northern Nova Scotia

Tour 1: Halifax and Dartmouth

Numbers in the margin correspond to points of interest on the Nova Scotia and Halifax maps.

❶ Salty and urbane, learned and plain-spoken, **Halifax** is large enough to have the trappings of a capital city—symphonies and scandals, smart hotels and carnivorous consultants, spicy gossip and first-class air service—and yet small enough to retain the warmth and convenience of a small town. In their hearts, Haligonians know there is no better place to live.

They may be right, too.

❷ Begin your walking tour at **Purdy's Wharf**—twin office towers shaped like milk cartons with feet, standing right in the harbor. Much of downtown Halifax is connected by overhead pedways, making it convenient for executives in Purdy's Wharf to shop, lunch, meet with bankers and brokers, and greet out-of-town guests without venturing outdoors. Take the pedway to the Sheraton, built low to match the historic ironstone buildings next door. If the weather is fine, try the Sheraton's outdoor bar, right on the water, and admire the schooner *Bluenose II* (*see* Guided Tours, *above*) and the ketch *White Heather,* moored alongside and awaiting charter parties.

❸ Next door are the warehouses of **Historic Properties,** dating from the early 19th century when trade and war made Halifax prosperous. They were built by such raffish characters as Enos Collins, who did business in the Collins Bank building. A privateer, smuggler, and shipper whose vessels defied Napoleon's blockade to bring American supplies to the Duke of Wellington, Collins was also a prime mover into the Halifax Banking Company, which evolved into the Royal Bank of Canada, the country's largest bank. Look up and to the right: There's the Royal Bank's office tower, three blocks away. When Collins died in 1871, at 99, he was said to be the richest man in Canada. The buildings have been taken over by quality shops and restaurants, boisterous pubs, and chic offices.

Walk along the water behind the modern Law Courts to the **❹** **Dartmouth ferry terminal,** jammed with commuters during the rush hour. Beyond lies the Cable Wharf, so named because it was once home to the ships that laid the undersea telegraph and telephone cables to Europe. There's a fishmarket here and a floating restaurant.

Pass the offices of the federal Department of Fisheries (other government offices are in the Central Guaranty Trust tower, **❺** across the street) and you'll arrive at the **Maritime Museum of the Atlantic,** housed in a restored chandlery and warehouse. The exhibits include an assortment of small boats once used around the coast, as well as displays describing Nova Scotia's proud heritage of sail—when the province, on its own, was one of the world's foremost shipbuilding and trading nations. *1675 Lower Water St., tel. 902/424–7490 or 902/424–7491. Admission free. Open year-round but times vary so call ahead.*

The wharves outside the museum are favorite berths for visiting transatlantic yachts and sail-training ships; at any time you may find South American and European square-riggers, classic yachts, and even Viking longships. The hydrographic steamer *Acadia* is moored here permanently, after a long life of charting the coasts of Labrador and the Arctic.

At the next wharf, in summer, is Canada's naval memorial, HMCS *Sackville,* the sole survivor of a fleet of doughty little corvettes (highly maneuverable warships) that escorted convoys of ships from Halifax to England during World War II. An interpretation center (open mid-June–Sept., Mon.–Sat. 10–5, Sun. 1–5), adjacent to the ship, explains that the convoys assembled in Bedford Basin, Halifax's vast inner harbor, where the first ships were launched in the early morning and others would follow in a steady stream all day long. The last ones would still be steaming out late at night.

Time Out   Between the Maritime Museum and Cornwallis Place (the modern office building just to the south) is an open square and playground at the bottom of Sackville Street. The square is a favorite lunchtime promenade for Halifax office workers, and a setting for concerts associated with the Atlantic Jazz Festival. This is a perfect people-watching or picnic spot. Coffee shops and restaurants are within a few blocks, mostly back the way we came.

6 Just south of the square is the **tugboat terminal,** which is about to become world famous: Andrew Cochran Associates—a local film company—recently produced an animated television series called *Theodore Tugboat,* based on the ships' fictional adventures.

Leave the tugboats and walk up to Water Street and enter the
7 **Brewery Market,** a sprawling ironstone complex that was once Keith's Brewery (named for its Alexander Keith, a 19th-century brewer) but now houses boutiques, offices, restaurants, and a Farmers' Market. This area is a favored haunt of knowledgeable Haligonians on Saturday mornings.

Take the elevator at the office-end of the complex, and emerge on Hollis Street. Turn left, past several elegant Victorian townhouses—notably Keith Hall (1475 Hollis St.)—once the executive offices of the brewery. Turn right on Bishop Street and walk up to Barrington Street, Halifax's main downtown thoroughfare. Ahead of you is the **Technical University of Nova Scotia,** one of six Halifax universities; it offers degrees in engineering, architecture, and similar fields.

Turn right on Barrington. The stone mansion on your right is
8 **Government House,** the official residence of Nova Scotia's Lieutenant-Governor, built in 1799 for Sir John Wentworth, the Loyalist governor of New Hampshire and his racy wife, Fanny. Thomas Raddall's novel *The Governor's Lady* tells their story. Across the street is **The Old Burying Ground,** the city's first cemetery, dating from 1749. One of its residents is General Robert Ross, leader of the attack on Baltimore in 1814 that inspired the anthem *The Star-Spangled Banner.* Its Sebastopol Monument honors two Halifax heroes of the Crimean War (1853–1856).

Beyond Government House is **St. Matthew's Church** (1859), and **Maritime Centre,** a towering office block above a shopping mall. Turn left on Spring Garden Road and go past the Catholic cathedral church to **St. Mary's Basilica** (1833), with the tallest polished-granite spire in the world.

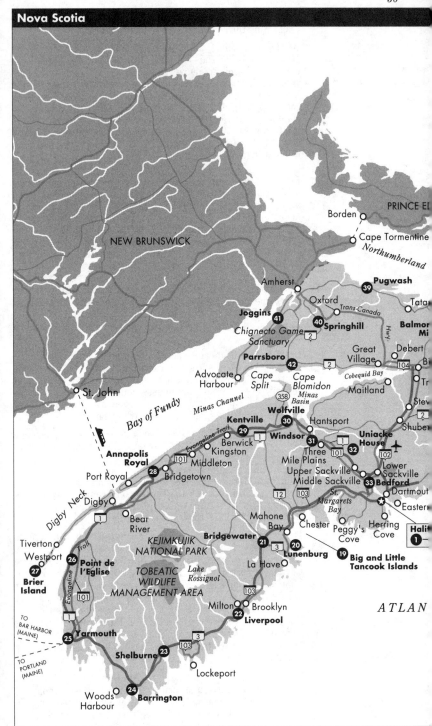

Nova Scotia

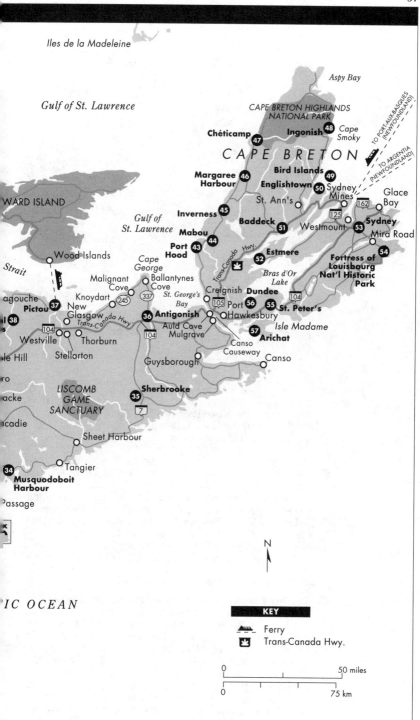

Iles de la Madeleine

Gulf of St. Lawrence

Aspy Bay

CAPE BRETON HIGHLANDS
NATIONAL PARK

Chéticamp 47   **Ingonish** 48   *Cape Smoky*

C A P E   B R E T O N

TO PORT AUX BASQUES
(NEWFOUNDLAND)

TO ARGENTIA
(NEWFOUNDLAND)

Margaree Harbour 46   **Bird Islands**   **Englishtown** 50   Sydney Mines

Englishtown 49

St. Ann's   Glace Bay

WARD ISLAND

Gulf of St. Lawrence

Inverness 45   **Baddeck** 51   162   **Sydney** 53

Mabou 44   125   Westmount   Mira Road

Port Hood 43   *Bras d'Or Lake*   **Estmere** 52

Wood Islands   *Cape George*   Ballantynes Cove   **Dundee**   **Fortress of Louisbourg Nat'l Historic Park** 54

Strait   Malignant Cove   245   *St. George's Bay*   Creignish   104

agouche   Knoydart   337   105   Port Hawkesbury   **St. Peter's** 55

Pictou 37   New Glasgow   **Antigonish** 36   **Dundee** 56

38   Trans-Canada Hwy   Auld Cove   *Isle Madame*

Westville   104   104   Mulgrave   **Arichat** 57

le Hill   Thorburn   Canso Causeway   Canso

Stellarton   Guysborough   Canso

ro

acke   LISCOMB GAME SANCTUARY   **Sherbrooke**

acadie   35

7

34   Sheet Harbour

Musquodoboit Harbour   Tangier

Passage

IC OCEAN

N

KEY

🚌 Ferry

🔽 Trans-Canada Hwy.

0 ————————— 50 miles

0 ————————— 75 km

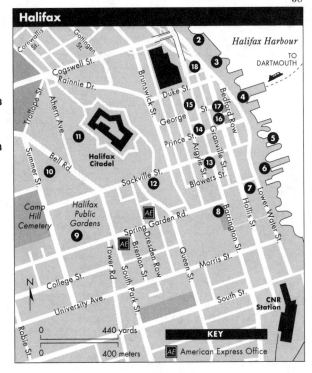

Time Out In the summer, the front lawn of the public library is crowded with people listening to street singers and snacking on french fries bought from **Bud the Spud,** a chip-wagon parked at the curb. Surrounding the lawn are plenty of opportunities for a more substantial take-out lunch.

9 From the library walk west on Spring Garden Road to the South Park Street entrance of the **Halifax Public Gardens,** where the statues of Robbie Burns and Sir Walter Scott face one another from across Spring Garden Road. The gardens were first laid out in 1753, but the present design was created in 1889 by Richard Power, who had been gardener to the Duke of Devonshire. Power's descendants cared for the gardens until the 1960s. Gravel paths wind among ponds, trees, and flower beds, revealing an astonishing variety of plants from all over the world. The centerpiece is a filigreed bandstand erected in 1887 for Queen Victoria's Golden Jubilee.

10 The **Nova Scotia Museum of Natural History,** on the South Commons, holds collections of human and natural-history artifacts and administers them to the smaller provincial museums throughout Nova Scotia. The museum is best known for its exhibits and events honoring tiny frogs known as "spring peepers." A huge fiberglass frog is mounted on the corner of the building, beginning in May and lasting until the real creatures fall silent in the autumn. *1747 Summer St., tel. 902/424–7353. Admission: $2.25 adults, 50¢ children 5–16. Open mid-May–Oct., Mon., Tues., Thurs.–Sun. 9:30–5:30 and Wed. 9:30–8; Nov.–early May, Tues., Thurs.–Sun. 9:30–5, Wed. 9:30–8.*

⑪ Between the Commons and the compact downtown rises the green bulk of **Citadel Hill,** topped by its star-shaped fort. The Citadel was the heart of the city's fortifications, and was linked to smaller forts and gun emplacements on the harbor islands and on the bluffs above the entrance. It is now a National Historic Site, with kilted soldiers drilling in front of the **Army Museum,** once the barracks. Every day at noon a cannon is fired; some local businesspeople in the towers below time their negotiations so the cannon's blast will throw their associates offstride. *Citadel Hill, tel. 902/426–5080. Admission: mid-June–Labor Day, $2 adults, $1 children, senior citizens free. Open July–Labor Day, daily 9–6; Labor Day–mid-June, daily 10–5.*

Most of the city's secondary fortifications have been turned into public parks. **Point Pleasant Park,** a favorite recreation spot, encompasses 186 wooded acres, veined with walking trails and seafront paths. The park was leased from the military by the city for 999 years, at a shilling a year. Its major military installation is a massive round Martello tower dating from the late 18th century. Point Pleasant is about 12 blocks down South Park Street from Spring Garden Road.

The handsome four-sided **Town Clock** on Citadel Hill was given to Halifax by Prince Edward, Duke of Kent, military commander from 1794 to 1800. The prince was enamored of round buildings, of which two survive: **St. George's Church,** downtown at Brunswick and Cornwallis streets, and **Julie's Music Room,** on a knoll beside the Bedford Highway. "Julie" was the prince's French mistress, with whom he lived for more than 20 years before being summoned to marry a princess and produce an heir to the British throne. He did his duty, and the result was Queen Victoria.

Pause over the view from the Citadel, and take in the details: the spiky downtown crowded between the hilltop and the harbor; the wooded islands at the harbor's mouth; and the naval dockyard under the Angus L. MacDonald Bridge, the nearer of the two bridges connecting Halifax with its sister city of Dartmouth.

⑫ From the Citadel, walk down Sackville Street toward the harbor. On your right is the **Royal Artillery Park,** with its little-known but excellent military library. The School Board building at Sackville and Brunswick streets is the old Halifax Academy, attended by author Hugh MacLennan.

⑬ Farther down Sackville, where it meets Argyle Street, is the **Neptune Theatre,** Canada's first professional repertory theater, which offers full summer and winter seasons. Argyle Street is the center of the Halifax dining and nightlife scene and a lively place on a Saturday night. A block north of the theater is the **Carleton Hotel,** built of cut stone from the original Fortress of Louisbourg. The hotel, which dates from 1760, was once the home of Richard Bulkeley, one of Halifax's founders, and it later served as a Court of Admiralty.

⑭ Turn left on Barrington Street. A block north is **St. Paul's Church** (1749), Canada's oldest Protestant church, Britain's first overseas cathedral, and the burial site of many colonial notables. Inside, on the north end, a piece of metal is embedded in the wall. It is a fragment of the *Mont Blanc,* one of the two ships whose collision caused the Halifax Explosion of December 1917, the greatest manmade explosion prior to Hiroshima. The blast flattened a square mile of the North End and left 2,000 dead, another 2,000 seriously injured, and 6,000 homeless.

⑮ Leaving St. Paul's, you will find yourself on the **Grand Parade,** facing City Hall. Musicians perform here at noon on fine summer days. From here, look uphill: The tall, stylish brick building is the **World Trade and Convention Centre** and is attached to the 10,000-seat **Halifax Metro Centre**—the site of hockey games, rock concerts, and political conventions. Farther to the right are the office towers above **Scotia Square,** the leading downtown shopping mall.

⑯ Walk downhill a block, and you'll see **Province House,** "a gem of Georgian architecture," according to Charles Dickens. The provincial legislature still meets in this lovely sandstone building, erected in 1819. *Hollis St., tel. 902/424–5982. Admission free. Open weekdays 9–6, Sat. 9–4.*

Across Hollis, on Cheapside—a pedestrian-way directly oppo-
⑰ site Province House—is the **Art Gallery of Nova Scotia,** which features work by Canadian and international artists. The gallery, housed in a renovated four-story building, displays extensive collections of maritime, Canadian, and folk art, and hosts contemporary traveling exhibitions from around the world. *1741 Hollis St. at Cheapside, tel. 902/424–7542. Admission: $2.50 adults, $1.25 students and senior citizens, children under 12 free, $5.50 families. Open June–Oct., Tues., Wed., Fri., Sat. 10–5:30, Thurs. 10–9, Sun. noon–5:30; Sept.–May, Tues–Fri. 10–5, Sat.–Sun. noon–5.*

Return to Province House, turn left, and go one block back to Historic Properties, where this tour began. In addition to owning the warehouses near Purdy's Wharf, Historic Properties also owns the 19th-century buildings between Granville, Duke, and Lower Water streets, at Duke. The upper floors of most of these buildings are used by the **Nova Scotia College of Art and Design** (NSCAD)—the first degree-granting arts university in Canada and a formidable influence in the world of art.

Go up the hill a block to Granville Street, past NSCAD's unobtrusive main entrance and turn right at the Split Crow pub, into the one-block **pedestrian mall** with its iron park benches, outdoor cafés, and chic shops. Near the end of the block is the
⑱ **Anna Leonowens Gallery,** which belongs to NSCAD, and often shows the most challenging exhibits in Halifax. The gallery is named for the College's founder, a remarkable Victorian woman who served the King of Siam as governess and wrote a book about the experience; Rodgers and Hammerstein eventually turned it into the Broadway production of *The King and I*, starring Yul Brynner and Deborah Kerr. *1891 Granville St., tel. 902/422–7381. Admission free. Open Tues.–Fri. 11–5, Sat. noon–4.*

Turn right when you leave the gallery. At the end of the block, look toward the harbor: Just across the street is the Sheraton, *Bluenose II*, and Privateer's Warehouse. Welcome back to the beginning of the tour. From here, the tour continues on to two areas: the Northwest Arm and Dartmouth. To continue the tour it will be necessary to travel by car.

"The Arm" is Halifax's recreational secondary harbor, with a popular park, many elegant waterfront homes, and two yacht clubs. From Historic Properties, follow either Duke Street or Cogswell Street (both converge at the Commons) to Quinpool Road, a busy shopping street. Quinpool takes you to a traffic circle called the Armdale Rotary, which heads the Northwest Arm. Take the exit for Purcell's Cove Road (Rte. 253), which winds along the Arm to the pretty village of **Purcell's Cove,** and passes the Armdale Yacht Club, Flemming Park, the Royal Nova Scotia Yacht Squadron, and the historic cliff-top fortifications of York Redoubt, before ending at the tiny fishing harbor of **Herring Cove.** There is no similar shorefront drive on the Halifax side of the Arm, though several Halifax streets terminate at the Arm's shores.

Dartmouth is Nova Scotia's second city, but it has always been overshadowed by the capital. It was first settled by Quaker whalers from Nantucket, and boasts Canada's largest Coast Guard base and Nova Scotia's most successful industrial park, at Burnside. The 23 lakes within Dartmouth's boundaries provided the Micmacs with a canoe route to the province's interior and to the Bay of Fundy. A 19th-century canal system connected the lakes for a brief time, but today there are only ruins, which have been partially restored as heritage sites.

Halifax-Dartmouth has North America's third-largest concentration of marine scientists, mostly due to the **Bedford Institute of Oceanography,** off Windmill Road just under the A. Murray Mackay Bridge. The institute also has a substantial fleet of specialized ships and submersibles. Visitors can take self-guided walking tours of the facility, or guided tours by reservation; call ahead. *Challenger Dr., tel. 902/426–4093. Admission free. Open weekdays 9–4.*

Tour 2: The South Shore and Annapolis Valley

Mainland Nova Scotia is a long, narrow peninsula; no point in the province is more than 56 kilometers (35 miles) from salt water. The South Shore is on the Atlantic side, the Annapolis Valley on the Fundy side, and though they are less than an hour apart by car, the two destinations seem like different worlds.

The South Shore is rocky coast, island-dotted bays, fishing villages, and shipyards; the Valley is lumber, farms, vineyards, and orchards. The South Shore is German, French, and Yankee; the Valley is stoutly British. The South Shore is Lutheran, Catholic, and Puritan and boasts a Catholic university; the Valley university is Baptist. The sea is everywhere on the South Shore; in the Valley the sea is blocked from view by a ridge of mountains.

Highway 103, Route 3, and various secondary roads form the province's designated **Lighthouse Route,** which leads from Halifax down the South Shore. It touches the heads of several big bays and small harbors, revealing an ever-changing panorama of shoreline, inlet, and island. Charming little towns are spaced out every 50 kilometers (30 miles) or thereabouts. This tour mostly focuses on the towns along the route, but you should follow the side roads whenever the inclination strikes; the South Shore rewards slow, relaxed exploration.

Leave Halifax on Route 3 or 103—or 333, the scenic road around the shore. **St. Margaret's Bay**, just minutes from Halifax, has always been a favorite summer haunt for Haligonians and is rapidly becoming an outer suburb.

Peggy's Cove, on Route 333, stands at the mouth of the bay facing the open Atlantic. The cove, with its houses huddled around the narrow slit in the boulders, is probably the most-photographed village in Canada. It also has the only Canadian post office located in a lighthouse (open April–November). Be careful exploring the bald, rocky shore. Incautious visitors have been swept to their deaths by the towering surf that sometimes breaks here.

Chester, with just over 1,100 people, is the first stop on Lunenburg County's Mahone Bay. The bay has literally hundreds of islands and, according to local claims, there is one for every day of the year. In summer Chester swells with its well-established population of U.S. visitors and Haligonians and with the sailing and yachting community. In mid-August the town celebrates **Chester Race Week,** the largest regatta in Atlantic Canada.

⓳ A passenger-only ferry runs from the dock in Chester to **Big and Little Tancook Islands,** 8 kilometers (5 miles) out in the bay. The boat runs four times daily Monday–Thursday; six times daily Friday; and twice daily on weekend days, and costs $1 for the 45-minute trip. Reflecting its part-German heritage, Big Tancook claims to make the best sauerkraut in Nova Scotia.

Take Route 12 inland from Chester to the **Ross Farm** at New Ross. The restored 19th-century farm-cum-museum illustrates the evolution of agriculture from 1600 to 1925. *Rte. 12, New Ross, tel. 902/689–2210. Admission: $2.25 adults, 50¢ children 5–16, $5.50 families. Open June–mid-Oct., daily 9:30–5:30.*

The town of **Mahone Bay** presents a dramatic face to visitors: Three tall wooden churches—of different denominations—stand side by side, their images reflected in the harbor water. Once a shipbuilding community, Mahone Bay is now a crafts center and also home to the **Wooden Boat Festival,** held during the first week of August, when the works of some of Lunenburg County's top wooden-boat builders are displayed.

⓴ **Lunenburg,** about 9½ kilometers (6 miles) away, is a feast of ornate German architecture, wooden boats, steel draggers (a fishing boat that operates a trawl), historic inns, and good restaurants. In the center of town is a national historic district, and the fantastic old school on the hilltop is the finest remaining example of Second Empire architecture, an ornate style that began in France.

Lunenburg also boasts being homeport to ***Bluenose*** and ***Bluenose II*** (*see* Guided Tours, *above*), the great racing schooner and its replica. Both were built at the Smith and Rhuland yard here, as was the replica of HMS *Bounty,* used in the film *Mutiny on the Bounty.*

The **Fisheries Museum of the Atlantic,** part of the Nova Scotia Museum complex, is housed in a renovated waterfront building and includes a traditional fishing schooner, the *Theresa E. Connor;* and a steel-hulled stern trawler, *Cape Sable;* as well as an aquarium; dory shop; and a wide range of displays. *Blue-*

nose Dr., tel. 902/634–4794. Admission: $2.25 adults, 50¢ children 5–16, $5.50 families. Open daily June–mid-Oct. 9:30–5:30.

Before leaving Lunenburg, you may want to visit the **Houston North Gallery,** which represents both trained and self-taught Nova Scotian artists and Inuit (Eskimo) soapstone carvers and printmakers. The gallery, in a large converted house, overlooks the harbor and is near the Fisheries Museum. *110 Montague St., tel. 902/634–8869. Open Feb.–Dec., Mon.–Sat. 10–6 and Sun. 1–6.*

㉑ **Bridgewater,** located at the head of navigation on the La Have River, is the main market town of the South Shore. Another of those towns whose focus was shipping and shipbuilding, Bridgewater, with its more than 7,000 residents, is now sustained by the large Michelin Tire plant nearby.

Just west of Bridgewater, on Route 325, is the **Wile Carding Mill,** which was built in 1860 and retains its original machinery. The mill itself was once powered by an overshot waterwheel. *242 Victoria Rd., tel. 902/543–8233. Admission free. Open June–Sept., Mon.–Sat. 9:30–5:30, Sun. 1–5:30.*

Farther down the La Have River, at La Have on Route 331, is **Fort Point Museum,** a former lighthouse-keeper's house that's open daily in the summer.

㉒ The Lighthouse Route winds on to **Liverpool,** on the estuary of the Mersey River. This community, settled around 1760 by New Englanders, is a fishing and paper-milling town and also serves as a convenient base for the 381-square-kilometer (147-square-mile) **Kejimkujik National Park,** an inland wilderness reached in about 45 minutes via Route 8. The Mersey is the oldest documented canoe route on the continent; it drains Lake Rossignol, Nova Scotia's largest freshwater lake. The interior of the province here is almost entirely unsettled and is ideally explored by canoe. There is also good trout and salmon fishing. For outfitters, go into the town of Greenfield, on Route 210, off Route 8.

During the American Revolution and the War of 1812, Liverpool was a privateering center; later, it became an important shipping and trading port. In the center of town is the **Simeon Perkins House** (109 Main St., tel. 902/354–4058; open June–mid-Oct., Mon.–Sat. 9:30–5:30, Sun. 1–5:30), built in 1766, which was the former home of a prominent early settler who kept an extensive and revealing diary. The house is now part of the Queens County Museum.

The Perkins diary was used extensively by Thomas Raddall, whose internationally successful novels and stories are sometimes set in and around Liverpool. *His Majesty's Yankees* (1944) is a vivid account of a local family's deeply divided loyalties during the American Revolution, when many Nova Scotians sympathized with the rebels, not the Crown. Raddall still lives in Liverpool.

㉓ The high noon of **Shelburne** occurred right after the Revolution, when 16,000 Loyalists briefly made it one of the largest communities in North America. Today it is a fishing and shipbuilding town situated on a superb harbor at the mouth of the Roseway River. Many of its homes date back to the Loyalists, including the **Ross-Thomson House** (9 Charlotte La., tel.

902/875–3141; open June–mid-Oct., daily 9:30–5:30), which is
now a provincial museum. Also in Shelburne, and worth a stop
is the **Dory Shop** (Dock St.; open mid-June–mid-Sept., daily
9:30–5:30), a provincial museum property that was officially
opened in 1983 by Prince Charles and Princess Diana. Dories
are flat-bottom boats with flaring sides and a sharp bow, well-
suited to North Atlantic waters. Until last year, 97 year-old
Sidney Mahaney built dories at the shop twice weekly. Although he may not be up to building more dories in 1994, he
will still occasionally be welcoming visitors interested in his
trade.

South of Shelburne, from Barrington to Digby, is the most
prosperous fishing region in the province. With a noticeably
milder climate than the rest of Nova Scotia and easy access to
the rich fishing grounds of George's Bank, fishermen can work
almost all year to bring in a rich harvest of lobster, scallops,
and groundfish.

㉔ **Barrington,** with only 349 residents, was the home of Captain
Benjamin Doane, whose book *Following the Sea* is a fine, lucid
account of 19th-century whaling and trading. Visit the **Barrington Woolen Mill,** built in 1884 and now a provincial museum,
with the original machinery intact and exhibits on weaving
wool into bolts of twills and flannels, blankets and suitings. *2368
Rte. 3, tel. 902/637–2185. Admission free. Open mid-June–Sept.,
Mon.–Sat. 9:30–5:30, Sun. 1:30–5:30.*

Now turn off for **Cape Sable Island,** Nova Scotia's southern-
most extremity. Like Barrington, Cape Sable Island is a Yankee community, as common family names attest; everyone
seems to be named "Smith" or "Nickerson." Interestingly,
there is a bewildering variety of small evangelical churches,
which presumably reflects the Puritan enthusiasm for irrecon-
cilable disagreements over fine points of doctrine. The largest
community on Cape Sable is **Clark's Harbour** (locally pronounced "Cla'k's Ha'bah," sounding more like a town in Massachusetts), named for Michael Swim, an early settler who
could read and write. He was thus described as a clerk or, to
the British, a "clark."

The famous Cape Islander fishing boat was developed here. By
now you have seen hundreds of examples of them: Sitting high
on the water, with its pilothouse forward and its high, flaring
bow and low stern, the Cape Islander is Nova Scotia's standard
inshore fishing boat. Boatbuilding (in fiberglass as well as
wood) is still a thriving occupation along these shores. Successful fishermen buy new boats and sell the older ones to less-fa-
vored regions such as the Eastern Shore and Cape Breton, and
many boats eventually turn up as spacious, inexpensive pleasure craft.

Upon reaching **Pubnico** you enter the Acadian milieu; from
here to Digby the communities are mostly French-speaking.
Favorite local fare includes fricot, a stew made mostly of vegetables but sometimes has rabbit meat; and rappie pie, made of
meat or poultry with potatoes from which much of the starch
has been removed.

You'll no doubt notice that there are no fewer than seven Pub-
nicos: Lower West Pubnico, Middle West Pubnico, and West
Pubnico, all on the west shore of Pubnico Harbour; three East
Pubnicos on the eastern shore; and just plain Pubnico, at the

top of the harbor. These towns were founded by Phillipe Muis D'Entremont, and they once constituted the only barony in French Acadia. He was a prodigious progenitor: To this day, many of the people in the Pubnicos are D'Entremonts, and most of the rest are D'Eons or Amiraults.

You'll also notice the Acadian flag, tricolored with a gold star representing *stella maris*, the star of the sea. The star guides the Acadians during troubled times, which have been frequent. In 1755, after residing for a century and a half in Nova Scotia, chiefly in the Annapolis Valley, the Acadians were expelled by the British—an event that inspired Longfellow's famous *Evangeline*. Some eluded capture and others slowly crept back, and many settled in New Brunswick and along this shore of Nova Scotia.

㉕ The next stop en route is **Yarmouth,** the largest town in southern Nova Scotia, the biggest port west of Halifax, and the point of entry for travelers arriving by ferry from Maine. Its population is relatively big, as well, with 8,500 people. The ferries are a major reason for Yarmouth's prosperity, as they pull in much revenue by providing quick, inexpensive access for merchants and consumers going to the Boston market for fish, pulpwood, boxes and barrels, knitwear, Irish moss, Christmas trees, and berries.

In the 19th century Yarmouth was an even bigger shipbuilding center than most, and its location put the port on all the early steamship routes. The award-winning **Yarmouth County Museum,** housed in a late-19th-century church, does a fine job of unraveling the region's history with its displays of period furniture, costumes, tools, and toys, as well as a significant collection of ship models and paintings. *22 Collins St., tel. 902/742–5539. Admission: $1 adults, 50¢ students, 25¢ children under 14, $2.50 families. Open June–mid-Oct., Mon.–Sat. 9–5, Sun. 1–5; mid-Oct.–May, Tues.–Sat. 2–5.*

Yarmouth has another museum that's surprisingly interesting: The **Firefighters Museum of Nova Scotia,** located one block from the waterfront, presents the evolution of fire fighting through its displays of equipment from the leather bucket to the chemical spray. *451 Main St., tel. 902/742–5525. Admission: $1 per person, $2 families. Open June, Mon.–Sat. 9–5; July–Aug., Mon.–Sat. 9–9, Sun. 10–5; Sept., Mon.–Sat. 9–5; Oct.–May, Mon.–Fri. 10–noon and 2–4.*

The Lighthouse Route ends here, and the **Evangeline Trail** begins, winding along the shore of St. Mary's Bay, through a succession of Acadian villages collectively known as the French Shore. The villages blend seamlessly into one another for about 32 kilometers (nearly 20 miles), each one, it seems, with its own wharf, fish plant, and enormous Catholic church. Hence, this part of Route 1 is sometimes called "the longest main street in the world."

Along this shore and through Nova Scotia as far east as Truro are nondescript shops called Frenchy's. "Frenchy" refers to Ed Theriault of Meteghan, who hit upon the idea of importing quality used clothing in bulk from Boston and selling it at flat-rate bargain prices. Normally it costs as much to dry-clean the clothes as it does to buy them. Today, even well-heeled Nova Scotians root through the tables at Frenchy's.

26 **Point de l'Eglise** (Church Point), past Meteghan River, is the site of **Université Ste-Anne,** the only French-language institution among Nova Scotia's 17 degree-granting colleges and universities. Founded in 1891, this small university is a focus of Acadian studies and culture in the province.

St. Mary's Church (1905) at Point de l'Eglise is the tallest and largest wooden church in North America, at 58 meters (190 feet) long and 56 meters (185 feet) high. The steeple requires 40 tons of rock ballast to keep it steady in the ocean winds. **St. Bernard,** just a few miles farther and marking the end of the French Shore, has an equally impressive granite gothic church, which seats 1,000 people. Built entirely by local people, beginning in 1910, this monument took 40 years to complete.

The other side of St. Mary's Bay is known as Digby Neck. To explore it, drive on to Digby and follow Route 217. Digby Neck is actually a long basalt peninsula extended seaward by two **27** narrow islands, Long Island and **Brier Island.** On the far side is the mouth of the Bay of Fundy; ferries going between the islands have to crab sideways against the ferocious Fundy tidal streams that course back and forth through the narrow gaps. The ferries operate hourly, 24 hours a day, and cost $1 for cars, but are free to pedestrians. One of the boats is called *Joshua Slocum* and the other is *Spray;* the former is named for Westport's most famous native, and the latter for the 11-meter (36-foot) oyster sloop, which he rebuilt and in which he became the first man to single-handedly circumnavigate the world, in 1894–96. At the southern tip of Brier Island is a cairn commemorating the voyage.

An important stop on the Atlantic Flyway, Brier Island is an excellent spot for bird-watching; because the surrounding waters are rich in plankton they attract a variety of whales, including fins, humpbacks, minkes, and right whales, as well as harbor porpoises. Whale-watching tours are available through several companies, including **Pirate's Cove Whale Cruises** (Rte. 217, Tiverton, Long Island, tel. 902/839–2242), which operates June–October and costs $33 for adults, $16.50 for children 6–14.

Digby is the terminus of the ferry service from Saint John, New Brunswick, and an important fishing port with several good restaurants and a major resort, The Pines. The town is particularly famous for its scallops and for smoked herring known as "Digby Chicks." Digby is located on the almost-landlocked Annapolis Basin, into which the Annapolis River flows after its long course through the valley that bears its name.

Swing inland to **Bear River,** a jewel of a village with a large arts-and-crafts community and many gift stores; or follow the shore of the Basin to the **Upper Clements Park,** a theme park that celebrates Nova Scotia's crafts and heritage and has a variety of rides and attractions, including a waterslide, carousel, and roller coaster. *Box 99, Clementsport, tel. 902/532–7557 or 800/565–PARK in Atlantic provinces. Admission free, but visitors pay for rides. Open June, Sat.–Sun. 10–7; July–Aug., daily 10–7; Sept., Sat.–Sun. 10–7.*

28 At the head of the Annapolis Basin is **Annapolis Royal,** the oldest European settlement in Canada, founded in 1605. Samuel de Champlain called it Port Royal and established his settlement 8 kilometers (5 miles) down the opposite side of the Basin;

the settlement has been reconstructed and is now **Port Royal National Historic Site.** *Tel. 902/532–2898. Admission free. Open mid-May–mid-Oct., daily 9–6; closed rest of year.*

Fort Anne National Historic Site was fortified in 1643; the present structures are the remains of the fourth fort erected here and garrisoned by the British as late as 1854. The officers' quarters are now a museum, with exhibits on the site's history. *On the waterfront, tel. 902/532–2397. Admission free. Open mid-May–mid-Oct., daily 9–6; mid-Oct.–mid-May, weekdays 9–6.*

Annapolis Royal was Nova Scotia's first capital and first military base. Local businesses (or the tourist information center, located in the Annapolis Royal Tidal Power Building; *see below*) can provide *Footprints with Footnotes*, a self-guided walking tour of the town; guided tours leave from the lighthouse on St. George Street, daily at 10 AM and 2:30.

Don't miss the **Annapolis Royal Historic Gardens,** 10 acres of magnificent themed gardens connected to the wildlife sanctuary, maintained by Ducks Unlimited. *441 St. George St., tel. 902/532–7018. Admission: $3.50 adults, $3 children and senior citizens, $9.75 families. Open mid-May–mid-Oct., 8–dusk.*

Located just 1/4 mile from Annapolis Royal, on the causeway that crosses the Annapolis River to the Granville Ferry is the **Annapolis Royal Tidal Power Project.** Designed to test the feasibility of generating electricity from tidal energy, this pilot project is the only saltwater generating station in existence. The interpretation center explains the process. *Tel. 902/532–5454. Admission free. Open mid-May–mid-June, daily 9–5:30; mid-June–Aug., daily 9–8; Sept.–mid-Oct. 9–5:30.*

The **Annapolis Valley** runs northeast like a huge trench, flat on the bottom, sheltered on both sides by the long ridges of the North and South Mountains. Occasional roads over the South Mountain lead to the South Shore; short roads over the North Mountain lead to the Fundy shore. The rich soil of the valley bottom supports dairy herds, hay, grain, root vegetables, tobacco, grapes, plums, strawberries, peaches, pears, cherries, and apples, apples, apples. The best time to visit? Apple blossom season: late May and early June.

Like the South Shore, the Valley is punctuated with pleasant small towns, each with a generous supply of extravagant Victorian homes and churches. (Annapolis Royal is particularly well supplied with imposing mansions, particularly along the upper end of St. George Street.) For most visitors, the Valley towns go by like charming milestones, among them: Bridgetown, Lawrencetown, Aylesford, Greenwood, Berwick. Each has its distinctions: the Gallery at Saratoga in **Bridgetown** features the paintings of Kenneth Tolmie, whose works reveal Valley scenes and hang in many leading galleries, including the National Gallery of Canada; **Lawrencetown** is the site of the Nova Scotia College of Geographical Sciences, which offers internationally recognized training in cartography, surveying, and various applications of high-technology to geography. **Aylesford** has a farm zoo; **Greenwood** is the home of Canada's antisubmarine aircraft squadrons; **Berwick** is the birthplace (1885) of Alfred Fuller, the original Fuller Brush man. Most of the Valley towns have small museums. But the major impression of the region is one of tranquillity: lush farmland and a settled agricultural society.

Kentville, New Minas, Greenwich, and Wolfville run into one another almost like the towns of the French Shore; their more-than-12,000 residents form the Valley's largest urban cluster.

㉙ At **Kentville, Agriculture Canada** (tel. 902/678–1093) maintains an important research station on horticulture and poultry; the grounds are beautiful, and free guided tours can be arranged from June through August, weekdays 8–4:30.

㉚ **Wolfville,** a bucolic college town, is the seat of Acadia University. The school's **Beveridge Art Centre** (Acadia University, Highland Ave., tel. 902/542–2201; open Sept.–May, Tues.–Fri. 11–5, weekends 1–4; June–Aug., daily 12–5) includes several works by Alex Colville, the internationally celebrated magical realist painter who lives on Wolfville's main thoroughfare and has served as Acadia's Chancellor.

At Greenwich, take Route 358 to Cape Blomidon via Port Williams and Canning for a spectacular view of the Valley and the Bay of Fundy from **The Lookoff.** Cape Blomidon itself rises 231 meters (760 feet) from the Bay. Continue to **Scots Bay,** where rock shelves contain ribbons of amethyst, jasper, and carnelian. A popular hiking trail leads from the end of Route 358 to the dramatic cliffs of Cape Split.

Beyond Wolfville is **Grand Pré,** once a major Acadian site, where a small stone church, at the Grand Pré National Historic Site (open mid-May–mid-Oct., daily 9–6), commemorates Longfellow's heroine Evangeline, and houses an exhibit on the 1755 deportation of the Acadians from the Valley. While here, visit **Grand Pré Vineyards** (tel. 902/542–1470), an estate winery with 150 acres of grapes under cultivation. Free tours can be arranged, and the estate has a wine salesroom and crafts shop.

㉛ **Windsor,** the last of the Valley towns, was settled in 1703 as an Acadian community, and **Fort Edward** (no tel.; open mid-June–Labor Day, daily 10–6)—one of the assembly points for the expulsion of the Acadians—still stands as the only remaining colonial blockhouse in Nova Scotia. Flora MacDonald, the Scottish heroine who helped Bonnie Prince Charlie escape to France, spent the winter of 1779 in Windsor while her husband was posted at the fort.

Windsor is also the home of Judge Thomas Chandler Haliburton—lawyer, politician, historian, and humorist. His best-known work, *The Clockmaker,* which is still in print, pillories Nova Scotian follies from the viewpoint of a Yankee clockmaker. **Haliburton's Home** (Clifton Ave., tel. 902/798–2915; open mid-May–mid-Oct., Mon.–Sat. 9:30–5:30, Sun. 1–5:30), set on a manicured 25-acre estate, now belongs to the Nova Scotia Museum.

The tide's average rise and fall at Windsor is over 40 feet, and you can see the tidal bore (the leading edge of the incoming tide) rushing up the Meander River and sometimes reaching a height of 3 feet. The local tourist office (902/798–2690) can tell you estimated tide times.

Continuing along the Evangeline Trail, Halifax is only about 45 minutes away, but one site 30 miles (18 miles) from Windsor
㉜ deserves attention: **Uniacke House,** built about 1815 for Richard John Uniacke. During the American Revolution Uniacke, who was fighting on the rebel side, was captured in Cumberland County, just across the Bay of Fundy. The young Irishman

was released through some hazy politics and came to Nova Scotia seeking his fortune. He eventually found it as Attorney-General and Advocate-General to the Admiralty Court, where his fees in one three-year period during the War of 1812 amounted to the stupendous sum of £50,000. Some of that money went into Uniacke House, a superb example of colonial architecture, situated on spacious grounds near a lake. The house, which is now part of the Nova Scotia Museum, is preserved in its original condition with many authentic furnishings. *758 Windsor Hwy., tel. 902/866–2560. Admission free. Open mid-May–mid-Oct., Mon.–Sat., 9:30–5:30, Sun. 1–5:30.*

③③ Highway 101 cuts across the peninsula through gypsum hills to **Bedford,** at the head of Bedford Basin. Once a toney summer resort, Bedford is now a favored suburb of Halifax. Follow the Bedford Highway to Halifax, noting **Julie's Music Room** (*see* Tour 1) as you pass through Prince's Lodge. If you take Windsor Street downtown, you will be following the 18th-century route between Windsor and Halifax—a proper conclusion to a memorable tour.

Tour 3: Northern Nova Scotia

This tour takes in parts of three of the official Scenic Trails, including **Marine Drive, The Sunrise Trail,** and **The Glooscap Trail.** Any one leg of the route could be done comfortably as an overnight trip from Halifax; for the whole tour, allow three or four days.

Pick up Route 7 at Dartmouth. The Eastern Shore—the Atlantic coast east of Halifax-Dartmouth—is perhaps the most scenic and unspoiled stretch of coastline in mainland Nova Scotia. Because it is unspoiled, of course, the Eastern Shore's facilities are relatively few and simple. The road winds along a deeply indented, glaciated coastline of rocky waters interspersed with pocket beaches, long narrow fjords, and fishing villages. Take the time to prowl the side roads and discover your own favorite rock pools and islets—there are plenty to find.

③④ **Musquodoboit Harbour,** with about 930 residents, is a substantial village at the mouth of the Musquodoboit River, not far east of Dartmouth. The river itself offers good trout and salmon fishing, and the village touches on two slender and lovely harbors. One of the Eastern Shore's best beaches, **Martinique Beach,** is about 12 kilometers (8 miles) south of the village, and other fine beaches are at Clam Bay and Clam Harbour, several kilometers (a few miles) east of Martinique.

The pretty villages slip by: Jeddore, Salmon River, Lake Charlotte. An increasingly important part of their economies is aquaculture; nearby, in **Ship Harbour,** the provincial Department of Fisheries has developed an aquaculture **Demonstration Centre** (Rte. 7, tel. 902/845–2991; admission free; open May–Sept., weekdays 9–3), with a small interpretive center on the hatchery, open to the public. As you travel a bit farther, take note of the strings of white buoys in Ship Harbour, marking North America's largest cultivated mussel farm.

This part of the shore experienced a small gold rush during the first part of this century, complete with a 1936 mine disaster, during which the first live, on-the-spot radio newscasts were made throughout Canada and the world. A small local museum at **Moose River Gold Mines,** about 30 kilometers (19 miles) north of Tangier, commemorates the period. *Rte. 224, tel. 902/384–2630. Admission free. Open late-June–Labor Day, Tues.–Sat. 10–5, Sun. 1–6.*

Time Out   Don't fail to stop in Tangier for some delicious smoked salmon, eel or mackerel from **Willy Krauch's Danish Smokehouse** (Rte. 7, tel. 902/772–2188; open Apr.–Christmas, daily 8–7; Christmas–Apr., daily 8–5).

Sheet Harbour is the major service center for the Eastern Shore, with a bank, hospital, accommodations, and campgrounds. Like Musquodoboit, this town straddles two harbors, from one of which is shipped pulpwood to Europe.

The road winds on through a string of uniquely named villages: Necum Teuch, Ecum Secum, Marie Joseph, Spanish Ship Bay. The latter was named for a ghostly galleon, which is said to enter the harbor in flames every seven years. Just beyond, at Liscomb Mills, is Liscomb Lodge, a full-service resort with a very respectable restaurant.

❸❺   The next major center is **Sherbrooke,** which has fewer than 400 residents, but is the Shore's leading tourist center. The St. Mary's River, which flows through the hamlet, is one of Nova Scotia's best salmon rivers, and much of the village itself has been rebuilt by the Nova Scotia Museum to its late 19th-century character, with a blacksmith shop, water-powered sawmill, horse-drawn wagons, tearooms, and stores. Twenty-five buildings have been restored on their original sites for the living history village. *Tel. 902/522–2400. Admission: $2.25 adults, 50¢ children under 16. Open June–mid-Oct., daily 9:30–5:30.*

From Sherbrooke you'll have to decide in which direction you wish to continue. Marine Drive continues down the shore through wild, harsh, lovely country rarely visited by tourists. To see Nova Scotia unbuttoned, as it were, follow the Drive down to **Canso,** pick up the Trans-Canada Highway via Guysborough, and talk to people at every stop. You will find few tourist attractions, although Canso itself has a stirring history and a National Historic Site; in this part of the province you'll come closer to traditional Nova Scotian ways of life than you will anywhere else.

The alternative is to stay on Route 7, which turns inland up the St. Mary's River through spruce woods and rolling farmland to Antigonish, an hour's drive away. The drive takes you from the Atlantic to the Northumberland Strait, part of the Gulf of St. Lawrence: from cold water and rocky shores to warm water and broad sandy beaches. If water sports are your thing, this is your shore: there are miles of wonderful beaches all along Northumberland Strait.

❸❻   **Antigonish** is the home of **St. Francis Xavier University,** a center for Gaelic studies and for the co-operative movement. Its Coady International Institute offers training to co-op and credit union workers from foreign countries. It's also a cathedral town with a population of about 5,200.

Follow Route 337, the Sunrise Trail, for a glorious drive along St. George's Bay with its many good swimming beaches, before the road abruptly climbs 1,000 feet up and over to **Cape George.**

Time Out There's a little take-out shop on the wharf at **Ballantyne's Cove,**
a tiny artificial harbor near the tip of Cape George, that is said
to have the best fish-and-chips in Nova Scotia. Grab an order
and enjoy the views.

After following the Cape, high above the sea, the road runs
along Northumberland Strait through lonely farmlands and
tiny villages such as Arisaig and Lismore. If, after hearing
those names, you have any doubt about the Scottish origin of
the people, they will be laid to rest by a stone cairn in Lismore
that commemorates Bonnie Prince Charlie's Highland rebels,
slaughtered by the English at Culloden in 1746.

Much of the rest of the road runs inland, but the turnoff to
Merigomish leads into a maze of inlets, beaches, and islands
that are well worth exploring. Either way you go, you'll eventually emerge at Highway 104, the Trans-Canada. Turn right
a kilometer and a half (a mile) later, and follow the shore road
to **Melmerby Beach**—a favorite local spot—and continue on to
New Glasgow by a circuitous shoreside road. Alternatively,
stay on the Trans-Canada to reach New Glasgow a few kilometers (2 miles) away.

New Glasgow is one of five industrial towns on the three rivers
that flow into Pictou Harbour. Combined, the five towns have
a population of nearly 30,000, making this one of the largest
urban centers in the province. New Glasgow is a steel-fabricat-
ing and manufacturing center; **Trenton** manufactures railway
cars; **Westville** and **Stellarton** are coal-mining towns.

For the visitor, however, the most interesting town by far is
③ **Pictou,** somewhat sullied by a papermill across the harbor, but
nevertheless one of the most engaging communities in Nova
Scotia. Lining its streets are typically Scottish-style stone cottage homes and public buildings, and there's a good selection
of very attractive small hotels and restaurants. Using the main
highway system, Pictou can be reached in about two hours from
Halifax.

To Pictou Harbour in 1773 came the *Hector*—the nearest thing
to a Canadian *Mayflower*—inaugurating the torrent of Scottish immigration that permanently altered the character of the
province and the nation. A replica of the *Hector* is under construction at the *Hector Heritage Quay* (tel. 902/485–8028).

Under the inspired leadership of men such as the pioneering
educator Thomas McCulloch, Pictou quickly became a center
of commerce, education, theological disputation, and radical
politics. **McCulloch House,** a restored 1806 building with displays of McCulloh's scientific collection and personal items
such as furniture, is preserved as part of the Nova Scotia Museum. *Old Haliburton Rd., tel. 902/485–4563. Admission free.
Open June–mid-Oct., Mon.–Sat. 9:30–5:30, Sun. 11:30–5:30;
mid-Oct.–May, weekdays 9–5.*

Leave Pictou on Route 6, the Sunrise Trail. The road runs beside an apparently endless string of beaches, with many summer homes plunked in the adjoining fields. **River John** is a good
meal stop, especially May, June, and July, when the community
prepares lobster suppers; or in August, when chicken barbecues are on the menu.

At Brule, take Route 326, then turn right on Route 256 to reach
(38) the water-powered gristmill at **Balmoral Mills** (1860), the oldest operating mill in Nova Scotia, and one of five that once operated on this stream. It is now a museum with milling demonstrations, and the grounds include a picnic park. *Tel.
902/657–3016. Admission free. Open June–mid-Oct., Mon.–Sat.
9:30–5:30, Sun. 1–5:30; demonstrations 10–12.*

Follow Route 256 to Route 311 and turn right to rejoin the Sunrise Trail. **Tatamagouche,** a market center for farmers and fishermen, is beautifully situated on a ridge overlooking a small
estuarine harbor. Beyond Tatamagouche, turn right to Mala-
gash to find **Jost Vineyards** (tel. 902/257–2636 or 800/565–4567
in Canada), one of three farm wineries in the province. Jost
produces a surprisingly wide range of very acceptable wines,
and offers tours at 3 PM daily, during mid-June through September.

The road continues through the small community of Wallace,
(39) on another small harbor, to **Pugwash.** This was the home of
Cleveland industrialist Cyrus Eaton, at whose estate numerous Thinkers' Conferences brought together leading intellec-
tual figures from the West and the Soviet Union during the
1950s and 1960s. Pugwash is still Scottish terrain, as attest the
Gaelic street signs. The town is also the home of **Seagull Pewter**
(Durham St., tel. 902/243–2516) a husband-and-wife crafts operation that has grown into a $25-million business by exporting
pewter vessels, picture frames, and other artifacts worldwide.
The showroom fronts on the main highway.

From Pugwash a half-hour drive will take you to Amherst,
through rolling hills and along the edge of Amherst Marsh,
part of the Tantramar Marsh. The Tantramar covers most of
the Isthmus of Chignecto, the narrow neck of land that joins
Nova Scotia to the rest of North America, and it is said to be
the largest marsh in the world. If you have not yet had your fill
of sandy beaches, however, an attractive alternative route
leads through Northport, Lorneville, and Tidnish Dock.

Amherst stands on one of the glacial ridges that borders the
Tantramar Marsh. Like New Glasgow, Truro, Oxford, and several other towns along what is now the Canadian National main
line, Amherst was once a thriving manufacturing center for
many products, including pianos and furnaces. During World
War II, Amherst's aerospace factories (which still survive, but
on a much smaller scale) built hundreds of Anson bombers;
they flew off to war from a now-vanished airport. The town is
historically significant for another reason: In 1917, en route
from New York to Russia, the Communist leader Leon Trotsky
was confined here for a month in a prisoner-of-war camp.

From Amherst, a two-hour drive via Highways 104 and 102 will
return you directly to Halifax. However, the Glooscap Trail
from Amherst through Parrsboro to Truro is much more interesting and takes only about an hour longer. Relatively few tourists travel the latter route, which provides some of the most
striking scenery in Nova Scotia.

If you opt for the Glooscap Trail, there are several roads that
connect Amherst and Parrsboro. Route 2 leads through the
(40) coal-mining town of **Springhill,** the site of the famous mine disaster immortalized in the folk song "The Ballad of Springhill"
by Peggy Seeger and Ewen McColl, and hometown of singer

Anne Murray, whose career is celebrated in the **Anne Murray Centre** (Main St., tel. 902/597-8614; open May–Oct., daily 9–5). Routes 2 and 302 offer the most direct passage to Parrsboro, running through tall hills and farmland to join Route 2 at Southampton.

❹ An alternative—and better—option is to take the Glooscap Trail, which branches off via Route 242 to **Joggins,** where coal age fossils are embedded in 150-foot sandstone cliffs. Visit the **Joggins Fossil Centre,** where you can learn about the region's geological and archaeological history. Also, guided tours of the fossil cliffs are available, but departure times depend on the tides. *30 Main St., tel. 902/251-2727. Admisson to center: $3.50 adults, $3 senior citizens, $2 children 5–18. Admission for tours: $10 adults, $8 senior citizens, $4 children 5–18. Open June–Sept., daily 9–6:30.*

From Joggins, the Glooscap Trail runs along the shore of Chignecto Bay through Shulie and Sand River to Apple River. You are now on the Bay of Fundy, the third coastline of this tour, where stupendous volumes of water rushing into a narrow shelving bay create the world's highest tides, which sometimes reach heights of 50 feet. **Advocate Harbour** was named by Champlain for his friend Marc Lescarbot, who was a lawyer or "avocat." Built on flat shore land with a tall ridge behind it and a broad harbor in front of it, Advocate is eerily beautiful. The road continues past the spectacular lighthouse at **Cape d'Or,** a piece of land that juts out and divides the waters of the main Bay of Fundy from the narrow enclosure of the Minas Basin. As the tides change, fierce riptides create spectacular waves and overfalls. The view from the ridge down to the lighthouse is superb; the view from the lighthouse itself is almost equally magnificent, but the road down is rather primitive and should only be attempted in four-wheel drives.

Route 209 continues through the 19th-century shipbuilding communities of **Spencer's Island** and **Port Greville.** A cairn at Spencer's Island commemorates the construction of the famous *Mary Celeste,* which was found in 1872, sailing in the mid-Atlantic without a crew. She had been abandoned at sea with the table still set for dinner—a story that is one of the enduring mysteries of the sea.

❷ **Parrsboro,** a center for rockhounds and fossil hunters, is the main town on this shore, and hosts the annual **Rockhound Roundup,** held every August. Among the exhibits and festivities are geological displays, concerts, and other special events. To sustain geologists' interests year-round will be the **Fundy Geological Museum** (Two Island Rd.; tel. 902/254-3814 open summer, daily 9–7; winter weekdays 9–5), scheduled to open in August 1993. The spacious museum will house exhibits on geology, from the days of the dinosaurs to present. Parrsboro is an appropriate setting for the new museum since it's not far from the site where the world's smallest dinosaur fossil was found; these tiny fossils will also be displayed at the new venue. Also, a favorite pastime of the town's visitors is to hunt for amethysts and agates that constantly wash out of the nearby cliffs.

Fossils are Parrsboro's claim to fame, but this harbor town was also a major shipping and shipbuilding port, and its history is described at the **Ottawa House Museum-by-the-Sea.** Ottawa

House, which occupies a striking location overlooking the Bay of Fundy, was the summer home of Sir Charles Tupper, a former Premier of Nova Scotia who was briefly Prime Minister of Canada. *Whitehall Rd., tel. 902/254–2376. Admission: $1. Open July–early Sept., daily 10–8.*

From Parrsboro, Route 2 runs along the shore of the Minas Basin to Truro; almost 5 kilometers (about 3 miles) from Parrsboro is the 125-foot-high **Hidden Falls** (tel. 902/254–2505; admission free; open mid-May–Nov.), on private property but open to the public. The adjoining gift shop is a jumble of antique furniture, books, crockery, and bric-a-brac that warrants a visit.

Among the most beautiful scenic areas along Route 2 is **Five Islands,** which, according to Micmac legend, was created when the god Glooscap threw handfuls of sod at Beaver. A provincial park on the shore of Minas Bay includes a campground, a beach, hiking trails, and some interpretation of the region's unusual geology.

Route 2 rejoins the Trans-Canada (Highway 104) at **Glenholme.** From here it is a 75-minute drive to Halifax.

Tour 4: Cape Breton Island

Allow three or four days for this meandering tour that begins by entering the cape via the Canso Causeway on Highway 104; turn left at the rotary, and take Route 19, the Ceilidh Trail. The road winds along the mountainside, with fine views across St. George's Bay to Cape George. This western shoreline of Cape Breton faces the Gulf of St. Lawrence, and is famous for its sandy beaches and warm salt water.

If Halifax is the heart of Nova Scotia, Cape Breton is its soul, complete with soul music: flying fiddles, boisterous rock, velvet ballads. Cape Breton musicians—weaned on Scottish jigs and reels—are among Canada's finest, and you can hear them all over the island, all summer long, at dozens of local festivals and concerts (*see* Festivals and Seasonal Events in Chapter 1).

43 **Port Hood** is the first stop on this tour because of its particularly good beaches and because it's a pleasant excursion: **Port Hood Island,** whose 17 traditional homes are now used primarily as a summer retreat by urban refugees. The island has scenic hills, rock formations on the shore, sandy beaches, and is surrounded by warm water. It's accessible only by an informal ferry operated by Bertie Smith (tel. 902/787-2515), the island's last year-round resident.

44 On the way from Port Hood to **Mabou,** the land lies low until Mabou Harbour, where it rises abruptly to the tall hills of the Mabou Highlands. Mabou itself has been called "the prettiest village in Canada," and it is also perhaps the most Scottish, with its Gaelic signs and a deep tradition of Scottish music and dancing. This is the hometown of innumerable great fiddlers such as John Allan Cameron, and the Rankin Family; stop at a local gift shop and pick up some tapes to play as you drive down the long fjord of Mabou Harbour to **Mabou Mines.** The mines is a place so hauntingly exquisite that you expect to meet the *sidhe*, the Scottish fairies, capering on the hillsides. Within these hills is some of the finest hiking in the province, and above the land fly bald eagles, plentiful in this region. Inquire locally or at the tourist office on Margaree Forks for information about trails.

The Ceilidh Trail winds on through green wooded glens and hidden farms to **Glenora Distillers** in **Glenville,** North America's only distillers of single-malt whisky. The distillery is built around a courtyard bisected by MacLellan's Brook, and includes a bar, a restaurant, and a small inn. *Rte. 19, tel. 902/258–2662. Tours: $2. Open June–Oct., daily 11–4.*

45 The road continues through **Inverness,** a fishing port and former coal-mining town with many services, and on to **Broad Cove,** the site of one of the most venerable Cape Breton Scottish concerts, held annually in late July. The road forks at **Dunvegan,** the home of Alastair MacLeod, whose powerful short stories pierce deeply into the life of these Scottish communities. Look for his collections *The Lost Salt Gift of Blood* or *As Birds Bring Forth the Sun* for a better understanding of the region.

Take Route 219 at Dunvegan, following the coast through **Chimney Corner** and **Whale Cove.** One of the beaches near Chimney Corner has "sonorous sands": When you step on the sand or drag a foot through it, it squeaks and moans. The
46 Ceilidh Trail joins the Cabot Trail at **Margaree Harbour** at the mouth of the Margaree River, a famous salmon-fishing stream and a favorite canoe route. Stop at the schooner *Marion Elizabeth,* now the Schooner Village restaurant and free museum, with many small shops and a good selection of books about Cape Breton. On the grounds is writer Farley Mowat's schooner *Happy Adventure,* featured in his book *The Boat That Wouldn't Float.*

The Margaree River is a cultural dividing line: South of the river the settlements are Scottish, up the river they are largely Irish, and north of the river they are Acadian French. The Cabot Trail crosses the river and runs along the shore through Belle Cote and **Cap Le Moine.** Don't miss Joe Delaney's whimsical scarecrow farm and gift shop at Cap Le Moine (Cabot Trail, tel. 902/235–2108). Most of the harbors on this bold, straight coast are the estuaries of small rivers, with treacherous sandbars at their mouths. Stop at **Friar's Head** and look over the cliff: The tiny cleft in the rocks below was long used as a fishing harbor.

47 **Cheticamp,** an Acadian community, is the best harbor and the largest settlement on the shore. With its tall silver steeple towering over the village, it stands exposed on a wide lip of flat land below a range of bald green hills, behind which lies the high plate 1 of the Cape Breton Highlands. Cheticamp is famous for its hooked rugs, available at many local gift shops, and for whale cruises, which depart in June, once daily; July and August, three times daily from the government wharf. **Whale Cruisers Ltd.** (tel. 902/224–3376) is one of the reliable charter companies in the area. Cruises cost $25 for adults, $10 for children 6–12.

At the outskirts of Cheticamp begins **Cape Breton Highlands National Park,** a 597-square-kilometer (370-square-mile) wilderness of wooded valleys, plateau barrens, and steep cliffs that stretches across the northern peninsula of Cape Breton from the Gulf Shore to the Atlantic. The highway through the park is magnificent, as it rises to the tops of the coastal mountains and descends through tight switchbacks to the sea. For wildlife watchers there's much to see, including moose, eagle, deer, bear, fox, and bobcat. *Tel. in summer 902/285–2535, in winter 902/285–2270. Admission June–Sept.: $5 per vehicle per day, $10 for 4-day pass, $20 for annual pass. Admission free in winter. No charge for vehicles passing through on Cabot Trail. Camping fees: $11 for tent camping, $17 for full hookup.*

Pleasant Bay is a tiny village in a cleft of the mountains, where the Grande Anse River reaches the sea. A spur road creeps along the cliffs to Red River, beyond which is **Gampo Abbey—** the only Tibetan Buddhist monastery in America—situated on a broad flat bench of land high above the sea. The main road climbs North Mountain, past the trail to **Lone Shieling,** a re-creation of a Scottish crofter's cottage. The cottage, about a 20-minute scenic walk from the highway, includes displays about the region's history and flora. Its name is taken from the anonymous "Canadian Boat Song," which expresses yearnings for the emigrants' lost Scottish home:

From the lone sheiling on the misty island
Mountains divide us, and the waste of seas;
But still the blood is strong, the heart is Highland
And we in dreams behold the Hebrides.

The most northerly tip of the island is not part of the National Park; turn off to discover **Bay St. Lawrence** and **Meat Cove,** set in an amphitheatre of bare green hills, and looking northward to the killer island of **St. Paul's,** site of more than 60 charted shipwrecks. Whale-watching cruises are available June through August, three times daily, through **Whale Watch Bay St. Lawrence** (tel. 902/383– 2981); the cost is $22 for adults, $11 for children 6–12.

The main road reenters the park near **Cabot's Landing,** the long sandy beach in Aspy Bay where Cape Breton folks believe that John Cabot made his landfall in 1497; this theory, however, is vigorously denied in Newfoundland. Dingwall, in the center of the bay, is an archetypal fishing village; so are White Point, New Haven, and Neil's Harbour.

48 **Ingonish,** one of the leading holiday destinations on the island, is actually several villages on two bays, divided by a long narrow peninsula called Middle Head. Each bay has a sandy beach, and Middle Head includes the provincially owned **Keltic Lodge,** a first-class hotel and resort complex. The hamlet offers a wide range of activities, among them, downhill and cross-country skiing, golfing, swimming, and hiking. Stop at **Lynn's Craft Shop and Art Gallery** (on Hwy., tel. 902/285–2735), which offers the work of noted local artist Christopher Gorey and others.

The road serpentines up Cape Smokey and along the face of the mountains, offering spectacular views from high above the sea. **Wreck Cove** is the headquarters of *Cape Breton's Magazine,* an award-winning oral-history publication whose home-spun appearance belies its essential sophistication. Look for it on newsstands throughout the island.

49 Notice the small islands on the far side of the mouth of St. Ann's Bay: These are the **Bird Islands,** breeding grounds for Atlantic puffins, black guillemots, razor-billed auks, and cormorants. Landing on the islands is forbidden, but boat tours are available from **Bird Islands Boat Tour** (tel. 902/674-2384) in Big Bras d'Or. The road descends at last to the flatlands around the mouth of the bay.

If you'd like to extend your drive, take the short ferry ride **50** (runs 24 hours and costs 50¢) to **Englishtown,** home of the celebrated Cape Breton Giant, Angus MacAskill. A museum holds the remains of a 7'9" man. *Tel. 902/929–2875. Admission: $1 adults, 50¢ children. Open May–Oct., 9–6.*

This alternative route around the head of the bay brings you to **St. Ann's,** home of North America's only **Gaelic College** (tel. 902/295–3441), with the Great Hall of the Clans and a Scottish gift shop. The college offers courses in Gaelic language and literature, Scottish music, and dancing, weaving, and other Scottish arts. In the first week of August Gaelic College hosts the **Gaelic Mod,** a week-long festival of games, theater, and music.

51 Turn right on Highway 105 for **Baddeck,** the most highly developed tourist center in Cape Breton, with more than 1,000 motel beds, a golf course, many fine gift shops, and numerous restaurants. Baddeck is the main town on the **Bras d'Or Lakes,** a vast, warm, almost-landlocked inlet of the sea, which occupies the entire center of Cape Breton. The coastline of the Lakes is more than 967 kilometers (600 miles) long, and yachtspeople sail from all over the world to cruise their serene, unspoiled coves and islands. Four of the largest communities along the shore are Micmac Indian reserves.

Baddeck's attractions include the **Centre Bras d'Or Festival of the Arts,** which offers live music and drama every evening during the summer, and the annual regatta of the Bras d'Or Yacht Club, held in the first week of August. Sailing tours and charters are available locally, as are bus tours along the Cabot Trail. A free ferry (passengers only) shuttles between the government wharf and the sandy beach, by the lighthouse at Kidston Island.

The **Alexander Graham Bell National Historic Site** commemorates the great inventor who spent his summers here and is buried on the mountaintop above his mansion, still owned by his family and visible from the town. The site contains displays and detailed records of Bell's research into an astonishing range of subjects. *Chebucto Rd., tel. 902/295–2069. Admission free. Open July–Sept, daily 9–9, Oct.–June, daily 9–5.*

Continue along the lake shore through several Indian villages to **Little Narrows,** then take the ferry (runs 24 hours and costs **52** 25¢) to the Washabuck Peninsula. Take Route 223 to **Estmere** and **Iona,** site of the **Nova Scotia Highland Village,** set high on a mountainside, with a spectacular view of two major Bras d'Or Lakes and the narrow Barra Strait, which joins them. The village's 10 historic buildings were assembled from all over Cape Breton to depict Highland Scots' way of life from their origins in the Hebrides to the present day. Among the participants at this living-history museum are a smith in the blacksmith shop and a clerk in the store. *Rte. 233, tel. 902/725–2272. Admission: $3 adults, $2.50 senior citizens, $1 students, $6 families. Open mid-June–mid-Sept., Mon.–Sat. 9–5, Sun. 11–6.*

A ferry carries you from Iona to Grand Narrows, and a few kilometers (about 2 miles) from the ferry, bear right toward Eskasoni and East Bay. (If you miss this turn, don't worry:

you'll have just as scenic a drive along St. Andrews Channel.) The East Bay route runs through the Micmac village of **Eskasoni,** the largest native community in the province. This is one of the friendliest villages in the province, with a fascinating cultural heritage: Find an excuse to stop and talk, perhaps at a gift shop or a general store.

Farther on, East Bay becomes a prosperous outer suburb of **⑤** **Sydney,** the heart of Nova Scotia's second-largest urban cluster. "Industrial Cape Breton" encompasses villages, unorganized districts, and half-a-dozen towns—most of which sprang up around the coal mines, which fed the steel plant at Sydney. These are warmhearted, interesting communities with a diverse ethnic population, including Ukraines, Welsh, Polish, Lebanese, West Indians, Italians; most residents descended from the miners and steelworkers who arrived a century ago when the area was booming. Sydney is also the only significantly industrialized district in Atlantic Canada, and it has suffered serious environmental damage.

Industrial Cape Breton has the island's only real airport, its only university, and a lively entertainment scene that specializes in Cape Breton music. The **University College of Cape Breton** offers many facilities for the public, such as a theater, art gallery, the Cape Breton Archives, and the Beaton Institute of Cape Breton Studies. The campus is located on the Sydney-Glace Bay Highway, not far from the airport.

Sydney is also a popular departure point: Fast ferries leave from **North Sydney** for Newfoundland, and scheduled air service to Newfoundland and the French islands of St. Pierre and Miquelon departs from Sydney Airport.

⑤ Situated about 30 minutes from Sydney, on Route 22, is **Fortress of Louisbourg National Historic Park,** the most remarkable site in Cape Breton. Louisbourg tends to be chilly, so pack a warm sweater or windbreaker. After the French were forced out of mainland Nova Scotia in 1713, they established their headquarters here, in a walled and fortified town on a low point of land at the mouth of Louisbourg Harbour.

The fortress was twice captured by the British and once returned; after the second siege, in 1758, it was razed to the ground. Its capture essentially ended the French Empire in America. During the past 30 years, a quarter of the original town has been rebuilt on its foundation, just as it was in 1744, before the first siege. Costumed actors re-create the lives and activities of the original inhabitants; you can watch a military drill, see nails and lace being made, and eat food prepared from 18th-century recipes in the town's two inns. Plan on spending at least half a day. Tours available. *Tel. 902/733–2280. Admission: $6.25 adults, $3.25 children 5–16, senior citizens free, $16 families. Open June and Sept., daily 9:30–5; July–Aug., daily 9–6.*

While in Louisbourg, consider stopping at the railway museum at the **Sidney and Louisburg Historical Society,** or the **Atlantic Statiquarium,** a marine museum devoted largely to underwater treasure. *Railway Museum: 7336 Main St., tel. 902/733–2720. Admission free. Open June–Sept., weekdays 9–5, July–Aug., daily 9–7. Statiquarium: 7523 Main St., tel. 902/733–2220. Admission: $2.50 adults, $1 children 5–16, $5 families. Open June–Sept., daily 10–8.*

To return, you must retrace your tracks, via Route 22, Highway 125, and Route 4 to East Bay; continue down the east side of the Bras d'Or Lakes.

Time Out On your return route, you'll come to **Big Pond**, home of singer/songwriter Rita MacNeil, who operates a tearoom here. Stop for tea and oatcakes, and pick up one of her tapes. *Rte. 4. Open June, daily 10–6; July–Aug., daily 10–8; Sept.–Oct., daily 10–6.*

Route 4 continues along the lake, sometimes close to the shore and sometimes high in the hills. The **Chapel Island Reserve** is the site of a major Micmac spiritual and cultural celebration, which draws 5,000 visitors every year during the last weekend in July. The event combines native and Roman Catholic ceremonies, and non-natives are welcome.

55 From St. Peter's to Port Hawkesbury the population is largely Acadian French. At **St. Peter's** the Atlantic Ocean is connected with the Bras d'Or Lakes by the century-old St. Peter's Canal, still heavily used by pleasure craft and fishing vessels. The town is a service center for the surrounding region, and offers such amenities as a marina, hotels, restaurants, and a liquor store. From St. Peter's, Route 247 leads through the Acadian villages of Grand Greve and L'Ardoise to a fine beach at Point Michaud.

56 The road onward along the Bras d'Or Lakes leads through pretty Acadian villages along the twisting channel of St. Peter's Inlet, with many coves and islands, and then along the main body of the lake to **Dundee,** a large resort with a spectacular hilltop golf course overlooking the island-studded waters of West Bay. The alternative route, equally engaging, leads along the Atlantic coast, through coves and islands past River Tillard and River Bourgeois to Louisdale.

Turn off on Route 320 for Isle Madame, a 27-square-kilometer (17- square-mile) island named for Madame de Maintenon, second wife of Louis XIV. Route 320 leads through the villages of Poulamon and D'Escousse, and overlooks the protected waterway of Lennox Passage, with its spangle of islands. Route 206 meanders through the low hills to a maze of land and water at West Arichat. Together, the two routes encircle the island, meeting at Arichat, the principal town of **Isle Madame.**

57 **Arichat** was once the seat of the local Catholic diocese; **Notre Dame de l'Assumption church,** built in 1838, still retains the grandeur of its former cathedral status. The bishop's palace, the only one in Cape Breton, is now a law office. The two cannons overlooking the harbor were installed after the town was sacked by John Paul Jones, founder of the U.S. Navy, during the American Revolution. When Jones returns, Arichat will be prepared. The town was an important shipbuilding and trading center during the 19th century, and some fine old houses from that period still remain, along with the 18th-century **LeNoir Forge** (902/226–9364; open May–Sept., weekdays 9–5, Sat. 10–3).

A dead-end road leads to the Acadian villages of Petit de Grat, Sampson's Cove, and **Little Anse;** with its rocky red bluffs, cobble shores, tiny harbor, and brightly painted houses, the latter is particularly attractive to artists and photographers.

From Louisdale, Route 104 speeds through the woods and crosses the Inhabitants River to **Port Hawkesbury,** a new industrial center around the deep-water port created when, in 1955, the Canso Causeway blocked the once-fierce currents from the Gulf of St. Lawrence. Port Hawkesbury has a paper mill, an electrical generating station, a gypsum wallboard plant, and an oil-transshipment depot. It also has all the usual services, including a number of motels.

Eight kilometers (5 miles) farther on is **Port Hastings,** at the Cape Breton end of the Canso Causeway. Many visitors find this presents them with the greatest decision they've had to face in Cape Breton thus far: When the time comes to leave, should they stay? The choice is yours. You don't have to cross the Causeway. If you do, Halifax is a three-hour drive away.

Shopping

You may claim a refund of Nova Scotia's 10% sales tax (nonrefundable on accommodations, meals, and alcohol) paid on goods you transport home. Refund claims must be filed within 90 days of leaving Nova Scotia and must be in excess of $15. (Refunds of the national Goods and Services Tax must be applied for separately; *see* Shopping in Chapter 1). For refund forms and information, contact the **Provincial Tax Commission** (Tax Refund Unit, Box 755, Halifax, NS B3J 2V4, tel. 902/424–5946 or 1/424–6708 in Nova Scotia).

Halifax The Spring Garden Road area has two new, stylish shopping malls, with shops selling everything from designer clothing to fresh pasta. **Jennifers of Nova Scotia** (5635 Spring Garden Rd., tel. 902/425–3119) sells locally made jewelry, pottery, wool sweaters, and soaps. You can also find fine crafts in Historic Properties and the Barrington Inn complex, near the waterfront, at such shops as **Pewter House** (1875 Granville St., tel. 902/423–8843) and the **Stornoway** (1873 Granville St., tel. 902/422–9507). The **Plaid Place** (1903 Barrington Pl., tel. 902/429–6872) has a dazzling array of tartans and Highland accessories. The **Wool Sweater Outlet** (1870 Hollis St., tel. 902/422–9209) offers wool and cotton sweaters at good prices.

Elsewhere in Nova Scotia Shopping malls in Nova Scotia are similar to those in other parts of Canada or in the United States. The two largest malls
Shopping Malls are the **MicMac Mall** in Dartmouth, off the A. Murray Mackay Bridge; and the **Halifax Shopping Centre** on Mumford Road. On Route 4 in Sydney you'll find the **Mayflower Mall** on the way to Glace Bay.

Specialty Shops Antiques, gifts, and crafts are especially popular in Cape Breton, but shops selling these items appear in numbers throughout the province. You'll find everything from blacksmithing in East Dover and silversmithing in Waverley to leaded glass ornaments in Purcells Cove, hooked rugs in Cheticamp, woolens in Yarmouth, wooden toys in Middletown, pewter in Wolfville, pottery in Arichat, and apple dolls in Halifax. A good shoppers' guide is the *Buyers Guide to Art and Crafts in Nova Scotia,* from the Department of Tourism and Culture (*see* Important Addresses and Numbers in Essential Information, *above*).

Sports and the Outdoors

The Department of Tourism and Culture (*see* Important Addresses and Numbers in Essential Information, *above*) publishes *Nova Scotia Outdoors*, a comprehensive guide to aviation, diving, kayaking, river rafting, rockhounding, windsurfing, skiing, and many others. They also publish a Sportsman's Calendar and *Master Guides*, a full catalog of outfitters.

Biking *Bicycle Tours in Nova Scotia* (US$21.95, C$24.95) is published by **Bicycle Nova Scotia** (5516 Spring Garden Rd., Box 3010, Halifax B3J 3G6, tel. 902/425–5450). The organization also conducts a variety of excursions around the province. **Backroads** (1516 5th St., Suite Q333, Berkeley, CA 94710, tel. 510/527–1555 or 800/245–3874) offers five- and six-day bike trips on the Evangeline Trail.

Bird-watching Nova Scotia is located on the Atlantic "flyway" and is an important staging point for migrating species. An excellent, beautifully illustrated book, *Birds of Nova Scotia*, by Robie Tufts, is a must on every ornithologist's reading list. One of the highest concentrations of bald eagles in North America—about 250 nesting pairs—is located in Cape Breton, along the Bras d'Or Lake region or in Cape Breton Highlands National Park. July and August are the best eagle-watching times. MacNabs Island, in Halifax harbor, has a large osprey population. The Bird Islands, off the coast of Cape Breton, are home to a variety of sea birds, including the rare Atlantic puffin.

Canoeing Nova Scotia is seamed with small rivers and lakes, by which the Micmac Indians roamed both Cape Breton and the peninsula. Especially good canoe routes are within Kejimkujik National Park (*see* National Parks, *below*). The publication *Canoe Routes of Nova Scotia* and a variety of route maps are available from the Nova Scotia Government Bookstore (Box 637, 1 Government Pl., Halifax B3J 2T3, tel. 902/424–7580).

Fishing Nova Scotia has more than 9,000 lakes and 100 brooks; practically all lakes and streams are open to visitors. The catch includes Atlantic salmon (June–September), brook and sea trout, bass, rainbow trout, and shad. You can get a nonresident fishing license from any Department of Natural Resources office in the province and at most sporting-goods stores.

Golf Nova Scotia and Cape Breton have 38 golf courses, as well as driving ranges and miniature golf courses. The 9-hole course at Parrsboro and the 18-hole links at Dundee offer spectacular views of the Minas Basin and Bras d'Or Lake, respectively. One of Canada's finest courses is at The Pines Resort Hotel, in Digby (*see* Lodging, *below*), offering 18 challenging holes amid a pine forest.

Hiking The province has a wide variety of trails along the rugged coastline and inland through forest glades, which enable you to experience otherwise inaccessible scenery, wildlife, and vegetation. Maps of Nova Scotia trails are available through the **Canadian Hostelling Association** (5516 Spring Garden Rd., Box 3010, Halifax B3J 3G6, tel. 902/425–5450).

Windsurfing Wind and water conditions are often excellent for windsurfing, the fastest-growing aquatic summer sport in Nova Scotia. Lessons and equipment rentals are available from retail outlets throughout the province.

Beaches

The province is one big seashore. The warmest beaches are found on the Northumberland Strait shore and include Heather Beach, Caribou, and Melmerby, all in provincial parks. The west coast of Cape Breton and the Bras d'Or Lakes also offer fine beaches and warm salt water.

National Parks

Nova Scotia has two national parks: **Cape Breton Highlands National Park** (*see* Tour 4, *above*), through which the Cabot Trail runs; and **Kejimkujik National Park** (*see* Tour 2, *above*), in the interior of the western part of the province. Essentially a wilderness area with many lakes, Kejimkujik offers well-marked canoe routes into the interior, with primitive campsites. Nature trails are marked for hikers, boat rentals are available, and there's freshwater swimming. One precaution: Check for ticks after hiking in the deep woods. *To Kejimkujik: Take Hwy. 8 from Liverpool or Annapolis Royal, Box 36, Maitland Bridge, B0T 1N0, tel. 902/682–2770. Park fee: $4 per vehicle per day, $9 for 4-day pass, $25 for annual pass. Camping fee: $8.50–$13 per day.*

Dining and Lodging

Dining

Many of Halifax's restaurants are set in refurbished historic homes or other restored quarters. The menus almost always center on seafood, including Malpeque oysters, Fundy lobster, and Digby scallops. Unless otherwise noted, dress is casual; only in expensive restaurants is a jacket required.

Along the main highways, your best bet for a meal will be at truck stops, particularly the **Irving Big Stops.** Expect nothing fancy, just generous helpings of plain, solid food at reasonable prices.

Highly recommended restaurants in each price category are indicated by a star ★.

Category	Cost*
Very Expensive	over $50
Expensive	$35–$50
Moderate	$15–$35
Inexpensive	under $15

per person, excluding drinks, service, 7% GST, and 10% sales tax on meals more than $3.

Lodging

Nova Scotia has a superb computerized system called **Check In** (tel. 800/565–0000; in Halifax-Dartmouth, 902/425–5781; in the continental U.S., 800/341–6096; in Maine, 800/492–0643), which provides information and makes reservations with more than 700 hotels, motels, inns, campgrounds, and car-rental agencies. Check In also represents most properties in Prince Edward Island and some in New Brunswick.

Several hotel and motel chains operate in Nova Scotia. **Best Western** (tel. 800/528–1234) and **Wandlyn Inns** (in eastern Canada, tel. 800/561–0000; in the U.S., 800/561–0006) are mid-range chains, quite suitable for families. **Journey's End** (tel. 800/668–4200) is a chain of new budget hotels with clean and pleasant rooms, but no facilities.

In addition to the reliable chains, Halifax-Dartmouth has a number of excellent hotels, and reservations are necessary year-round, and can be made by calling **Check In** (*see above*). Expect to pay considerably more in the capital district than elsewhere. Those on a budget might try a hostel, country inn, or bed-and-breakfast.

Highly recommended lodgings in each price category are indicated by a star ★.

Category	Cost*
Very Expensive	over $80
Expensive	$65–$80
Moderate	$45–$65
Inexpensive	under $40

*All prices are for a standard double room, excluding 10% service charge.

Halifax-Dartmouth

Dining **Clipper Cay.** This restaurant gets the prize for the best
★ location in the city: It overlooks Privateer's Wharf and the entire harbor. Request a table with a window view and choose the smoked salmon from the menu. In summer the downstairs eatery, **The Cay Side,** serves seafood lunches outside on the wharf. *1869 Upper Water St., tel. 902/432–6818. Reservations advised. AE, DC, MC, V. Expensive.*

Ryan Duffy's. Steaks are the specialty at this spot, in the Spring Garden Place shopping mall, where you can select your own cut by the ounce; other options include an array of seafood and lamb. Upstairs, corner window seats allow you to watch the world walk by from inside this brass and wood-paneled dining room. The green-and-burgundy color scheme adds to Ryan Duffy's old-time atmosphere. *5640 Spring Garden Rd., tel. 902/421–1116. Reservations advised for dining room. AE, MC, V. Moderate–Expensive.*

Daily Catch. Don't be fooled by appearances: This small, nondescript neighborhood restaurant in a working-class section of town serves fabulous food. The menu, scribbled on a blackboard on the wall, features Italian seafood. Try the lobster Fra Diavolo—lobster, squid, mussels, shrimp, clams, and scallops served over linguini, in a cast-iron skillet. *2590 Agricola St., tel. 902/429–2223. Reservations advised. AE, MC, V. Moderate.*

Da Maurizio. This popular northern Italian restaurant, in the Brewery Center, and the adjoining wine bar, **Baccus,** are under the same management. Chef-owner Maurizio serves pastas with olive oil; ravioli stuffed with duck or rabbit; grilled fish and meats; and the only risotto in town. The brewery's enormously high ceilings—15 and 20 feet—and its stone-and-brick walls are warmed by fresh flowers, gleaming silver and linen, and a Venetian carnival theme, with paintings and masks adorning the walls. There's a wide wine selection by the bottle and by the glass, and food is served in the wine bar, too. *1496 Lower Water St., tel. 902/423–0859. Reservations recommended. Closed Sat. lunch and Sun. AE, MC, V. Moderate.*

★ **Old Man Morias.** Authentic Greek specialties at this turn-of-the-century Halifax townhouse include lamb on a spit and moussaka. Greek music, tapestries, and archways set the mood for a traditionally Greek evening, and full-flavored dishes enrich the spirit. Sample the fried squid and Greek fried cheese appetizers. *1150 Barrington St., tel. 902/422–7960. Reservations advised. Closed Sun. AE, DC, MC, V. Moderate.*

Scanway. Scandinavian dishes are the specialty of this bright, pretty restaurant, decorated with pine wood and orange-and-yellow drapes. Try the *sjokreps* (Danish scampi with garlic and parsley butter). The dessert menu alone makes Scanway worth a visit: homemade ice cream, King Olav's cake (chocolate truffle torte), marzipan cake filled with fresh fruit. *1569 Dresden Row, tel. 902/422–3733. Reservations advised. AE, MC, V. Moderate.*

Privateer's Warehouse. Inside this building are three restaurants, all sharing the early 18th-century stone walls and hewn beams, and serving food in descending order of elegance. **Bradley's Upper Deck,** a comfortably elegant place with great views of the harbor, specializes in regional Nova Scotian cooking, with fresh ingredients and lots of seafood. The **Middle Deck** has a bistro-style, casual atmosphere and serves pan-fried haddock and barbecued ribs, among other items, until 10 PM and snacks until midnight; on Thursday, Friday, and Saturday maritime folk music fills the air. The **Lower Deck** is a boisterous pub with long trestle tables, a patio, beer mugs for thumping, and lots of hand-holding and singing of traditional maritime, Irish, and Scottish songs; fish and chips and other pub food is served. *Historic Properties, tel. 902/422–1289. Reservations advised for Upper Deck. Upper Deck closed Sat. lunch and Sun.; Middle and Lower Decks closed Sun. AE, DC, MC, V. Moderate–Inexpensive.*

Satisfaction Feast. This small, vegetarian restaurant and bakery is informal, friendly, and usually packed at lunchtime. The food is simple and wholesome, with a truly homemade flavor. Try the fresh whole wheat bread and one of the daily curries. No smoking permitted. *1581 Grafton St., tel. 902/422–3540. MC, V. Inexpensive.*

Lodging **Cambridge Suites.** You can get "a suite for the price of a room" is this hotel's motto . . . and a good one it is. Choose among three suite sizes, but all have sitting room and kitchenette. What makes this lodging even more desirable is its convenient location near the Citadel and the Spring Garden Road shopping district, and it's only a short walk from downtown. Complimentary Continental breakfast is served. *1583 Brunswick St., B3J 3P5, tel. 902/420–0555 or 800/565–1263 in Canada. 200 mini-suites and one-bedrooms. Facilities: whirlpool, sauna, rooftop sundeck, exercise room. AE, MC, V. Very Expensive.*

Chateau Halifax. This first-class Canadian Pacific hotel offers large, pretty rooms in a perfect location, near Scotia Square and Historic Properties. There's a good dining room and an upbeat bar with live entertainment. *1990 Barrington St., B3J 1P2, tel. 902/425–6700. 279 rooms, 21 suites. Facilities: restaurant, coffee shop, lounge, pool, sauna. AE, DC, MC, V. Very Expensive.*

Citadel Inn. Situated at the base of Citadel Hill, this business-oriented hotel is still within walking distance of the action. Rooms with a harbor view are recommended, though they will cost more than those without. Free parking is an asset in car-clogged Halifax. *1960 Brunswick St., B3J 2G7, tel. 902/422–1391. 261 rooms, 6 suites. Facilities: restaurant, indoor pool, fitness center, sauna, whirlpool, and exercise room. AE, DC, MC, V. Very Expensive.*

Delta Barrington. This traditional-style hotel was built in 1979 using the original facade of an entire city block. It has a prime downtown location, and the rooms are spacious. All-weather walkways connect the hotel to Scotia Square shops. *1875 Barrington St., B3J 3L6, tel. 902/429–7410. 200 rooms, 1 suite. Facilities: restaurant, lounge, piano bar, sauna, whirlpool, and pool. AE, DC, MC, V. Very Expensive.*

The Halifax Hilton. This wonderful, spacious old hotel, formerly the Nova Scotian, was recently bought by Hilton International and totally renovated. It's down by the harbor near the end of Lower Water Street. There's ample parking, a tennis court, and a roof terrace where you can sit in the evening and look out over the city. This Hilton is a popular site for meetings and conventions, with its 13 conference rooms and lavish breakfast buffet. *1181 Hollis St., B3H 2P6, tel. 902/423–7231 or 800/445–8667; fax 902/422–9465. 307 rooms. Facilities: 2 restaurants, indoor pool, sauna, ballroom, tennis court, roof terrace. AE, D, DC, MC, V. Very Expensive.*

Halliburton House Inn. A registered heritage property, this hotel is an elegant renovation of several 19th-century townhouses. All units are furnished with period antiques, lending a homey ambience to the inn. Continental breakfast is included in the room rate. *5184 Morris St., B3J 1B3, tel. 902/420–0658. 30 rooms, jr. suites and suites. Facilities: private garden courtyard, conference rooms. AE, DC, MC, V. Very Expensive.*

Holiday Inn Halifax Centre. This first-class property overlooks Halifax Commons, and is 1 kilometer (½ mile) west of Scotia Square, and features standard Holiday Inn decor with modern amenities. *1980 Robie St., B3H 3G5, tel. 902/423–1161. 228 rooms, 3 suites. Facilities: restaurant, piano bar, pool, sauna, whirlpool, gift shop, free parking. AE, DC, MC, V. Very Expensive.*

Prince George Hotel. The Prince George is a luxurious and understated business-oriented hotel. The contemporary mahogany furnishings include a writing desk. The building is conveniently connected by underground tunnel to the World Trade and Convention Center. *1725 Market St., B3J 3N9, tel. 902/425–1986 or 800/565–1567 in Canada. 208 rooms, 3 suites. Facilities: restaurant, café, 2 lounges, pub, pool, whirlpool, fit-*

ness center, concierge, children's playroom, roof deck and gardens. *AE, DC, MC, V. Very Expensive.*

Sheraton Halifax. The convenient location, in Historic Properties, contributes to the elegance of this waterfront hotel. Other assets include the hotel's indoor pool with a summer sun deck and spa facilities. There's also docking space for yachts. In summer you can sit on an outdoor terrace at the **Café Maritime** restaurant and eat lobster while you watch the ships go by. *1919 Upper Water St., B3J 3J5, tel. 902/421–1700 or 800/325–3535. 332 rooms, 24 suites. Facilities: restaurant, 24-hr. room service, concierge, shops, meeting facilities, boat slips, skywalk to shopping and office complexes. AE, DC, MC, V. Very Expensive.*

Ramada Renaissance. Located in Dartmouth's Burnside Industrial Park, this new luxury hotel is aimed squarely at the business traveler, with modern amenities. *240 Brownlow Ave., B3B 1X6, tel. 902/468–8888 or 800/268–8998. 178 rooms, suites available. Facilities: restaurant, lounge, bar, 24-hr. room service, pool, whirlpool, sauna, exercise room, gift shop, meeting and banquet facilities. AE, DC, MC, V. Very Expensive.*

Waken'n Eggs B&B. Situated across the Common from the Citadel is this Victorian, built as two homes side-by-side, but is now a single house. The comfortable, eclectic furnishings include antiques and folk art and the helpful service makes this a hospitable B&B. *2114 Windsor St., B3K 5B4, tel. 902/422–4737. 3 rooms with 1 private, 1 shared bath. No credit cards. Moderate.*

Mainland Nova Scotia

Annapolis Royal **Wandlyn Royal Anne Motel.** Offering clean rooms at reason-
Lodging able rates is this modern, no-frills motel that was renovated and enlarged several years ago. Enjoy the pleasant quiet country setting by taking a walk on the motel's 20 acres of land. *Box 628, B0S 1A0, tel. 902/532–2323. 30 rooms. Facilities: whirlpool, sauna, conference room. AE, DC, MC, V. Moderate.*

The Moorings B&B. This tall, beautiful home overlooking Annapolis Basin was formerly the home of author H. R. Percy and comes complete with fireplace, tin ceilings, and antiques and contemporary art. *Box 118, Granville Ferry B0S 1K0, tel. 902/532–2146. 3 rooms, 2 w/half-baths, 2 shared full baths. V. Inexpensive.*

Antigonish **Lobster Treat Restaurant.** Once a two-room schoolhouse, this
Dining property has since been converted into a cozily decorated brick, pine, and stained-glass restaurant. Located on the Trans-Canada Highway, it's convenient for travelers following the Sunrise Trail. The menu features fresh seafood and vegetables year-round, as well as bread and pies baked on the premises. Because of a relaxed atmosphere and a varied menu, including a separate list for the children, families like to frequent this restaurant. *241 Post Rd., tel. 902/863–5465. Reservations advised in summer. AE, DC, MC, V. Closed Jan. Moderate.*

Chester **The Galley.** Decked out in nautical bric-a-brac and providing a
Dining spectacular view of the ocean, this restaurant offers a pleasant, relaxed atmosphere. The menu features seafood: Smoked salmon and mussel dishes are the local favorites, but save room for the homemade blueberry pie. *Hwy. 3, on the Marina, tel. 902/275–4700. Reservations advised. AE, MC, V. Closed mid-Dec.–mid-Mar. Inexpensive.*

Debert
Lodging

Shady Maple Inn B&B. Here's a unique property: a working dairy farm where you can breakfast on fresh eggs, the farm's own maple syrup, jams, and jellies. Enjoy the smoke-free rooms and sun-dried linen, and take a dip in the pool. One of the three rooms is a deluxe suite with a water bed. *R.R. 1, B0M 1G0, tel. 902/662–3565. MC, V. Moderate–Expensive.*

Digby
Dining and Lodging

The Pines Resort Hotel. Complete with fireplaces, sitting rooms, a colossal dining room, and a view of Digby Harbor, this elegant property offers myriad amenities. Seafood with a French touch is served daily in the restaurant, and there is live entertainment in the lounge nightly. *Box 70, Shore Rd., B0V 1A0, tel. 902/245–2511. 90 rooms in main lodge, 60 in cottages. Facilities: restaurant, lounge, tennis, outdoor pool, golf. AE, DC, MC, V. Closed mid-Oct.–May. Expensive.*

Lorneville
Dining and Lodging
★

Amherst Shore Country Inn. Located 32 kilometers (20 miles) from Amherst on Route 366 is this superb inn with four rooms in-house and a rustic seaside cottage with fireplace. The comfortable decor includes quilts and antiques. Four new units, featuring Jacuzzi baths, efficiencies, and canopy beds will be added in early 1994. Incredibly well-prepared four-course dinners are served at one daily seating, at 7:30 PM (reservations required). *R.R. 2, Amherst, B4H 3X9, tel. 902/661–4800. 5 rooms. Facilities: restaurant. AE, DC, MC, V. Open May–Oct. Expensive.*

Lunenburg
Lodging

Bluenose Lodge. This 130-year-old mansion has nine large bedrooms and offers a full complimentary breakfast featuring treats such as freshly baked muffins, stewed rhubarb, and quiche. The bedrooms and sitting areas are furnished with distinctive antiques. The lodge also arranges deep sea fishing, biking, and whale watching excursions. *Box 339, 10 Falkland St., B0J 2C0, tel. 902/634–8851. 9 rooms. MC, V. Closed Nov.–Apr. Moderate–Expensive.*

Boscawen Inn. Antiques and fireplaces decorate this elegant century-old mansion, located in the center of town. The inn has views of this historic town's harbor. An annex, with four suites, is scheduled to open in 1994. *150 Cumberland St., Box 1343, B0J 2C0, tel. 902/634–3325. 17 rooms. AE, MC, V. Closed New Year's–Easter. Moderate–Expensive.*

Pictou
Lodging

The Walker Inn. A hospitable and energetic Swiss couple run this downtown inn in their brick Georgian-style townhouse, built in 1865. Every room is different, the dining room is fully licensed, and there's a new library-conference room where guests have an opportunity to meet each other. A Continental breakfast buffet is included in room rate. *34 Coleraine St., Box 629, B0K 1H0, tel. 902/485–1433. 10 rooms with bath. Facilities: restaurant, meeting room. AE, MC, V. Moderate.*

Salmon River
Lodging

Salmon River House. About 35 minutes east of Dartmouth, where Route 7 crosses the Salmon River, is this unpretentious white-frame inn, situated on 30 acres and offering glorious views. The home has a licensed dining room, sun room, wheelchair-accessible guest room, and one room with a water bed and whirlpool bath. *R.R. 2, head of Jeddore, B0J 1P0, tel. 902/889–3353 or 800/341–6096. 6 rooms with bath or shower. Facilities: dining room, canoe and boat rentals, fishing arranged. MC, V. Moderate–Expensive.*

Wolfville
Dining and Lodging

Blomidon Inn. Rooms at this elegant 19th-century sea-captain's mansion, restored in 1981, are uniquely decorated in

authentic colonial and Victorian fashion. The inn is located on
2½ acres of terraced land shaded by century-old elms, chest-
nuts, and maples. The dining room serves local cuisine cooked
in traditional style, using fresh seasonal produce. Complimentary tea is served every day at 4 PM. *127 Main St., B0P 1X0, tel.
902/542-2291. 27 rooms. Facilities: dining room, conference
room, tennis court. MC, V. Closed Dec. 24–26. Expensive.*

Yarmouth
Dining and Lodging

Manor Inn. With superior rooms and good food in pleasant surroundings, this colonial mansion on Highway 1 is a nice find.
There are three settings to choose from: a lakeside cottage, the
main estate, or the more secluded side wing. Steak and lobster
are the specialties in the dining room; reservations are required. *Box 56, Hebron, B0W 1X0, tel. 902/742-2487. 54 rooms.
Facilities: 2 dining rooms, 2 bars, whirlpool, heated pool, tennis
court, fireplaces. AE, DC, MC, V. Moderate.*

Cape Breton Island

Baddeck
Lodging

Inverary Inn Resort. These pleasant accommodations, in a 100-
year-old inn, cottages, motel units, and duplex cabins are all
situated within a waterfront complex on the island's scenic central drive. The property offers boating and swimming and close
proximity to the village, but the resort remains tranquil. Families will appreciate the on-site children's playground, and most
guests appreciate the wharfside restaurant. The main lodge
with its paneled walls, stone fireplace, and polished horse
brasses, has a strong Scottish flavor. *Box 190, B0E 1B0, tel.
902/295-2674. 137 rooms. Facilities: restaurant, chapel, indoor
and outdoor pools, fitness and games room, tennis, sauna. AE,
MC, V. Very Expensive.*

Iona
Lodging and Dining

Highland Heights Inn. The rural surroundings, the Scottish
homestyle cooking served near the dining room's huge stone
fireplace, and the unspoiled view of the lake substitute nicely
for the Scottish Highlands. The inn is located on a hillside beside the Nova Scotia Highland Village, overlooking the village
of Iona, where some residents still speak the Gaelic language
of their ancestors. Enjoy the salmon (or any fish in season),
fresh-baked oat cakes, and homemade desserts. *Box 19, Iona,
tel. 902/725-2360. 26 rooms. Facilities: dining room. AE, MC, V.
Closed mid-Oct.–mid-May. Moderate.*

Margaree Valley
Lodging

Normaway Inn. This secluded, 1920s inn is nestled in the hills
of the river valley, on 250 acres. Many of the cabins have wood-
burning stoves. Take advantage of the recreation barn and the
nightly traditional entertainment, including square dancing.
The inn is known for its gourmet country food, all of which is
prepared on the premises. The owners will organize salmon-
fishing trips for interested guests. *Box 326, B0E 2C0, tel.
902/248-2987. 9 rooms, 17 cabins. Facilities: restaurant, tennis,
bicycles. AE, MC, V. Closed Oct. 16–mid-June. Moderate.*

Northeast
Margaree
Lodging

Heart of Hart's Tourist Farm. This 100-year-old rural farmhouse on the Cabot Trail is within walking distance of the village. The theme is "very country," with wood stove, antiques,
and old-fashioned deep tubs in two of the bathrooms. Hot
homemade oatmeal and Red River cereal are a favorite part of
the full breakfast that is included in the room rate. Salmon and
trout-fishing trips can be arranged. *On Cabot Trail, B0E 2H0,
tel. 902/248-2765. 5 rooms. No credit cards. Open May–Oct. Inexpensive.*

Sydney **Joe's Warehouse.** For excellent food in the heart of town, stop
Dining here, where the specialties include local seafood and prime rib.
The porridge rolls and homemade scones also win rave reviews.
In summer, when the patio is open, the restaurant seats 200
people. Dress is casual and the atmosphere fun. After dinner
head downstairs for live music and dancing at Smooth Herman's. *424 Charlotte St., tel. 902/539–6686. AE, DC, MC, V. Moderate.*

Lodging **Delta Sydney.** This new hotel is located on the harbor, beside
the yacht club and close to the center of town. The attractively
decorated guest rooms have all the amenities, and each has a
view of the harbor. The intimate dining room specializes in seafood and Continental cuisine. *300 Esplanade, B1P 6J4, tel. in
Canada, 902/562–7500 or 800/268–1133; in U.S., 800/887–1133;
152 rooms. Facilities: restaurant, lounge, indoor pool, sauna,
fitness center. AE, DC, MC, V. Expensive.*

The Arts and Nightlife

The Arts

Theater Canada's oldest professional repertory theater, the **Neptune
Theatre** (5216 Sackville St., Halifax, tel. 902/429–7300), presents a full season each summer and winter of performances
from classics to contemporary Canadian drama. The **Mulgrave
Road Co-Op Theatre** (tel. 902/533–2092) is a small but active
professional company performing all over the Maritime Provinces, producing original plays based on local history. **Mermaid Theatre** (tel. 902/798–5841), based in Windsor, travels the
world with original children's plays that make extensive use of
masks and puppets.

The **Atlantic Fringe Festival** presents 40 shows in eight venues
during the first week of September. Dinner theaters in Halifax
include the **Historic Feast Company** (tel. 902/420–1840), which
presents shows set in the 19th century at Historic Properties
Thursday, Friday, and Saturday evenings; and the **Grafton
Street Dinner Theatre** (1741 Grafton St., tel. 902/425–1961),
where shows run Wednesday through Saturday.

Parrsboro's professional **Ship's Company Theatre** (tel.
902/254–2003) offers a summer season of plays based on historical events of the region, performed aboard the MV *Kipawo*,
a former Minas Basin ferry. The **Chester Summer Theatre** (tel.
902/275–2933) operates throughout the summer. Among the
best of Nova Scotia's thriving amateur companies are the **Kipawa Show Boat Company** (tel. 902/542–3500), which performs
in Wolfville on summer weekends, and **Theatre Antigonish** (tel.
902/867–3954), which performs at St. Francis Xavier University in Antigonish.

Many other towns have theaters that present touring shows
and occasional local productions, notably Chester, Liverpool,
Yarmouth, Annapolis Royal, Middle Musquodoboit, Pictou,
and Sydney. Glace Bay's opulent old opera house, the **Savoy
Theatre,** is the home of the summer-long Festival on the Bay.

Music Live concerts and musical presentations are held in Halifax at
the **Metro Centre** (Brunswick and Duke Sts., tel. 902/451–1202)
and the **Rebecca Cohn Auditorium** (6101 University Ave., tel.

902/494–2646). **Symphony Nova Scotia** normally appears at "the Cohn."

Scotia Festival of Music (tel. 902/429–9469) presents internationally recognized classical musicians in concerts and master classes each May and June at various locations in Halifax. **Musique Royale** hosts an August series of superb Renaissance and baroque concerts in historic buildings around the province. The **Atlantic Jazz Festival** takes place in Halifax in mid-July.

Talented musicians abound in Nova Scotia, ranging from traditional fiddlers to folk singers and rock bands. They appear in clubs, concerts, dances and a constant stream of open-air festivals. Names to watch for include The Rankin Family, The Barra MacNeills, the Minglewood Band, Sam Moon, Rita MacNeil, David MacIsaac, Scott Macmillan, and John Allan Cameron, as well as traditional fiddlers such as Buddy MacMaster, Ashley MacIsaac, Sandy MacIntyre, Lee Cremo, Jerry Holland, and Natalie MacMaster. An annual **Nova Scotia Bluegrass** and **Oldtime Music Festival** is held in Ardoise the last weekend in July; the **Lunenburg Folk Harbour Festival,** devoted to acoustic instruments and authentic folk music, takes place in early August; many leading fiddlers appear at Cape Breton's **Big Cove Concert** in mid-July.

Film

Halifax has a dynamic and growing film industry, which presents current work during the **Atlantic Film Festival,** held in Halifax the third week in September. The festival also showcases feature films, TV movies, and documentaries made elsewhere in the Atlantic Provinces. **Wormwood's Dog** and **Monkey Cinema** (2015 Gottingen St., tel. 902/422–3700) shows Canadian, foreign-language, and experimental films. Its associated video store, Critic's Choice, specializes in hard-to-find films on videotape.

Nightlife

The multilevel entertainment center in Historic Properties, **Privateer's Warehouse** (tel. 902/422–1289), is a popular nighttime hangout. At the ground-level Lower Deck tavern you can quaff a beer to Celtic music or enjoy jazz riffs at the Middle Deck on the second floor. There is a cover for both decks, and they are packed on weekends, so get there early.

Other popular Halifax night spots include **Cheers** (1743 Grafton St., tel. 902/421–1655), with bands and entertainment nightly, and **O'Carroll's** (1860 Upper Water St., tel. 902/423–4405), a restaurant, oyster bar, and lounge where you can hear live Irish music nightly.

The **Flamingo Café and Lounge** (1505 Barrington St., tel. 902/420–1051) features a wide variety of live entertainment, including open-mike night on Mondays.

3 Excursions from Nova Scotia to Coastal Maine

By David Laskin

The travel writings of David Laskin have appeared in the New York Times and Travel and Leisure, and 1990 saw publication of his book Eastern Islands: Accessible Islands of the East Coast.

Updated by Hilary Nangle

Maine is a likely excursion from Nova Scotia thanks to two ferry systems that make commuting easy. Boats depart form Yarmouth, Nova Scotia, and arrive in either Portland or Bar Harbor, Maine. Consider taking your car across, so you can travel up the Maine coast, taking in history, seafood, and fine shopping in the many outlet shops.

Getting There by Ferry

Marine Atlantic (tel. 800/341–7981) makes the 6½-hour trip from Yarmouth to Bar Harbor Sunday, Tuesday, and Thursday at 8 AM; boats return from Bar Harbor Monday, Wednesday, and Friday at 8 AM. One-way fares are $28.50 adults and $15.80 children 5–12; a $3 tax must be paid for children under 5. Cars cost an additional $47. Marine Atlantic also offers overnight and weekend packages (Maine to Nova Scotia), which include ferry transportation, hotels, and meals. Call for details. All ferries have a snack bar and full-buffet dining room, and it's advisable to make reservations for travel one week in advance.

Prince of Fundy Cruises (tel. 800/341–7540) takes passengers and cars on an 11-hour journey from Yarmouth to Portland, Maine, from early May until late October. Ferries depart from Nova Scotia every day except Wednesday at 9 PM; ferries depart from Maine every day except Tuesday at 9 PM. Peak season extends from late June through late September, at which time one-way fares are $75 adults and $38 children 5–14; children under 5 ride free. Cars cost an additional $98. During the rest of the operational year, one-way fares are $55 adults and $28 children; cars are an additional $80. All ferries have a dining room with a full menu and a coffee shop, and it's advisable to make reservations for travel one week in advance.

The Coast: Portland to Pemaquid Point

Maine's largest city, yet small enough to be seen with ease in a day or two, Portland is undergoing a cultural and economic renaissance. New hotels and a bright new performing arts center have joined the neighborhoods of historic homes; the Old Port Exchange, perhaps the finest urban renovation project on the East Coast, balances modern commercial enterprise with a salty waterfront character in an area bustling with restaurants, shops, and galleries. The piers of Commercial Street abound with opportunities for water tours of the harbor and excursions to the Calendar Islands.

Freeport, north of Portland, is a town made famous by the L. L. Bean store, whose success led to the opening of scores of other clothing stores and outlets. Brunswick is best known for Bowdoin College; Bath has been a shipbuilding center since 1607, and the Maine Maritime Museum preserves its history.

The Boothbays—the coastal areas of Boothbay Harbor, East Boothbay, Linekin Neck, Southport Island, and the inland town of Boothbay—attract hordes of vacationing families and flotillas of pleasure craft. The Pemaquid peninsula juts into the Atlantic south of Damariscotta and just east of the Boothbays, and near Pemaquid Beach one can view the objects unearthed at the Colonial Pemaquid Restoration.

Important Addresses and Numbers

Visitor Information **Convention and Visitors Bureau of Greater Portland** (305 Commercial St., tel. 207/772–5800).

Boothbay Harbor Region Chamber of Commerce (Box 356, Boothbay Harbor, tel. 207/633–2353).

Brunswick Area Chamber of Commerce (59 Pleasant St., Brunswick, tel. 207/725–8797).

Bath Area Chamber of Commerce (45 Front St., Bath, tel. 207/443–9751).

Freeport Merchants Association (Box 452, Freeport, tel. 207/865–1212).

Greater Portland Chamber of Commerce (145 Middle St., Portland, tel. 207/772–2811).

Getting Around Portland to Pemaquid Point

By Car The Congress Street exit from I–295 will take you into the heart of Portland. Numerous city parking lots have hourly rates of 50¢ to 85¢; the Gateway Garage on High Street, off Congress, is a convenient place to leave your car while exploring downtown. North of Portland, I–95 takes you to Exit 20 and Route 1, Freeport's Main Street, which continues on to Brunswick and Bath. East of Wiscasset you can take Route 27 south to the Boothbays, where Route 96 is a good choice for further exploration.

By Bus Portland's **Metro** (tel. 207/774–0351) runs seven bus routes in Portland, South Portland, and Westbrook. The fare is $1 for adults and 50¢ for senior citizens, people with disabilities, and children; exact change is required. Buses operate from 5:30 AM to 11:45 PM.

Exploring Portland

Numbers in the margin correspond to points of interest on the Southern Maine Coast and Portland maps.

❶ Congress Street, **Portland**'s main street, runs the length of the peninsular city from the Western Promenade in the southwest to the Eastern Promenade in the northeast, passing through the small downtown area. A few blocks southeast of downtown, the bustling Old Port Exchange sprawls along the waterfront.

❷ One of the notable homes on Congress Street is the **Neal Dow Memorial,** a brick mansion built in 1829 in the late Federal style by General Neal Dow, a zealous abolitionist and prohibitionist. The library has fine ornamental ironwork, and the furnishings include the family china, silver, and portraits. Don't miss the grandfather clocks and the original deed granted by James II. *714 Congress St., tel. 207/773–7773. Admission free. Open for tours weekdays 11–4. Closed holidays.*

❸ Just off Congress Street, the distinguished **Portland Museum of Art** has a strong collection of seascapes and landscapes by

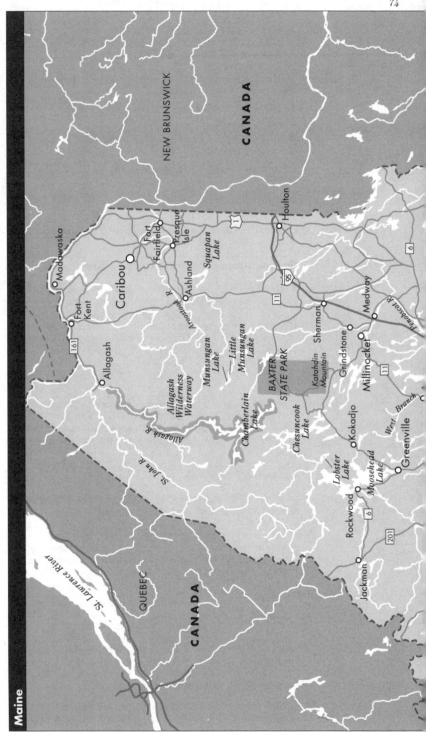

Maine

NEW HAMPSHIRE

ATLANTIC OCEAN

N

40 miles
60 km

Passamaquoddy Bay
Campobello Island
Grand Manan Island

West Gouldsboro
Hancock

Frenchman Bay

Passadumkeag
Passadumkeag

Old Town

Bangor

Ellsworth

Bar Harbor
ACADIA NAT'L PARK
Mt. Desert Island

Castine
Islesboro
Penobscot Bay
Deer Isle
Stonington
Vinalhaven Island
Isle au Haut

Dead R.

Newport

Belfast

Camden

Rockland

Damariscotta

Muscongus Bay

Kennebec R.

Waterville

Augusta

Newcastle

Bath

Georgetown

Freeport

Phippsburg

Casco Bay

Farmington

Androscoggin R.

Lewiston

Brunswick

495

Portland

Rangeley Lake
Rangeley
Mooselookmeguntic Lake

17

Bethel

26

Auburn

WHITE MOUNTAIN NAT'L FOREST

Lovell

Sebago Lake

Biddeford

Kennebunkport

Kennebunk

95

1

Portsmouth

9

1

1

1

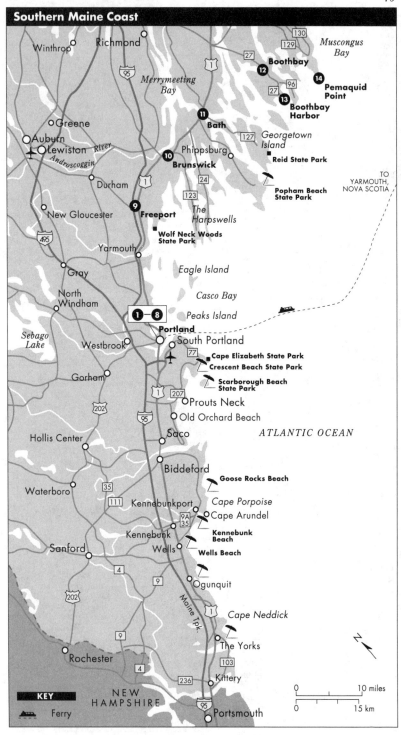

Southern Maine Coast

Winthrop

Richmond

130
129

Muscongus Bay

27

Boothbay ⑫

⑭ **Pemaquid Point**

27 96

⑬ **Boothbay Harbor**

Merrymeeting Bay

1

Greene

Auburn
Lewiston

Androscoggin River

⑪ **Bath**

Georgetown Island

127

■ **Reid State Park**

Durham

Phippsburg

⑩ **Brunswick**

1

24

123

Popham Beach State Park

TO YARMOUTH, NOVA SCOTIA

New Gloucester

⑨ **Freeport**

The Harpswells

Wolf Neck Woods State Park

Yarmouth

Eagle Island

Gray

North Windham

Casco Bay

Peaks Island

①—⑧

Sebago Lake

Portland

Westbrook

South Portland

77

■ **Cape Elizabeth State Park**

■ **Crescent Beach State Park**

Gorham

1 207

Scarborough Beach State Park

202

Prouts Neck

Old Orchard Beach

ATLANTIC OCEAN

Hollis Center

Saco

Biddeford

Waterboro

35

Goose Rocks Beach

111

Kennebunkport

Cape Porpoise

Cape Arundel

9A
35

Kennebunk Beach

Kennebunk

Sanford

Wells

Wells Beach

4

9

Ogunquit

202

Cape Neddick

1

9

The Yorks

Rochester

4

103

Kittery

236

KEY

▲ Ferry

0   10 miles

0   15 km

NEW HAMPSHIRE

95

Portsmouth

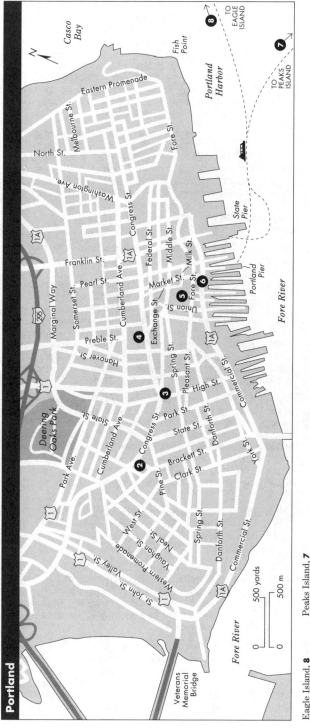

Portland

Casco Bay

N

Eastern Promenade

Fish Point

Portland Harbor

Melbourne St.

North St.

Washington Ave.

Fore St.

Congress St.

State Pier

Franklin St.

1A

Pearl St.

Cumberland Ave.

Federal St.

Middle St.

Milk St.

Somerset St.

Market St.

Fore St.

Portland Pier

Marginal Way

Exchange St.

Union St.

295

Preble St.

Hanover St.

Spring St.

1A

Deering Oaks Park

1

Pleasant St.

Congress St.

Park St.

High St.

Commercial St.

State St.

Danforth St.

Cumberland Ave.

State St.

1

Pine St.

Brackett St.

Clark St.

York St.

Park Ave.

West St.

Spring St.

Danforth St.

Vaughan St.

Neal St.

Western Promenade

1

1A

St. John St.

Valley St.

Commercial St.

1

Fore River

Fore River

Veterans Memorial Bridge

TO EAGLE ISLAND

TO PEAKS ISLAND

❽

❼

❻

❺

❹

❸

❷

0   500 yards
0   500 m

Eagle Island, **8**
Mariner's Church, **6**
Neal Dow Memorial, **2**
Old Port Exchange, **5**

Peaks Island, **7**
Portland Museum of Art, **3**
Wadsworth Longfellow House, **4**

such masters as Winslow Homer, John Marin, Andrew Wyeth, and Marsden Hartley. Homer's *Pulling the Dory* and *Weather-beaten,* two quintessential Maine coast images, are here. The Joan Whitney Payson Collection includes works by Monet, Picasso, and Renoir. The strikingly modern Charles Shipman Payson wing was designed by Harry N. Cobb, an associate of I. M. Pei, in 1983. *7 Congress Sq., tel. 207/775–6148 or 773–2787 for recorded information. Admission: $5 adults, $4 senior citizens and students, $2.50 children 6–18, free Sat. 10–noon. Open Tues.–Sat. 10–5, Thurs. 10–9, Sun. noon–5.*

❹ Walk east on Congress Street to the **Wadsworth Longfellow House** of 1785, the boyhood home of the poet and the first brick house in Portland. The late Colonial-style structure sits well back from the street and has a small portico over its entrance and four chimneys surmounting the hip roof. Most of the furnishings are original to the house. *485 Congress St., tel. 207/772–1807 or 207/774–1822. Admission: $3 adults, $1 children. Open June–Columbus Day weekend, Tues.–Sat. 10–4. Closed July 4. Garden open daily 9–5.*

❺ Although you can walk from downtown to the **Old Port Exchange,** you're better off driving and parking your car either at the city garage on Fore Street (between Exchange and Union streets) or opposite the U.S. Customs House at the corner of Fore and Pearl streets. Like the Customs House, the brick buildings and warehouses of the Old Port Exchange were built following the Great Fire of 1866 and were intended to last for ages. When the city's economy slumped in the middle of the present century, however, the Old Port declined and seemed slated for demolition. Then artists and craftspeople began opening shops here in the late 1960s, and in time restaurants, chic boutiques, bookstores, and gift shops followed.

The Old Port is best explored on foot. Allow a couple of hours to wander at leisure on Market, Exchange, Middle, and Fore **❻** streets. The **Mariner's Church** (376 Fore St.) has a fine facade of granite columns, and the Elias Thomas Block on Commercial Street demonstrates the graceful use of bricks in commercial architecture. Inevitably the salty smell of the sea will draw you to one of the wharves off Commercial Street; Custom House Wharf retains some of the older, rougher waterfront atmosphere.

Island Excursions The brightly painted ferries of **Casco Bay Lines** (tel. 207/774–7871) are the lifeline to the Calendar Islands of Casco Bay, which number about 136, depending on the tides and how one defines an island.

❼ **Peaks Island,** nearest Portland, is the most developed, and some residents commute to work in Portland. Yet you can still commune with the wind and the sea on Peaks, explore an old fort, and ramble along the alternately rocky and sandy shore. One bed-and-breakfast has overnight accommodations (*see* Peaks Island Lodging, *below*).

❽ The 17-acre **Eagle Island,** owned by the State of Maine and open to the public for day trips in summer, was the home of Admiral Robert E. Peary, the American explorer of the North Pole. Peary built a stone and wood house on the island as a summer retreat in 1904, then made it his permanent residence. The house remains as it was when Peary was here with his stuffed Arctic birds and the quartz he brought home set into the fieldstone fireplace. The *Kristy K.*, departing from Long Wharf, makes a four-hour narrated tour. *Long Wharf, tel. 207/774–6498. Excursion tour: $15 adults, $12 senior citizens, $9 children 5–9. Departures mid-June–Labor Day, daily 10.*

Exploring North of Portland

❾ Freeport, on Route 1, 15 miles northeast of Portland, has charming back streets lined with old clapboard houses and even a small harbor on the Harraseeket River, but the over-whelming majority of visitors come to shop, and L. L. Bean is the store that put Freeport on the map. Founded in 1912 as a small mail-order merchandiser of products for hunters, guides, and fisherfolk, L. L. Bean now attracts some 3.5 million shoppers a year to its giant store in the heart of Freeport's shopping district on Route 1. Here you can still find the original hunting boots, along with cotton, wool, and silk sweaters; camping and ski equipment; comforters; and hundreds of other items for the home, car, boat, or campsite. Across the street from the main store, a Bean factory outlet has seconds and discontinued mer-chandise at marked-down prices. *Rte. 1, Freeport, tel. 800/341–4341. Open 24 hrs.*

All around L. L. Bean, like seedlings under a mighty spruce, some 70 outlets have sprouted, offering designer clothes, shoes, housewares, and toys at marked-down prices (*see* Shopping, *below*).

❿ It's 9 miles northeast on Route 1 from Freeport to **Brunswick.** Follow the signs to the Brunswick business district, Pleasant Street, and—at the end of Pleasant Street—Maine Street, which claims to be the widest (198 feet across) in the state. Friday from May through October sees a fine farmer's market on the town mall, between Maine Street and Park Row.

Maine Street takes you to the 110-acre campus of **Bowdoin College,** an enclave of distinguished architecture, gardens, and grassy quadrangles in the middle of the city. Campus tours (tel. 207/725–3000) depart weekdays from Moulton Union. Among the historic buildings are Massachusetts Hall, a stout, sober, hip-roofed brick structure that dates from 1802, and Hubbard Hall, an imposing 1902 neo-Gothic building that houses **The Peary-MacMillan Arctic Museum.** The museum contains pho-tographs, navigational instruments, and artifacts from the first successful expedition to the North Pole, in 1909, by two of Bow-doin's most famous alumni, Admiral Robert E. Peary and Don-ald B. MacMillan. *Tel. 207/725–3416. Admission free. Open Tues.–Sat. 10–5, Sun. 2–5. Closed holidays.*

Don't miss the **Bowdoin College Museum of Art,** a splendid limestone, brick, and granite structure in a Renaissance Re-vival style, with three galleries upstairs, and five more down-stairs, radiating from a rotunda. Designed in 1894 by Charles F. McKim, the building stands on a rise, its facade adorned with classical statues and the entrance set off by a triumphal arch. The collections encompass Assyrian and Classical art and that of the Dutch and Italian old masters, including Pieter Brueghel's *Alpine Landscape*; a superb gathering of Colonial and Federal paintings, notably the Gilbert Stuart portraits of Madison and Jefferson; and paintings and drawings by Winslow Homer, Mary Cassatt, John Sloan, Rockwell Kent,

Jim Dine, and Robert Rauschenberg. *Walker Art Bldg., tel. 207/725–3275. Admission free. Open Tues.–Sat. 10–5, Sun. 2–5. Closed holidays.*

Before going on to Bath, you may elect to drive down Route 123 or Route 24 to the peninsulas and islands known collectively as the **Harpswells.** The numerous small coves along Harpswell Neck shelter the boats of local lobstermen, and summer cottages are tucked away amid the birch and spruce trees.

⓫ **Bath,** 7 miles east of Brunswick on Route 1, has been a shipbuilding center since 1607. Today the Bath Iron Works turns out guided-missile frigates for the U.S. Navy and merchant container ships.

The **Maine Maritime Museum** in Bath (take the Bath Business District exit from Route 1, turn right on Washington Street, and follow the signs) has ship models, journals, photographs, and other artifacts to stir the nautical dreams of old salts and young. The 142-foot Grand Banks fishing schooner *Sherman Zwicker,* one of the last of its kind, is on display when in port. You can watch apprentice boatbuilders wield their tools on classic Maine boats at the restored Percy & Small Shipyard and Apprentice Shop. The outdoor shipyard is closed in winter, but the indoor exhibits, videos, and activities are enhanced. *243 Washington St., tel. 207/443–1316. Admission: $6 adults, $5.40 senior citizens, $2.50 children 6–15. Open daily 9:30–5. Closed Thanksgiving, Dec. 25, Jan. 1.*

From Bath it's 10 miles northeast on Route 1 to Wiscasset, where the huge rotting hulls of the schooners *Hester* and *Luther Little* rest, testaments to the town's once-busy harbor. Those who appreciate both music and antiques will enjoy a visit to the **Musical Wonder House** to see and hear the vast collection of antique music boxes from around the world. *18 High St., tel. 207/882–7163. Admission free. 1-hr tour of main floor: $8 adults ($15 for 2), $6 children under 12 and senior citizens; 3-hr tour of entire house: $25 ($40 for 2). Open May 15–Oct. 15, daily 10–6. 1-hr tours given Sept.–Oct. 15 at 11, 1, and 3; May 15–Aug., whenever enough people; 3-hr tours by appointment. Closed Oct. 16–May 14.*

Across the river, drive south on Route 27 to reach the **Boothbay**
⓬ **Railway Village,** about a mile north of **Boothbay,** where you can ride 1½ miles on a narrow-gauge steam train through a recreation of a turn-of-the-century New England village. Among the 24 village buildings is a museum with more than 50 antique automobiles and trucks. *Rte. 27, Boothbay, tel. 207/633–4727. Admission: $5 adults, $2.50 children 2–12. Open mid-June–mid-Oct., daily 9:30–5.* Continue south on Route 27 into Boothbay Harbor, bear right on Oak Street, and follow it to the
⓭ waterfront parking lots. **Boothbay Harbor** is a town to wander through: Commercial Street, Wharf Street, the By-Way, and Townsend Avenue are lined with shops, galleries, and ice-cream parlors. Excursion boats (*see* Sports and Outdoor Activities, *below*) leave from the piers off Commercial Street.

Time Out   The **P&P Pastry Shoppe** (6 McKown St.) is a welcome stop for a sandwich or a pastry.

Having explored Boothbay Harbor, return to Route 27 and head north again to Route 1. Proceed north to Business Route

1, and follow it through Damariscotta, an appealing shipbuilding town on the Damariscotta River. Bear right on the Bristol Road (Route 129/130), and when the highway splits, stay on Route 130, which leads to Bristol and terminates at **Pemaquid Point.**

About 5 miles south of Bristol you'll come to New Harbor, where a right turn will take you to Pemaquid Beach and the **Colonial Pemaquid Restoration.** Here, on a small peninsula jutting into the Pemaquid River, English mariners established a fishing and trading settlement in the early 17th century. The excavations at Pemaquid Beach, begun in the mid-1960s, have turned up thousands of artifacts from the Colonial settlement, including the remains of an old customs house, tavern, jail, forge, and homes, and from even earlier Native American settlements. The State of Maine operates a museum displaying many of the artifacts. *Rte. 130, Pemaquid Point, tel. 207/677–2423. Admission: $1.50 adults, 50¢ children 6–12. Open Memorial Day–Labor Day, daily 9:30–5.*

Route 130 terminates at the **Pemaquid Point Light,** which looks as though it sprouted from the ragged, tilted chunk of granite that it commands. The former lighthouse keeper's cottage is now the **Fishermen's Museum,** with photographs, models, and artifacts that explore commercial fishing in Maine. Here, too, is the Pemaquid Art Gallery, which mounts changing exhibitions from July 1 through Labor Day. *Rte. 130, tel. 207/677–2494. Museum admission by contribution. Open Memorial Day–Columbus Day, Mon.–Sat. 10–5, Sun. 11–5.*

Portland to Pemaquid Point for Free

Bowdoin College Museum of Art, Brunswick
Neal Dow Memorial, Portland
The Peary-MacMillan Arctic Museum, Brunswick

What to See and Do with Children

Boothbay Railway Village, Boothbay
Children's Museum of Maine. Touching is okay at this museum where little ones can pretend they are lobstermen, shopkeepers, or computer experts. *142 Free St., Portland, tel. 207/797–5483. Admission: $2.50 adults, $2 senior citizens and children over 1, 1/2 price Wed. Open daily 9:30–4:30.*

Off the Beaten Track

Stroudwater Village, 3 miles west of Portland, was spared the devastation of the fire of 1866 and thus contains some of the best examples of 18th- and early 19th-century architecture in the region. Here are the remains of mills, canals, and historic homes, including the Tate House, built in 1755 with paneling from England. It overlooks the old mastyard where George Tate, Mast Agent to the King, prepared tall pines for the ships of the Royal Navy. The furnishings date to the late 18th century. *Tate House, 1270 Westbrook St., tel. 207/774–9781. Admission: $3 adults, $1 children. Open July–Sept. 15, Tues.–Sat. 10–4, Sun. 1–4.*

Shopping

The best shopping in Portland is at the Old Port Exchange, where many shops are concentrated along Fore and Exchange streets. Freeport's name is almost synonymous with shopping, and shopping in Freeport means **L. L. Bean** and the 70 factory outlets that opened during the 1980s. Outlet stores are located in the Fashion Outlet Mall (2 Depot St.) and the Freeport Crossing (200 Lower Main St.), and many others crowd Main Street and Bow Street. The *Freeport Visitors Guide* (Freeport Merchants Association, Box 452, Freeport 04032, tel. 207/865–1212) has a complete listing. Boothbay Harbor, and Commercial Street in particular, is chockablock with gift shops, T-shirt shops, and other seasonal emporia catering to visitors.

Antiques
Portland

F. O. Bailey Antiquarians (141 Middle St., tel. 207/774–1479), Portland's largest retail showroom, features antique and reproduction furniture; jewelry, paintings, rugs, and china.
Mary Alice Reilley Antiques (83 India St., tel. 207/773–8815) carries china, glass, tins, primitives, and a large selection of English and Irish country pine furniture.

Boothbay Harbor

Maine Trading Post (Commercial St., tel. 800/788–2760) sells antiques and quilts, as well as period restorations and reproductions that include rolltop desks able to accommodate personal computers.

Freeport

Harrington House Gallery Store (45 Main St., tel. 207/865–0477) is a restored 19th-century merchant's home owned by the Freeport Historical Society; all the period reproductions that furnish the rooms are for sale. In addition, you can buy wallpaper, crafts, Shaker items, toys, and kitchen utensils.

Books and Maps
Portland

Carlson and Turner (241 Congress St., tel. 207/773–4200) is an antiquarian book dealer with an estimated 40,000 titles.
Raffles Cafe Bookstore (555 Congress St., tel. 207/761–3930) presents an impressive selection of fiction and nonfiction. Coffee and a light lunch are served, and there are frequent readings and literary gatherings.

Freeport

DeLorme's Map Store (Rte. 1, tel. 207/865–4171) carries an exceptional selection of maps and atlases of Maine and New England, nautical charts, and travel books.

Clothing
Portland

A. H. Benoit (188 Middle St., tel. 207/773–6421) sells quality men's clothing from sportswear to evening attire.
Joseph's (410 Fore St., tel. 207/773–1274) has elegant tailored designer clothing for men and women.

Boothbay Harbor

House of Logan (Townsend Ave., tel. 207/633–2293) has specialty clothing for men and women, plus children's togs next door at the Village Store.

Crafts
Edgecomb

Edgecomb Potters (Rte. 27, tel. 207/882–6802) sells glazed porcelain pottery and other crafts.
Sheepscot River Pottery (Rte. 2, tel. 207/882–9410) has original hand-painted pottery as well as a large collection of American-made crafts including jewelry, kitchenware, furniture, and home accessories.

Galleries
Portland

Abacus (44 Exchange St., tel. 207/772–4880) has unusual gift items in glass, wood, and textiles, plus fine modern jewelry.

The Pine Tree Shop & Bayview Gallery (75 Market St., tel. 207/773–3007 or 800/244–3007) has original art and prints by prominent Maine painters.

Stein Glass Gallery (20 Milk St., tel. 207/772–9072) specializes in contemporary glass, both decorative and utilitarian.

Sports and Outdoor Activities

Boat Trips
Portland — For tours of the harbor, Casco Bay, and the nearby islands, try **Bay View Cruises** (Fisherman's Wharf, tel. 207/761–0496), **The Buccaneer** (Long Wharf, tel. 207/799–8188), **Casco Bay Lines** (Maine State Pier, tel. 207/774–7871), **Eagle Tours** (Long Wharf, tel. 207/774–6498), or **Old Port Mariner Fleet** (Long Wharf, tel. 207/775–0727).

Boothbay Harbor — *Appledore* (tel. 207/633–6598), a 66-foot windjammer, departs from Pier 6 at 9, noon, 3, and 6 for voyages to the outer islands.

Argo Cruises (tel. 207/633–2500) runs the *Islander* for morning cruises, Bath Hellgate cruises, supper sails, and whale watching; the *Islander II* for 1½-hour trips to Seal Rocks; the *Miss Boothbay*, a licensed lobster boat, for lobster-trap hauling trips. Biweekly evening cruises feature R&B or reggae. Departures are from Pier 6.

Balmy Days II (tel. 207/633–2284) leaves from Pier 8 for its day trips to Monhegan Island; the *Maranbo II*, operated by the same company, tours the harbor and nearby lighthouses.

Bay Lady (tel. 207/633–6990), a 31-foot Friendship sloop, offers sailing trips of under two hours from Fisherman's Wharf. **Cap'n Fish's Boat Trips** (tel. 207/633–3244) offers sightseeing cruises throughout the region, including puffin cruises, trips to Damariscove Harbor, Pemaquid Point, and up the Kennebec River to Bath, departing from Pier 1.

Eastward (tel. 207/633–4780) is a Friendship sloop with six-passenger capacity that departs from Ocean Point Road in East Boothbay for one-day or half-day sailing trips. Itineraries vary with passengers' desires and the weather.

Deep-Sea Fishing
Half-day and full-day fishing charter boats operating out of Portland include *Anjin-San* (tel. 207/772–7168) and *Devils Den* (DeMillo's Marina, tel. 207/761–4466).

Operating out of Boothbay Harbor, **Cap'n Fish's Deep Sea Fishing** (tel. 207/633–3244) schedules daylong and half-day trips, departing from Pier 1, and **Lucky Star Charters** (tel. 207/633–4624) runs full-day and half-day charters for up to six people, with departures from Pier 8.

Nature Walks
Wolfe's Neck Woods State Park has self-guided trails along Casco Bay, the Harraseeket River, and a fringe salt marsh, as well as walks led by naturalists. Picnic tables and grills are available, but there's no camping. Follow Bow Street opposite L. L. Bean off Route 1. *Wolfe's Neck Rd., tel. 207/865–4465. Open Memorial Day–Labor Day.*

Beaches

Crescent Beach State Park (Rte. 77, Cape Elizabeth, tel. 207/767–3625), about 8 miles from Portland, has a sand beach, picnic tables, seasonal snack bar, and bathhouse.

Scarborough Beach State Park (Rte. 207, off Rte. 1 in Scarborough, tel. 207/883–2416) has a long stretch of sand beach with good surf. Parking is limited.

Popham Beach State Park, at the end of Route 209, south of Bath, has a good sand beach, a marsh area, and picnic tables. *Phippsburg, tel. 207/389–1335. Admission: $1.50 adults, 50¢ children, late Apr.–mid-Oct.*

Reid State Park, on Georgetown Island, off Route 127, has 1½ miles of sand on three beaches. Facilities include bathhouses, picnic tables, fireplaces, and snack bar. Parking lots fill by 11 AM on summer Sundays and holidays. *Georgetown, tel. 207/371–2303. Admission: $2 adults, 50¢ children, late Apr.–mid-Oct.*

Dining and Lodging

Many of Portland's best restaurants are in the Old Port Exchange district. Casual dress is the rule except where noted. Highly recommended restaurants and lodgings in each price category are indicated by a star ★.

Bath **Kristina's Restaurant & Bakery.** This frame house turned res-
Dining taurant, with a front deck built around a huge oak tree, turns out some of the finest pies, pastries, and cakes on the coast. A satisfying dinner menu features new American cuisine, including fresh seafood and grilled meats. Pastries can be packed to go. *160 Centre St., tel. 207/442–8577. Reservations accepted. D, MC, V. Closed Mon. No dinner Sun. Inexpensive–Moderate.*

Lodging **Fairhaven Inn.** This cedar-shingle house built in 1790 is set on 27 acres of woods and meadows sloping down to the Kennebec River. Guest rooms are furnished with handmade quilts and four-poster beds. The home-cooked breakfast offers such treats as peach soup and blintzes. *RR 2, Box 85, N. Bath, 04530, tel. 207/443–4391. 7 rooms, 5 with bath. Facilities: hiking and cross-country ski trails. Children welcome by prior arrangement. AE, MC, V. Rates include breakfast. Moderate.*

Boothbay **Kenniston Hill Inn.** The white-clapboard house with columned
Lodging porch offers comfortably old-fashioned accommodations in a country setting only minutes from Boothbay Harbor. Four guest rooms have fireplaces, some have four-poster beds, rocking chairs, and gilt mirrors. Full breakfasts are served family-style at a large wood table. *Box 125, 04537, tel. 207/633–2159. 10 rooms with bath. No pets. No smoking. MC, V. Expensive.*

Boothbay Harbor **Black Orchid.** The classic Italian fare includes fettuccine Al-
Dining fredo with fresh lobster and mushrooms, and *petit filet à la diabolo* (fillets of Angus steak with Marsala sauce). The upstairs and downstairs dining rooms sport a Roman-trattoria ambience, with frilly leaves and fruit hanging from the rafters and little else in the way of decor. In the summer there is a raw bar outdoors. *5 By-Way, tel. 207/633–6659. AE, MC, V. Closed Nov.–Apr. No lunch. Moderate–Expensive.*

Andrew's Harborside. The seafood menu is typical of the area—lobster, fried clams and oysters, haddock with seafood stuffing—but the harbor view makes it memorable. Lunch features lobster and crab rolls; children's and seniors' menus are available. You can dine outdoors on a deck during the summer. *8 Bridge St., tel. 207/633–4074. Dinner reservations accepted for 5 or more. MC, V. Closed mid-Oct.–mid-May. Moderate.*

Lodging **Fisherman's Wharf Inn.** All rooms overlook the water at this modern motel-style facility built 200 feet out over the harbor. The large dining room has floor-to-ceiling windows, and several day-trip cruises leave from this location. *40 Commercial St., 04538, tel. 207/633–5090 or 800/628–6872. 54 rooms with bath. Facilities: restaurant. AE, D, DC, MC, V. Closed Nov.–mid-May. Moderate–Very Expensive.*

The Pines. Families seeking a secluded setting with lots of room for little ones to run will be interested in this motel on a hillside a mile from town. Rooms have sliding glass doors opening onto private decks, two double beds, and small refrigerators. Cribs are free. *Sunset Rd., Box 693, 04538, tel. 207/633–4555. 29 rooms with bath. Facilities: all-weather tennis court, heated outdoor pool, playground. MC, V. Closed mid-Oct.–early May. Moderate.*

Brunswick **The Great Impasta.** This small, storefront restaurant is a great
Dining spot for lunch, tea, or dinner. Try the seafood lasagna, or match your favorite pasta and sauce to create your own dish. *42 Maine St., tel. 207/729–5858. No reservations. AE, D, DC, MC, V. Closed Sun. Inexpensive–Moderate.*

Lodging **Captain Daniel Stone Inn.** One of only two Someplace Different select hostelries in the United States, this Federal-style inn overlooks the Androscoggin River. While no two rooms are furnished identically, all offer executive-style comforts and many have whirlpool baths and pullout sofas in addition to queen-size beds. A guest parlor, 24-hour breakfast room, and excellent service in the Narcissa Stone Restaurant make this an upscale escape from college-town funk. *10 Water St., 04011, tel. 207/725–9898. Facilities: air-conditioning, cable TV, complimentary Continental breakfast, movies. No pets. No smoking. AE, DC, MC, V. Expensive.*

Freeport **Harraseeket Inn.** The formal, no-smoking dining room upstairs
Dining is a simply appointed, light and airy space with picture windows facing the inn's garden courtyard. The New England/Continental cuisine emphasizes fresh, local ingredients. Downstairs, the Broad Arrow Tavern appears to have been furnished by L. L. Bean, with fly rods, snowshoes, moose heads, and other hunting-lodge trappings. The fare is hearty, with less formal lunches and snacks and dinners of charbroiled skewered shrimp and scallops, ribs, burgers, pasta, or lobster. *162 Main St., tel. 207/865–9377 or 800/342–6423. Reservations advised. Collared shirt at dinner. AE, D, DC, MC, V. Expensive–Very Expensive.*

Harraseeket Lunch & Lobster Co. This no-frills, bare-bones, genuine lobster pound and fried seafood place is located beside the town landing in South Freeport. Seafood baskets and lobster dinners are what it's all about; there are picnic tables outside and a dining room inside. *Main St., South Freeport, tel. 207/865–4888. No reservations. No credit cards. Inexpensive.*

Lodging **Harraseeket Inn.** When two white-clapboard houses, one a fine Greek Revival home of 1850, found themselves two blocks from the biggest retailing explosion ever to hit Maine, the innkeepers added a four-story building that looks like an old New England inn—white clapboard with green shutters—and is in fact a steel and concrete structure with elevators and Jacuzzis. The Harraseeket strives to achieve the country inn experience, with afternoon tea in the mahogany drawing room and fireplaces throughout. Guest rooms (vintage 1989) have reproductions of Federal-period canopy beds and bright, coordinated

fabrics. The full breakfast is served buffet-style in an airy upstairs formal dining room facing the garden. *162 Main St.,
04032, tel. 207/865–9377 or 800/342–6423. 54 rooms with bath, including 6 suites. Facilities: restaurant, tavern, room service
until 11 PM, croquet, some rooms have a working fireplace. AE,
D, DC, MC, V. Very Expensive.*

Georgetown **The Osprey.** Located in a marina on the way to Reid State Park,
Dining this gourmet restaurant may be reached both by land and sea.
The appetizers alone are worth the stop: homemade garlic and
Sicilian sausages; artichoke strudel with three cheeses; and
warm braised duck salad with Oriental vegetables in rice
paper. Entrées might include such classics as saltimbocca or
such originals as salmon en papillote with julienne leeks, car-
rots, and fresh herbs. The wine list is excellent. The glassed-in
porch offers water views and breezes. *6 mi down Rte. 127, turn
left at restaurant sign on Robinhood Rd., tel. 207/371–2530. Reservations advised. MC, V. Open daily June–Labor Day; call for
schedule rest of year. Moderate–Expensive.*

Newcastle **Newcastle Inn.** The white-clapboard house, vintage mid-19th
Lodging century, has a homey living room with a red velvet sofa, books,
★ family photos on the mantel, and a sun porch with white wicker
furniture and ice-cream parlor chairs. Guest rooms are not
large, but they have been carefully appointed with old spool
beds, toys, and Victorian velvet sofas, minimizing clutter and
maximizing the light and the river views. Guests choose between bed-and-breakfast (a full gourmet meal, perhaps scram-
bled eggs with caviar in puff pastry, ricotta cheese pie, or
frittata) and Modified American Plan. *River Rd., 04553, tel.
207/563–5685 or 800/83–BUNNY. 15 rooms with bath. Facilities:
dining room. No smoking. MC, V. Expensive.*

Peaks Island **Keller's B&B.** This turn-of-the-century home offers rustic ac-
Lodging commodations with deck views of Casco Bay and the Portland
skyline. The beach is only steps away from your room. *20 Island
Ave., tel. 207/766–2441. 4 rooms with bath. MC, V. Moderate.*

Pemaquid Point **The Bradley Inn.** Within walking distance of the Pemaquid
Dining and Lodging Point lighthouse, beach, and fort, the 1900 Bradley Inn began
as a rooming house for summer rusticators and alternated be-
tween abandonment and operation as a B&B until its complete
renovation in the early 1990s. Rooms are comfortable and un-
cluttered; ask for one of the cathedral-ceilinged, waterside
rooms on the third floor, which offer breathtaking views of the
sun setting over the water. The Ship's Restaurant offers such
entrées as Moroccan chicken, filet mignon, and seafood alfredo;
there's light entertainment in the pub on weekends. *Rte. 130,
HC 61, 361 Pemaquid Point, New Harbor 04554, tel. 207/677–
2105. 12 rooms with bath, 1 cottage. Facilities: restaurant, pub,
cable TV and phones in rooms, croquet, bicycles, light entertainment on weekends. Continental breakfast included in rate. AE,
MC, V. Expensive–Very Expensive.*

Portland **The Back Bay Grill.** Mellow jazz, a mural of Portland, an im-
Dining pressive wine list, and wonderful, carefully prepared food
★ make this simple, elegant restaurant a popular spot. Appetizers such as pizza with capicola, three cheeses, peppers, and
shallots, and mixed greens with caramelized pecans in a gor-
gonzola-balsamic vinaigrette are followed by grilled chicken,
halibut, oysters, salmon, trout, pork chops, or steak. *65 Port-*

land St., tel. 207/772–8833. Reservations advised. Jacket advised. Closed Sun. AE, D, MC, V. Expensive–Very Expensive.

Alberta's. Small, bright, casual, and friendly, Alberta's specializes in what one waiter described as "electric American" cuisine: dishes like London broil spiced with garlic, cumin, and lime; pan-blackened rib-eye steak with sour cream and scallions; and Atlantic salmon fillet with orange-ginger sauce, grilled red cabbage, and apple salad. The two-tier dining room has photos mounted on salmon-hued walls, and the music ranges from country to classical. *21 Pleasant St., tel. 207/774–0016. No reservations. AE, DC, MC, V. Beer and wine only. Closed Thanksgiving, Dec. 25. No lunch weekends. Moderate–Expensive.*

★ **Cafe Always.** White linen tablecloths, candles, and Victorian-style murals by local artists set the mood for innovative cuisine. Begin with Pemaquid Point oysters seasoned with pink peppercorns and champagne, or chicken and wild rice in a nori roll, before choosing from vegetarian dishes, pasta, or more substantial entrées, such as grilled tuna with a fiery Japanese sauce or leg of lamb with goat cheese and sweet peppers. *47 Middle St., tel. 207/774–9399. Reservations advised. Dress: neat but casual. AE, MC, V. Closed Mon. Moderate–Expensive.*

Seamen's Club. Built just after Portland's Great Fire of 1866, and an actual sailors' club in the 1940s, this restaurant has become an Old Port Exchange landmark, with its Gothic windows and carved medallions. Seafood is an understandable favorite—moist, blackened tuna, salmon and swordfish prepared differently each day, and lobster fettuccini are among the highlights. *375 Fore St., tel. 207/772–7311. Reservations advised. Dress: neat but casual. AE, DC, MC, V. Moderate–Expensive.*

Katahdin. Somehow, the painted tables, flea-market decor, mismatched dinnerware, and faux-stone bar work together here. The cuisine, large portions of home-cooked New England fare, is equally unpretentious and fun: Try the chicken pot pie, fried trout, crab cakes, or the nightly Blue Plate special—and save room for a fruit-crisp for dessert. *108 Spring St., tel. 207/774–1740. No reservations. MC, V. Moderate.*

★ **Street & Co.** If the secret of a restaurant's success can be "keep it simple," Street & Co., the best seafood restaurant in Maine, goes one step further—"keep it small." You enter through the kitchen, with all its wonderful aromas, and dine amid dried herbs and shelves of staples on one of a dozen copper-topped tables (so your waiter can place a skillet of steaming seafood directly in front of you). Begin with lobster bisque or diavolo for two, crab sautéed with Oriental mushrooms and watercress, or grilled eggplant—vegetarian dishes are the only alternatives to fish. Choose from an array of superb entrées, ranging from calamari, clams, mussels, or shrimp served over linguine, to blackened, broiled, or grilled seafood. The desserts are top-notch. *33 Wharf St., tel. 207/775–0887. Reservations advised. AE, MC, V. No lunch. Inexpensive–Moderate.*

Lodging **Pomegranate Inn.** Clever touches such as faux marbling on the moldings and mustard-colored rag-rolling in the hallways give this bed-and-breakfast a bright, postmodern air. Most guest rooms are spacious and bright, accented with original paintings on floral and tropical motifs; the location on a quiet street in the city's Victorian Western Promenade district ensures serenity. Telephones and televisions, rare in an inn, make this a good choice for businesspeople. *49 Neal St., 04102, tel. 207/772–*

1006 or 800/356–0408. 7 rooms with bath, 1 suite. AE, DC, MC, V. Expensive–Very Expensive.

★ **Portland Regency Inn.** The only major hotel in the center of the Old Port Exchange, the Regency building was Portland's armory in the late 19th century and is now the city's most luxurious, most distinctive hotel. The bright, plush, airy rooms have four-poster beds, tall standing mirrors, floral curtains, and loveseats. The health club, the best in the city, offers massage and has an aerobics studio, free weights, Nautilus equipment, a large Jacuzzi, dry sauna, and steam room. 20 Milk St., 04101, tel. 207/774–4200 or 800/727–3436. *95 rooms with bath, 8 suites. Facilities: restaurant, health club, nightclub, banquet and convention rooms. AE, D, DC, MC, V. Expensive.*

Sonesta Hotel. Across the street from the art museum and in the heart of the downtown business district, the 12-story brick building, vintage 1927, looks a bit dowdy today. Rooms in the tower section (added in 1961) have floor-to-ceiling windows, and the higher floors have harbor views. The small health club offers Universal gym equipment, rowing machines, stationary bikes, and a sauna. *157 High St., 04101, tel. 207/775–5411 or 800/777–6246. 202 rooms with bath. Facilities: 2 restaurants, 2 bars, health club, banquet and convention rooms. AE, D, DC, MC, V. Moderate–Expensive.*

The Arts

Center for the Arts at the Chocolate Church (804 Washington St., tel. 207/422–8455) offers changing exhibits by Maine artists such as Douglas Alvord and Dahlov Ipcar, as well as performances by Marion McPartland, Livingston Taylor, a children's orchestra, and repertory theater groups. There is also a classic film series, classes, and workshops.

Portland Performing Arts Center (25A Forest Ave., Portland, tel. 207/761–0591) hosts music, dance, and theater performances.

Dance **Ram Island Dance Company** (25A Forest Ave., Portland, tel. 207/773–2562), the city's resident modern dance troupe, appears at the Portland Performing Arts Center.

Music **Bowdoin Summer Music Festival** (Bowdoin College, Brunswick, tel. 207/725–3322 Sept.–May or 914/664–5957 June–Aug.) is a six-week concert series featuring performances by students, faculty, and prestigious guest artists.

Carousel Music Theater ("The Meadows," Boothbay Harbor, tel. 207/633–5297) mounts musical revues from Memorial Day to Columbus Day.**Cumberland County Civic Center** (1 Civic Center Sq., Portland, tel. 207/775–3458) hosts concerts, sporting events, and family shows in a 9,000-seat auditorium.

Portland Symphony Orchestra (30 Myrtle St., Portland, tel. 207/773–8191) gives concerts October through August.

Theater **Mad Horse Theatre Company** (955 Forest Ave., Portland, tel. 207/797–3338) performs contemporary and original works.

Maine State Music Theater (Pickard Theater, Bowdoin College, Brunswick, tel. 207/725–8769 or 800/698–8769) stages musicals from mid-June through August.

Portland Stage Company (25A Forest Ave., Portland, tel. 207/774–0465), a producer of national reputation, mounts six productions, from November through April, at the Portland Performing Arts Center.

Theater Project of Brunswick (14 School St., Brunswick, tel. 207/729–8584) performs from late June through August.

Nightlife

Bars and Lounges **Cafe No** (20 Danforth St., Portland, tel. 207/772–8114) transports guests back to the '50s with coffeehouse poetry readings, beat music, and Middle Eastern food. There's live jazz Thursday through Saturday, with open jam sessions on Sunday from 4 until 8. *Closed Monday.*

Gritty McDuff's Brew Pub (396 Fore St., Portland, tel. 207/772–2739) attracts the young, the lively, and connoisseurs of the ales and bitters brewed on the premises. Steak and kidney pie and fish and chips are served.

Three Dollar Dewey's (446 Fore St., Portland, tel. 207/772–3310), long a popular Portland night spot, is an English-style ale house.

Top of the East (Sonesta Hotel, 157 High St., Portland, tel. 207/775–5411) has a view of the city and live entertainment—jazz, piano, and comedy.

Music **McSeagull's Gulf Dock** (Boothbay Harbor, tel. 207/633–4041) draws young singles with live music and a loud bar scene.

Raoul's Roadside Attraction (865 Forest Ave., tel. 207/775–2494), southern Maine's hippest nightclub/restaurant, books both local and name bands, especially R&B, jazz, and reggae groups.

The Coast: Penobscot Bay

Purists hold that the Maine coast begins at Penobscot Bay, where the vistas over the water are wider and bluer, the shore a jumble of broken granite boulders, cobblestones, and gravel punctuated by small sand beaches, and the water numbingly cold. Port Clyde in the southwest and Stonington in the southeast are the outer limits of Maine's largest bay, 35 miles apart across the bay waters but separated by a drive of almost 100 miles on scenic but slow two-lane highways.

Rockland, the largest town on the bay, is Maine's major lobster distribution center and the port of departure to several bay islands. The Camden Hills, looming green over Camden's fashionable waterfront, turn bluer and fainter as one moves on to Castine, the elegant small town across the bay. Deer Isle is connected to the mainland by a slender, high-arching bridge, but Isle au Haut, accessible from Deer Isle's fishing town of Stonington, may be reached by passenger ferry only: More than half of this steep, wooded island is wilderness, the most remote section of Acadia National Park.

Important Addresses and Numbers

Visitor
Information

Blue Hill Chamber of Commerce (Box 520, Blue Hill, 04614).

Castine Town Office (tel. 207/326–4502).

Deer Isle–Stonington Chamber of Commerce (Rte. 15, Little Deer Isle; Box 268, Stonington, 04681, tel. 207/348–6124).

Rockland–Thomaston Area Chamber of Commerce (Harbor Park, Box 508, Rockland, 04841, tel. 207/596–0376).

Rockport–Camden–Lincolnville Chamber of Commerce (Box 919, Camden, 04843, tel. 207/236–4404).

Searsport Chamber of Commerce (Box 468, Searsport, 04974, tel. 207/548–6510).

Emergencies **Island Medical Center** (Airport Rd., Stonington, tel. 207/367–2311).

Penobscot Bay Medical Center (Rte. 1, Rockland, tel. 207/596–8000).

Arriving and Departing by Plane

Bangor International Airport (tel. 207/947–0384), north of Penobscot Bay, has daily flights by major U.S. carriers.

Knox County Regional Airport (tel. 207/594–4131), 3 miles south of Rockland, has frequent flights to Boston.

Getting Around Penobscot Bay

By Car Route 1 follows the west coast of Penobscot Bay, linking Rockland, Camden, Belfast, and Searsport. On the east side of the bay, Route 175 (south from Route 1) takes you to Route 166A (for Castine) and Route 15 (for Blue Hill, Deer Isle, and Stonington). A car is essential for exploring the bay area.

Exploring Penobscot Bay

Numbers in the margin correspond to points of interest on the Penobscot Bay map.

From Pemaquid Point at the western extremity of Muscongus Bay to Port Clyde at its eastern extent, it's less than 15 miles across the water, but it's 50 miles for the motorist who must return north to Route 1 to reach the far shore.

Travelers on Route 1 can make an easy detour south through Tenants Harbor and Port Clyde before reaching Rockland. Turn onto Route 131 at Thomaston, 5 miles west of Rockland, and follow the winding road past waterside fields, spruce woods, ramshackle barns, and trim houses. **Tenants Harbor,** 7 miles from Thomaston, is a quintessential Maine fishing town, its harbor dominated by squat, serviceable lobster boats, its shores rocky and slippery, its town a scattering of clapboard houses, a church, a general store. The fictional Dunnet Landing of Sarah Orne Jewett's classic sketches of Maine coastal life, *The Country of the Pointed Firs,* is based on this region.

Route 131 ends at Port Clyde, a fishing town that is the point of departure for the *Laura B.* (tel. 207/372–8848 for schedules),

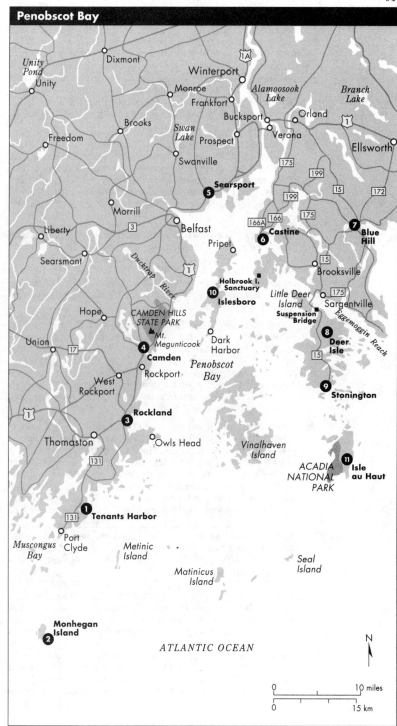

Penobscot Bay

2 the mailboat that serves Monhegan Island. Tiny, remote **Monhegan Island** with its high cliffs fronting the open sea was known to Basque, Portuguese, and Breton fishermen well before Columbus "discovered" America. About a century ago Monhegan was discovered again by some of America's finest painters, including Rockwell Kent, Robert Henri, and Edward Hopper, who sailed out to paint the savage cliffs, the meadows, the wild ocean views, and the shacks of fisherfolk. Tourists followed, and today Monhegan is overrun with visitors in summer.

Returning north to Route 1, you have less than 5 miles to go to **3** **Rockland** on Penobscot Bay. This large fishing port is the commercial hub of the coast, with working boats moored alongside growing flotilla of cruise schooners. Although a number of boutiques and restaurants have emerged in recent years, the town has retained its working-class flavor—you are more likely to find rusting hardware than ice-cream shops at the water's edge.

The outer harbor is bisected by a nearly mile-long breakwater, which begins on Waldo Avenue and ends with a lighthouse that was built in 1888. Next to the breakwater is **The Samoset Resort** (Warrenton St., tel. 207/594–2511 or 800/341–1650), a sprawling oceanside resort featuring an 18-hole golf course, indoor and outdoor swimming pools, tennis, racquetball, restaurant, and health club.

Also in Rockland is the **William A. Farnsworth Library and Art Museum.** Here are oil and watercolor landscapes of the coastal lands you have just seen, among them Andrew Wyeth's *Eight Bells* and N.C. Wyeth's *Her Room.* Jamie Wyeth is also represented in the collections, as are Winslow Homer, Rockwell Kent, and the sculptor Louise Nevelson. *19 Elm St., tel. 207/596–6457. Admission free. Open Mon.–Sat. 10–5, Sun. 1–5. Closed Mon. Oct.–May.*

4 From Rockland it's 8 miles north on Route 1 to **Camden,** "Where the mountains meet the sea"—an apt description, as you will discover when you step out of your car and look up from the harbor. Camden is famous not only for geography but for the nation's largest windjammer fleet; at just about any hour during the warmer months you're likely to see at least one windjammer tied up in the harbor, and windjammer cruises are a superb way to explore the ports and islands of Penobscot Bay.

Time Out   **Ayer's Fish Market** on Main Street has the best fish chowder in town; take a cup to the pleasant park at the head of the harbor when you're ready for a break from the shops on Bayview and Main streets.

The entrance to the 6,000-acre **Camden Hills State Park** (tel. 207/236–3109) is 2 miles north of Camden on Route 1. If you're accustomed to the Rockies or the Alps, you may not be impressed with heights of not much more than 1,000 feet, yet the Camden Hills are landmarks for miles along the vast, flat reaches of the Maine coast. The park contains 25 miles of trails, including an easy trail up Mount Megunticook, the highest of the group. The 112-site camping area, open May through November, has flush toilets and hot showers. Admission to the trails or the auto road up Mount Battie is $1.50 per person.

5 Farther north on Route 1, **Searsport**—Maine's second-largest deepwater port (after Portland)—claims to be the antiques capital of Maine. The town's stretch of Route 1 hosts a seasonal weekend flea market in addition to its antiques shops.

Searsport preserves a rich nautical history at the **Penobscot Marine Museum,** whose seven buildings display portraits of 284 sea captains, artifacts of the whaling industry (lots of scrimshaw), paintings and models of famous ships, navigational instruments, and treasures that seafarers collected. *Church St., tel. 207/548–2529. Admission: $4 adults, $3.50 senior citizens, $1.50 children 7–15. Open June–mid-Oct., Mon.–Sat. 9:30–5, Sun. 1–5.*

6 Historic **Castine,** over which the French, the British, and the Americans fought from the 17th century to the War of 1812, has two museums and the ruins of a British fort, but the finest thing about Castine is the town itself: the lively, welcoming town landing, the serene Federal and Greek Revival houses, and the town common. Castine invites strolling, and you would do well to start at the town landing, where you can park your car, and walk up Main Street past the two inns and on to the white Trinitarian Federated Church with its tapering spire.

Turn right on Court Street and walk to the town common, which is ringed by a collection of white-clapboard buildings that includes the Ives House (once the summer home of the poet Robert Lowell), the Abbott School, and the Unitarian Church, capped by a whimsical belfry that suggests a gazebo.

7 From Castine, take Route 166 north to Route 199 and follow the signs to **Blue Hill.** Castine may have the edge over Blue Hill in charm, for its Main Street is not a major thoroughfare and it claims a more dramatic perch over its harbor, yet Blue Hill is certainly appealing and boasts a better selection of shops and galleries. Blue Hill is renowned for its pottery, and two good shops are right in town.

8 The scenic Route 15 south from Blue Hill passes through Brooksville and on to the graceful suspension bridge that crosses Eggemoggin Reach to **Deer Isle.** The turnout and picnic area at Caterpillar Hill, 1 mile south of the junction of Routes 15 and 175, commands a fabulous view of Penobscot Bay, the hundreds of dark green islands, and the Camden Hills across the bay, which from this perspective look like a range of mountains dwarfed and faded by an immense distance—yet they are less than 25 miles away.

9 Route 15 continues the length of Deer Isle—a sparsely settled landscape of thick woods opening to tidal coves, shingled houses with lobster traps stacked in the yards, and dirt roads that lead to summer cottages—to **Stonington,** an emphatically ungentrified community that tolerates summer visitors but makes no effort to cater to them. Main Street has gift shops and galleries, but this is a working port town, and the principal activity is at the waterfront, where fishing boats arrive with the day's catch. The high, sloped island that rises beyond the archipelago of Merchants Row is Isle au Haut, accessible by mailboat from Stonington, which contains sections of Acadia National Park.

Island Excursions **Islesboro,** accessible by car-and-passenger ferry from Lin-
10 colnville Beach north of Rockland (Maine State Ferry Service,

tel. 207/789–5611), has been a retreat of wealthy, very private families for more than a century. The long, narrow, mostly wooded island has no real town to speak of; there are scatterings of mansions as well as humbler homes at Dark Harbor and at Pripet near the north end. Since the amenities on Islesboro are quite spread out, you don't want to come on foot. If you plan to spend the night on Islesboro, you should make a reservation well in advance (*see* Islesboro Lodging, *below*).

Time Out   **Dark Harbor Shop** (tel. 207/734–8878) on Islesboro is an old-fashioned ice-cream parlor where tourists, locals, and summer folk gather for sandwiches, newspapers, gossip, and gifts. Open June through August.

⓫ Isle au Haut thrusts its steeply ridged back out of the sea 7 miles south of Stonington. Accessible only by passenger ferry (tel. 207/367–5193), the island is worth visiting for the ferry ride alone, a half-hour cruise amid the tiny, pink-shore islands of Merchants Row, where you may see terns, guillemots, and harbor seals. More than half the island is part of Acadia National Park; 17½ miles of trails extend through quiet spruce and birch woods, along cobble beaches and seaside cliffs, and over the spine of the central mountain ridge. From late June to mid-September, the mailboat docks at Duck Harbor within the park. The small campground here, with five Adirondack-type lean-tos (open mid-May to mid-October), fills up quickly; reservations are essential, and they can be made only by writing to Acadia National Park (Box 177, Bar Harbor 04609).

Penobscot Bay for Free

Maine Coast Artists Gallery (Russell Ave., Rockport, tel. 207/236–2875) shows the work of Maine artists from June through September; lectures and classes are also scheduled.

Shore Village Museum exhibits U.S. Coast Guard memorabilia and artifacts, including lighthouse lenses, lifesaving gear, ship models, Civil War uniforms, and dolls. *104 Limerock St., Rockland, tel. 207/594–0311. Open June–mid-Oct., daily 10–4.*

What to See and Do with Children

Owls Head Transportation Museum, 2 miles south of Rockland on Route 73, shows antique aircraft, cars, and engines and stages weekend air shows. *Rte. 73, Owls Head, tel. 207/594–4418. Admission: $4 adults, $3.50 senior citizens, $2.50 children 5–12. Open May–Oct., daily 10–5; Nov.–Apr., weekdays 10–4, weekends 10–3.*

Off the Beaten Track

The Haystack Mountain School of Crafts, on Deer Isle, attracts an internationally renowned group of glassblowers, potters, sculptors, jewelers, and weavers to its summer institute. You can attend evening lectures or visit the studios of artisans at work (by appointment only). *South of Deer Isle Village on Route 15, turn left at Gulf gas station and follow signs for 6 miles, tel. 207/348–2306. Admission free. Open June–Sept.*

Shopping

The most promising shopping streets are Main and Bayview streets in Camden and Main Street in Stonington. Antiques shops are scattered around the outskirts of villages, in farmhouses and barns; yard sales abound in summertime.

Antiques
Brooklin
Creative Antiques (Rte. 175, tel. 207/359–8525) features painted furniture, hooked rugs, and prints.

Deer Isle Village
Old Deer Isle Parish House (Rte. 15, tel. 207/367–2455) is a place for poking around in the jumbles of old kitchenware, glassware, books, and linen.

Sargentville
Old Cove Antiques (Rte. 15, tel. 207/359–2031) has folk art, quilts, hooked rugs, and folk carvings.

Searsport
Billing itself the antiques capital of Maine, Searsport hosts a massive weekend flea market on Route 1 during the summer months. Indoor shops, most of them in old houses and barns, are also located on Route 1, in Lincolnville Beach as well as Searsport. Shops are open daily during the summer months, by chance or by appointment from mid-October through the end of May.

Art Galleries
Belfast
Gallery 68 (68 Main St., tel. 207/338–1558) carries contemporary art in all media.

Blue Hill
Leighton Gallery (Parker Point Rd., tel. 207/374–5001) shows oil paintings, lithographs, watercolors, and other contemporary art in the gallery, and sculpture in its garden.

Deer Isle Village
Blue Heron Gallery & Studio (Church St., tel. 207/348–6051) features the work of the Haystack Mountain School of Crafts faculty (*see* Off the Beaten Track, *above*).
Deer Isle Artist Association (Rte. 15, no tel.) has group exhibits of prints, drawings, and sculpture from mid-June through September.

Lincolnville
Maine's Massachusetts House Galleries (Rte. 1, tel. 207/789–5705) offers a broad selection of northern art, including bronzes, carvings, sculptures, and landscapes and seascapes in pencil, oil, and watercolor.

Books and Gifts
Belfast
Fertile Mind Bookshop (13 Main St., tel. 207/338–2498) sells a thoughtfully chosen selection of books, records, maps, and cards, including Maine-published works.

Crafts and Pottery
Blue Hill
Handworks Gallery (Main St., tel. 207/374–5613) carries unusual crafts, jewelry, and clothing.
Rackliffe Pottery (Rte. 172, tel. 207/374–2297) is famous for its vivid blue pottery, including plates, tea and coffee sets, casseroles, and canisters.
Rowantrees Pottery (Union St., tel. 207/374–5535) has an extensive selection of styles and patterns in dinnerware, tea sets, vases, and decorative items.

South Penobscot
North Country Textiles (Rte. 175, tel. 207/326–4131) is worth the detour for fine woven shawls, placemats, throws, and pillows in subtle patterns and color schemes.

Furniture
Lincolnville
The Windsor Chairmakers (Rte. 1, tel. 207/789–5188) sells custom-made, handcrafted beds, chests, china cabinets, dining tables, and highboys.

Sports and Outdoor Activities

Boat Trips Windjammers create a stir whenever they sail into Camden harbor, and a voyage around the bay on one of them is unforgettable. The season for the excursions is June through September.

Camden **Angelique** (Yankee Packet Co., Box 736, tel. 207/236–8873 or 800/282–9989) makes three- and six-day trips. **Appledore** (0 Lilly Pond Dr., tel. 207/236–8353) offers day sails as well as private charters. **Maine Windjammer Cruises** (Box 617CC, tel. 207/236–2938 or 800/736–7981) has three two-masted schooners making three- and six-day trips along the coast and to the islands. The Schooner **Roseway** (Box 696, tel. 207/236–4449 or 800/255–4449) takes three- and six-day cruises.

Rockland The **Vessels of Windjammer Wharf** (Box 1050, tel. 207/236–3520 or 800/999–7352) organizes three- and six-day cruises on the *Pauline* and the *Stephen Taber*.

Rockport **Timberwind** (Box 247, tel. 207/236–0801 or 800/759–9250) sails out of Rockport harbor.

Stonington **Palmer Day IV** (Stonington Harbor, tel. 207/367–2207) cruises Penobscot Bay in July and August, stopping at North Haven and Vinalhaven.

Biking **Maine Sport** (Rte. 1, Rockport, tel. 207/236–8797) rents bikes, canoes and kayaks, and camping gear.

Hiking **Country Walkers** (RR 2, Box 754, Waterbury, VT 05676–9754, tel. 802/244–1347) leads nature-oriented walking vacations from Blue Hill through Castine and the Schoodic Peninsula, from mid-May to mid-October.

Deep-Sea Fishing **Bay Island Yacht Charters** (Box 639, Camden, tel. 207/236–2776 or 800/421–2492) has charters by the day, week, and month.

Water Sports Eggemoggin Reach is a famous cruising ground for yachts, as are the coves and inlets around Deer Isle and the Penobscot Bay waters between Castine and Islesboro. For island camping and inn-to-inn tours, try **Indian Island Kayak** (16 Mountain St., Camden, tel. 207/236–4088). **Maine Sport** (Rte. 1, Rockport, tel. 207/236–8797) offers sea kayaking expeditions.

State Parks

Camden Hills State Park (*see* Exploring Penobscot Bay, *above*).

Holbrook Island Sanctuary (on Penobscot Bay in Brooksville, tel. 207/326–4012) has a gravelly beach with a splendid view; hiking trails through meadow and forest; no camping facilities.

Dining and Lodging

Camden has the greatest variety of restaurants and inns in the region. Highly recommended restaurants and lodgings in each price category are indicated by a star ★.

Blue Hill **Jonathan's.** The older downstairs room has captain's chairs,
Dining blue tablecloths, and local art; in the post-and-beam upstairs,
★ there's wood everywhere, candles with hurricane globes, and high-back chairs. The menu may include chicken breast in a

fennel sauce with peppers, garlic, rosemary, and shallots; shrimp scorpio (shrimp served on linguine with a touch of ouzo and feta cheese); and grilled strip steak. Chocolate bourbon pecan cake makes a compelling finale. The wine list has 250 selections from French and California vineyards. *Main St., tel. 207/374–5226. Reservations advised in summer. Dress: casual. MC, V. Closed Mon. Jan.–Apr. Inexpensive–Moderate.*

Lodging **The John Peters Inn.** The John Peters is unsurpassed for the
★ privacy of its location and the good taste in the decor of its guest rooms. The living room has two fireplaces, books and games, baby grand piano, and Empire furniture. Oriental rugs are everywhere. Huge breakfasts in the light and airy dining rooms include the famous lobster omelet, served complete with lobster-claw shells as decoration. The Surry Room, one of the best rooms (all are nice), has a king-size bed, a fireplace, curly-maple chest, gilt mirror, and six windows with delicate lace curtains. The Honeymoon Suite is immense, with wet bar and minifridge, white furniture, deck, and a view of Blue Hill Bay. The large rooms in the carriage house, a stone's throw down the hill from the inn, have dining areas, cherry floors and woodwork, wicker and brass accents, and a modern feel. Four have decks, kitchens, and fireplaces, a real plus here. *Peters Point, Box 916, Blue Hill, 04614, tel. 207/374–2116. 7 rooms with bath, 1 suite in inn; 6 rooms with bath in carriage house. Facilities: phones in carriage house rooms, fireplaces in 9 bedrooms; swimming pool, canoe, sailboats, pond, 2 moorings. No pets. MC, V. Closed Nov.–Apr. Very Expensive.*

Camden **The Belmont.** Round tables are set well apart in this dining
Dining room with smoke-colored walls and soft classical music or jazz.
★ The changing menu of new American cuisine might include sautéed scallops with Pernod leek cream; grilled pheasant with cranberry; chicken with a tomato coconut curry; or braised lamb shanks. *6 Belmont Ave., tel. 207/236–8053. Reservations advised. Dress: casual. MC, V. Closed Jan.–Apr., Mon. May–Columbus Day, Mon.–Wed. Columbus Day–Dec. Dinner only. Expensive.*

The Waterfront Restaurant. A ringside seat on Camden Harbor can be had here; the best view is from the outdoor deck, open in warm weather. The fare is seafood: boiled lobster, scallops, bouillabaisse, steamed mussels, Cajun barbecued shrimp. Lunchtime features are lobster salad, crabmeat salad, lobster and crab rolls, tuna niçoise, turkey melt, and burgers. *Bayview St., tel. 207/236–3747. No reservations. Dress: casual. MC, V. Moderate.*

Cappy's Chowder House. Lobster traps, a moosehead, and a barbershop pole decorate this lively but cozy tavern; the Crow's Nest dining room upstairs is quieter and has a harbor view. Simple fare is the rule here: burgers, sandwiches, seafood, and, of course, chowder. A bakery downstairs sells breads, cookies, and filled croissants to go. *1 Main St., tel. 207/236–2254. No reservations. MC, V. Inexpensive–Moderate.*

Dining and **Whitehall Inn.** Camden's best-known inn, just north of town on
Lodging Route 1, boasts a central white-clapboard, wide-porch ship captain's home of 1843 connected to a turn-of-the-century wing. Just off the comfortable main lobby with its faded Oriental rugs, the Millay Room preserves memorabilia of the poet Edna St. Vincent Millay, who grew up in Rockland. Rooms are sparsely furnished, with dark wood bedsteads, white bed-

spreads, and clawfoot bathtubs. Some rooms have ocean views. The dining room is open to the public for dinner and breakfast, offering traditional and creative American cuisine. Dinner entrées include Eastern salmon in puff pastry, swordfish grilled with roast red pepper sauce, and lamb tenderloin. *Box 558, 04843, tel. 207/236–3391. 50 rooms, 42 with bath. Facilities: restaurant, all-weather tennis court, shuffleboard, motorboat, golf privileges. AE, MC, V. Closed mid-Oct.–mid-May. Rates are MAP. Very Expensive.*

Lodging **Norumbega.** The stone castle amid Camden's elegant clapboard houses, built in 1886 by Joseph B. Stearns, the inventor of duplex telegraphy, was obviously the fulfillment of a fantasy. The public rooms boast gleaming parquet floors, oak and mahogany paneling, richly carved wood mantels over four fireplaces on the first floor alone, gilt mirrors, and Empire furnishings. At the back of the house, several decks and balconies overlook the garden, the gazebo, and the bay. The view improves as you ascend; the newly completed penthouse suite features a small deck, private bar, and a skylight in the bedroom. *61 High St., 04843, tel. 207/236–4646. 13 rooms with bath. AE, MC, V. Very Expensive.*

Windward House. A choice bed-and-breakfast, this Greek Revival house of 1854, situated at the edge of town, features rooms furnished with fishnet lace canopy beds, cherry highboys, curly-maple bedsteads, and clawfoot mahogany dressers. Guests are welcome to use any of three sitting rooms, including the Wicker Room with its glass-topped white wicker table where morning coffee is served. A small deck overlooks the back garden. Breakfasts may include quiche, apple puff pancakes, peaches-and-cream French toast, or soufflés. *6 High St., 04843, tel. 207/236–9656. 6 rooms with bath, 1 efficiency. MC, V. Expensive–Very Expensive.*

Castine **Gilley's Seafood.** This unpretentious harborside restaurant has
Dining just the kind of traditional dishes Downeasters love: a variety of chowders, lobster stew, subs, and tiny Maine shrimp or fresh clams. *Water St., tel. 207/326–4001. Reservations accepted. Dress: casual. MC, V. Closed Tues. off-season. Inexpensive.*

Dining and **The Pentagoet.** A recent renovation of the rambling, pale yel-
Lodging low Pentagoet gave each room a bath, enlarged the dining room, and opened up the public rooms. The porch wraps around three sides of the inn. Guest rooms are warmer, more flowery, more feminine than those of the Castine Inn across the street; they have hooked rugs, a mix of Victorian antiques, and floral wallpapers. Dinner in the deep rose and cream formal dining room (open to the public on a limited basis) is an elaborate affair; entrées might include lobster (usually prepared two different ways), grilled salmon with Dijon sauce, and pork loin braised in apple cider. Inn guests can expect a hearty breakfast. *Main St., 04421, tel. 207/326–8616. 16 rooms with bath. MC, V. Closed Nov.–Apr. Rates are MAP. Very Expensive.*

★ **The Castine Inn.** Dark wood pineapple four-poster beds, white upholstered easy chairs, and oil paintings are typical of the room furnishings here. The third floor has the best views: the harbor over the back garden on one side, Main Street on the other. The dining room, decorated with whimsical murals, is open to the public for breakfast and dinner; the menu features traditional New England fare—Maine lobster, crabmeat cakes with mustard sauce, roast leg of lamb, and chicken and leek pot pie. A snug, old-fashioned pub off the lobby has small tables and antique spirit jars over the mantel. *Main St., 04421, tel. 207/326–4365. 27 rooms with bath, 3 suites. Facilities: restaurant, pub. MC, V. Closed Nov.–mid-Apr. Rates include full breakfast. Moderate–Expensive.*

Deer Isle **Fisherman's Friend Restaurant.** Fresh salmon, halibut, monk-
Dining fish, lobster, and even prime rib and chicken are on the menu
★ here. Friday is fish-fry day: free seconds on fried haddock for $5.99. *School St., Stonington, tel. 207/367–2442. Reservations advised. Dress: casual. No credit cards. BYOB. Closed mid-Nov.–mid-Mar.; closed Mon. after Columbus Day. Inexpensive.*

Lodging **Goose Cove Lodge.** The heavily wooded property at the end of a back road has 2,500 feet of ocean frontage, two sandy beaches, a long sandbar that leads to the Barred Island nature preserve, nature trails, and sailboats for rent nearby. Some cottages and suites are in secluded woodlands, some on the shore, some attached, some with a single large room, others with one or two bedrooms. All but two units have fireplaces. In July and August the minimum stay is one week. *Box 40, Sunset 04683, tel. 207/348–2508. 11 cottages, 10 suites. Facilities: rowboat, canoe, volleyball, horseshoes. No credit cards. Closed mid-Oct.–Apr. Rates are MAP. Moderate–Expensive.*

Pilgrim's Inn. The bright red, four-story, gambrel-roof house dating from about 1793 overlooks a mill pond and harbor at the center of Deer Isle. The library has wing chairs and Oriental rugs; a downstairs taproom has pine furniture, braided rugs, and parson's benches. Guest rooms, each with its own character, sport Laura Ashley fabrics and select antiques. The dining room in the attached barn, an open space both rustic and elegant, has farm implements, French oil lamps, and tiny windows. The single-entrée menu changes nightly; it might include rack of lamb or fresh local seafood; scallop bisque; asparagus and smoked salmon; and poached pear tart for dessert. *Deer Isle 04627, tel. 207/348–6615. 13 rooms, 8 with bath, 1 cottage. Facilities: restaurant. No credit cards. Closed mid-Oct.–mid-May. Rates are MAP or bed-and-breakfast. Moderate–Expensive.*

Captain's Quarters Inn and Motel. Accommodations, as plain and unadorned as Stonington itself, are in the middle of town, a two-minute walk from the Isle au Haut mailboat. You have your choice of motel-type rooms and suites or efficiencies, and you can take your breakfast muffins and coffee to the sunny deck on the water. *Main St., Box 83, Stonington, 04681, tel. 207/367–2420. 13 units, 11 with bath. AE, MC, V. Inexpensive–Moderate.*

Isle au Haut **Keeper's House.** This converted lighthouse-keeper's house, set
Lodging on a rock ledge surrounded by thick spruce forest, has no electricity and limited access by road; guests dine by candlelight on seafood or chicken and read in the evening by kerosene lantern. Trails link the inn with the park trail network, and you can walk to the village, a collection of simple houses, a church, a tiny school, and a general store. The five guest rooms are spacious, airy, and simply decorated with painted wood furniture and local crafts. A separate cottage, the Oil House, has no indoor plumbing. *Box 26, Isle au Haut 04645, tel. 207/367–2261. 5 rooms with shared bath, 1 cottage. Facilities: dock. No credit cards. Closed Nov.–Apr. Rates include 3 meals. Expensive–Very Expensive.*

Islesboro *Lodging*	**Dark Harbor House.** The yellow-clapboard, neo-Georgian summer "cottage" of 1896 has a stately portico and a hilltop setting. Inside, an elegant double staircase curves from the ground floor to the bedrooms, which are spacious, some with balconies, half with fireplaces, one with an 18th-century four-poster bed. The dining room, open to the public for prix-fixe dinners, features seafood and West Indian specialties. *Box 185, 04848, tel. 207/734–6669. 10 rooms with bath. Facilities: restaurant. MC, V. Closed mid-Oct.–mid-May. Very Expensive.*
Lincolnville *Dining*	**Chez Michel.** This tiny restaurant, serving up a fine rabbit pâté, mussels marinière, steak au poivre, and poached salmon, might easily be on the Riveria instead of Ducktrap Beach. Chef Michel Hetuin creates bouillabaisse as deftly as New England chowder, and he welcomes special requests. *Rte. 1, tel. 207/789–5600. Reservations accepted for 6 or more. Dress: casual. MC, V. Closed Mon. off-season. Inexpensive–Moderate.*
North Brooklin *Lodging*	**The Lookout.** The stately white-clapboard building stands in a wide field at the tip of Flye Point, with a superb view of the water and the mountains of Mount Desert Island. Although the floors slope and a century of damp has left a certain mustiness, the rustic rooms are nicely furnished with country antiques original to the house and newer matching pieces. The larger south-facing rooms command the view. Six cottages have from one to four bedrooms each. With the dining room expanded onto the porch, seven tables enjoy a view of the outdoors. Entrées could include filet mignon, grilled salmon, and shrimp and scallops provençale; Wednesday night is the lobster cookout. *North Brooklin, 04661, tel. 207/359–2188. 6 rooms with shared bath, 6 cottages. Facilities: restaurant. MC, V. Closed mid-Oct.–mid-Apr. Moderate.*
Spruce Head *Dining and Lodging*	**The Craignair Inn.** Built in the 1930s as a boardinghouse for stonecutters and converted to an inn a decade later, the Craignair commands a coastal view of rocky shore and lobster boats. Inside the three-story gambrel-roof house you'll find country clutter, books, and cut glass in the parlor; braided rugs, brass beds, and dowdy dressers in the guest rooms. In 1986 the owners converted a church dating from the 1890s into another accommodation with six rooms—each with bath—that have a more modern feel. The waterside dining room, decorated with Delft and Staffordshire plates, serves such fare as bouillabaisse; lemon pepper seafood kebab; rabbit with tarragon and wine; and those New England standards: shore dinner, prime rib, and scampi. A bourbon pecan tart and crème brûlée are the dessert headliners. *Clark Island Rd., 04859, tel. 207/594–7644. 23 rooms, 8 with bath. Facilities: restaurant. AE, MC, V. Closed Feb. Moderate–Expensive.*
Tenants Harbor *Dining and Lodging*	**East Wind Inn & Meeting House.** On Route 131, 10 miles off Route 1 and set on a knob of land overlooking the harbor and the islands, the inn offers simple hospitality, a wraparound porch, and unadorned but comfortable guest rooms furnished with an iron bedstead, flowered wallpaper, and heritage bedspread. The dining room has a rustic decor; the dinner menu features duck with black currant sauce; seafood stew with scallops, shrimp, mussels, and grilled sausage; boiled lobster; and baked stuffed haddock. *Box 149, 04860, tel. 207/372–6366. 26 rooms, 12 with bath. Facilities: sailboat cruises in season. AE, MC, V. Moderate–Expensive.*

The Arts

Music   **Bay Chamber Concerts** (Rockport Opera House, Rockport, tel. 207/236–2823) offers chamber music Thursday and Friday nights during July and August; concerts are given once a month October through May.

Kneisel Hall Chamber Music Festival (Box 648, Blue Hill, tel. 207/374–2811) has concerts Sunday and Friday in summer.

Theater   **Cold Comfort Productions** (Box 259, Castine, no tel.), a community theater, mounts plays in July and August.

Nightlife

Bars and Lounges   **Dennett's Wharf** (Sea St., Castine, tel. 207/326–9045) has a long bar that can become rowdy after dark. Open May through October.

Peter Ott's Tavern (16 Bayview St., Camden, tel. 207/236–4032) is a steakhouse with a lively bar scene.

Thirsty Whale Tavern (Camden Harbour Inn, 83 Bayview St., Camden, tel. 207/236–4200) is a popular local drinking spot.

The Coast: Acadia

East of Penobscot Bay, Acadia is the informal name for the area that includes Mount Desert Island (pronounced dessert) and its surroundings: Blue Hill Bay; Frenchman Bay; and Ellsworth, Hancock, and other mainland towns. Mount Desert, 13 miles across, is Maine's largest island, and it harbors most of Acadia National Park, Maine's principal tourist attraction with more than 4 million visitors a year. The 34,000 acres of woods and mountains, lake and shore, footpaths, carriage paths, and hiking trails that make up the park extend as well to other islands and some of the mainland. Outside the park, on Mount Desert's east shore, an upper-class resort town of the 19th century has become a busy tourist town of the 20th century in Bar Harbor, which services the park with a variety of inns, motels, and restaurants.

Important Addresses and Numbers

Visitor   **Acadia National Park** (Box 177, Bar Harbor 04609, tel.
Information   207/288–3338).

Bar Harbor Chamber of Commerce (Box BC, Cottage St., Bar Harbor 04609, tel. 207/288–3393, 207/288–5103, or 800/288–5103).

Getting Around Acadia

By Car   North of Bar Harbor the scenic 27-mile Park Loop Road takes leave of Route 3 to circle the eastern quarter of Mount Desert Island, with one-way traffic from Sieur de Monts Spring to Seal Harbor and two-way traffic between Seal Harbor and Hulls Cove. Route 102, which serves the western half of Mount Desert, is reached from Route 3 just after it crosses onto the island or from Route 233 west from Bar Harbor. All these island roads pass in, out, and through the precincts of Acadia National Park.

Guided Tours

Acadia Taxi and Tours (tel. 207/ATT–4020) conducts half-day historic and scenic tours of the area.

National Park Tours (tel. 207/288–3327) offers a 2½-hour bus tour of Acadia National Park, narrated by a park naturalist, which departs twice daily across from Testa's Restaurant on Main Street in Bar Harbor.**Acadia Air** (tel. 207/667–5534), on Route 3 between Ellsworth and Bar Harbor at Hancock County Airport, offers aircraft rentals and aerial whale-watching trips.

Exploring Acadia

Numbers in the margin correspond to points of interest on the Acadia map.

Coastal Route 1 passes through Ellsworth, where Route 3 turns south to Mount Desert Island and takes you into the busy
❶ town of **Bar Harbor.** Although most of Bar Harbor's grand mansions were destroyed in the fire of 1947 and replaced by modern motels, the town retains the beauty of a commanding location on Frenchman Bay. Shops, restaurants, and hotels are clustered along Main, Mount Desert, and Cottage streets.

❷ The **Hulls Cove** approach to Acadia National Park is 4 miles northwest of Bar Harbor on Route 3. Even though it is often clogged with traffic in summer, the Park Loop Road provides the best introduction to Acadia National Park. At the start of the loop at Hulls Cove, the visitor center shows a free 15-minute orientation film and has maps of the hiking trails and carriage paths in the park.

❸ Follow the road to the parking area for **Sand Beach,** a small stretch of pink sand backed by the mountains of Acadia and the odd lump of rock known as the Beehive. The **Ocean Trail,** which parallels the Park Loop Road from Sand Beach to the Otter Point parking area, is a popular and easily accessible walk with some of the most spectacular scenery in Maine: huge slabs of pink granite heaped at the ocean's edge, ocean views unobstructed to the horizon, and Thunder Hole, a natural seaside cave in which the ocean rushes and roars.

Those who want a mountaintop experience without the effort
❹ of hiking can drive to the summit of **Cadillac Mountain,** at 1,523 feet the highest point along the eastern coast. From the smooth, bald summit you have a 360-degree view of the ocean, the islands, the jagged coast, and the woods and lakes of Acadia and its surroundings.

On completing the 27-mile Park Loop, you can continue your auto tour of the island by heading west on Route 233 for the villages on Somes Sound, a true fjord—the only one on the East
❺ Coast—which almost bisects Mount Desert Island. **Somesville,** the oldest settlement on the island (1621), is a carefully preserved New England village of white-clapboard houses and churches, neat green lawns, and bits of blue water visible behind them.

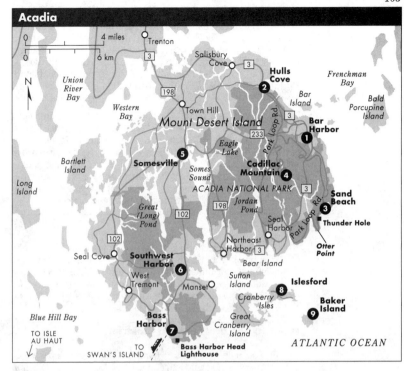

Acadia

N

Union River Bay

Western Bay

Bartlett Island

Long Island

Blue Hill Bay

TO ISLE AU HAUT

TO SWAN'S ISLAND

0 — 4 miles
0 — 6 km

Trenton

Salisbury Cove

Town Hill

Mount Desert Island

Somesville

Somes Sound

Great (Long) Pond

Seal Cove

Southwest Harbor

West Tremont

Manset

Bass Harbor

Bear Island

Sutton Island

Great Cranberry Island

Bass Harbor Head Lighthouse

Hulls Cove ❷

Bar Island

Bar Harbor ❶

Eagle Lake

Cadillac Mountain ❹

ACADIA NATIONAL PARK

Jordan Pond

Northeast Harbor

Seal Harbor

Sand Beach ❸

Thunder Hole

Otter Point

Islesford ❽

Cranberry Isles

Baker Island ❾

Frenchman Bay

Bald Porcupine Island

Park Loop Rd

ATLANTIC OCEAN

❻ Route 102 south from Somesville takes you to **Southwest Harbor,** which combines the rough, salty character of a working port with the refinements of a summer resort community. From the town's Main Street along Route 102, turn left onto Clark Point Road to reach the harbor.

Time Out At the end of Clark Point Road in Southwest Harbor, **Beal's Lobster Pier** serves lobsters, clams, and crab rolls in season at dockside picnic tables.

Those who want to tour more of the island will continue south on Route 102, following Route 102A where the road forks, and passing through the communities of Manset and Seawall. The Bass Harbor Head lighthouse, which clings to a cliff at the eastern entrance to Blue Hill Bay, was built in 1858. The tiny lob-
❼ stering village of **Bass Harbor** has cottages for rent, a gift shop, and a car-and-passenger ferry to Swans Island.

Island Excursions Situated off the southeast shore of Mount Desert Island at the entrance to Somes Sound, the five Cranberry Isles—Great Cranberry, Islesford (or Little Cranberry), Baker Island, Sutton Island, and Bear Island—escape the hubbub that engulfs Acadia National Park in summer. Great Cranberry and Islesford are served by the Beal & Bunker passenger ferry (tel. 207/244–3575) from Northeast Harbor; Baker Island is reached by the summer cruise boats of the Islesford Ferry Company (tel. 207/276–3717); Sutton and Bear islands are privately owned.

8 **Islesford** comes closest to having a village: a collection of houses, a church, a fishermen's co-op, a market, and a post office near the ferry dock. The Islesford Historical Museum, run by the national park, has displays of tools, documents relating to the island's history, and books and manuscripts of the writer Rachel Field (1894–1942), who summered on Sutton Island. Puddles on the Water (tel. 207/244–3177), on the Islesford Dock, serves three meals a day from June through September.

9 The 123-acre **Baker Island,** the most remote of the group, looks almost black from a distance because of its thick spruce forest. The cruise boat from Northeast Harbor makes a 4¹/₂-hour narrated tour, in the course of which you are likely to see ospreys nesting on a sea stack off Sutton Island, harbor seals hauled out on ledges, and cormorants flying low over the water. Because Baker Island has no natural harbor, the tour boat ties up off-shore and you take a fishing dory to reach the island.

Acadia for Free

Bar Harbor Historical Society Museum displays photographs of Bar Harbor from the days when it catered to the very rich. Other exhibits document the great fire of 1947, in which many of the Gilded Age cottages were destroyed. *34 Mt. Desert St., tel. 207/288–4245. Admission free. Open mid-June–Oct., Mon.–Sat. 1–4; by appointment in other seasons.*

What to See and Do with Children

Acadia Zoo, a 30-acre preserve and petting zoo, has pastures, streams, woods, and wild and domestic animals. *Rte. 3, Trenton, tel. 207/667–3244. Open May–Columbus Day.*
Mount Desert Oceanarium has exhibits in three locations on the fishing and sea life of the Gulf of Maine, as well as hands-on "touch tanks." *Clark Point Rd., Southwest Harbor, tel. 207/244–7330; Rte. 3, Bar Harbor, tel. 207/288–5005; Lobster Hatchery at Municipal Pier, Bar Harbor, tel. 207/288–2344. Call for admission fees. Open mid-May–mid-Oct., Mon.–Sat. 9–5; Lobster Hatchery open evenings July–Aug.*

Off the Beaten Track

Bartlett Maine Estate Winery offers tours, tastings, and gift packs. Wines are produced from locally grown apples, blueberries, raspberries, and other fruit. *Rte. 1 in Gouldsboro, north of Bar Harbor, tel. 207/546–2408. Open June–Oct., Tues.–Sun. 10–5.***Jackson Laboratory,** a center for research in mammalian genetics, studies cancer, diabetes, and heart disease. R *te. 3, 3¹/2 mi south of Bar Harbor, tel. 207/288–3371. Audiovisual presentations mid-June–Aug., Tues. and Thurs. at 2.*

Shopping

Bar Harbor in the summer is a good place for browsing for gifts, T-shirts, and novelty items; for bargains, head for the outlets that line Route 3 in Ellsworth, which have good discounts on shoes.

Antiques **E. and L. Higgins** (tel. 207/244–3983) has a good stock of wicker, *Bernard* along with pine and oak country furniture.

Southwest Harbor **Marianne Clark Fine Antiques** (Main St., tel. 207/244–9247) has an eclectic stock of formal and country furniture, American paintings, and accessories from the 18th and 19th centuries.

Crafts **Acadia Shops** (inside the park at Cadillac Mountain summit;
Bar Harbor Thunder Hole on Ocean Dr.; Jordan Pond House on Park Loop Rd.; and 85 Main St.) sell crafts and Maine foods.
Island Artisans (99 Main St., tel. 207/288–4214) is a crafts co-operative.
The Next Egg Gift Gallery (12 Mt. Desert St., tel. 207/288–9048) carries upscale, handcrafted baubles.

Sports and Outdoor Activities

Biking, Jogging, The network of carriage paths that wind through the woods
Cross-Country and fields of Acadia National Park is ideal for biking and jog-
Skiing ging when the ground is dry and for cross-country skiing in winter. Hulls Cove visitor center has a carriage-paths map.

Bikes for hire can be found at **Acadia Bike & Canoe** (48 Cottage St., Bar Harbor, tel. 207/288–9605); **Bar Harbor Bicycle Shop** (141 Cottage St., tel. 207/288–3886); and **Southwest Cycle** (Main St., Southwest Harbor, tel. 207/244–5856).

Boat Trips **Acadia Boat Tours & Charters** (West St., tel. 207/288–9505) em-
Bar Harbor barks on 1¹/₂-hour lobster fishing trips in summer. **Acadian Whale Watcher** (Golden Anchor Pier, tel. 207/288–9794) runs 2¹/₂-hour whale-watching cruises in summer. *Natalie Todd* (Inn Pier, tel. 207/288–4585) offers weekend windjammer cruises from mid-May through mid-October.

Northeast Harbor *Blackjack* (Town Dock, tel. 207/276–5043 or 207/288–3056), a 33-foot Friendship sloop, makes four trips daily, May through October, Monday through Saturday. *Sunrise* (Sea St. Pier, tel. 207/276–5352) does lobster fishing tours in the summer months.

Camping The two campgrounds in Acadia National Park (tel. 207/288–3338)—Blackwoods, open year-round, and Seawall, open late May to late September—fill up quickly during the summer season. Off Mount Desert Island, but convenient to it, the camp-ground at Lamoine State Park (tel. 207/667–4778) is open mid-May to mid-October; the 55-acre park has a great location on Frenchman Bay.

Canoeing and For canoe rentals and guided kayak tours, see **Acadia Bike &**
Kayaking **Canoe,** or **National Park Canoe Rentals** (Rte. 102, 2 mi west of Somesville, at the head of Long Pond, tel. 207/244–5854).

Hiking Acadia National Park maintains nearly 200 miles of foot and carriage paths, ranging from easy strolls along flatlands to rig-orous climbs that involve ladders and handholds on rock faces. Among the more rewarding hikes are the Precipice Trail to Champlain Mountain, the Great Head Loop, the Gorham Mountain Trail, and the path around Eagle Lake. The National Park visitor center has a trail guide and map.

Sailing **Harbor Boat Rentals** (Harbor Pl., 1 West St., tel. 207/288–3757)
Bar Harbor has 13-foot and 17-foot Boston whalers and some sailboats.

Southwest Harbor **Manset Boat Rental** (Manset Boatyard, just south of South-west Harbor, tel. 207/244–9233) rents sailboats.

Dining and Lodging

Bar Harbor has the greatest concentration of accommodations on Mount Desert Island. Much of this lodging has been converted from 19th-century summer cottages. A number of fine restaurants are also tucked away in these old homes and inns. Highly recommended restaurants and lodgings in each price category are indicated by a star ★.

Bar Harbor
Dining
★

George's. Candles, flowers, and linens grace the tables in four small dining rooms in an old house. The menu shows a distinct Mediterranean influence in the lobster streudel wrapped in phyllo, and in the sautéed veal; fresh chargrilled salmon and swordfish stand on their own. Couples tend to linger in the romantic setting. Jazz piano may be heard nightly July 4–Labor Day. *7 Stephen's La., tel. 207/288–4505. Reservations advised. Dress: casual. AE, D, DC, MC, V. Closed late Oct.–mid-June. Dinner only. Moderate–Expensive.*

Jordan Pond House. Oversize popovers and tea are a warm tradition at this rustic restaurant in the park, where in fine weather you can sit on the terrace or the lawn and admire the views of Jordan Pond and the mountains. The dinner menu offers lobster stew, seafood thermidor, and fisherman's stew. *Park Loop Rd., tel. 207/276–3316. Reservations one day in advance advised in summer. Dress: casual. AE, D, MC, V. Closed late Oct.–late May. Moderate.*

★ **124 Cottage Street.** The four dining rooms have the feel of a country inn, and the back room has a sliding glass door to a small garden and woods. The fare is seafood and pasta with an Oriental twist: Szechuan shrimp; pasta primavera with pea pods and broccoli; seafood pasta with mussels, shrimp, and scallops in tomato sauce. *124 Cottage St., tel. 207/288–4383. Reservations advised. Dress: casual. MC, V. Closed late Oct.–mid-June. Dinner only. Moderate.*

Lodging
Holbrook House. Built in 1876 as a boardinghouse with a wraparound porch for rocking and big shuttered windows to catch the breeze, the lemon-yellow Holbrook House sits right on Mount Desert Street, the main access route through Bar Harbor. In 1876 it was no doubt pleasant to listen to the horses clip-clop past, but today, the traffic noise can be annoying, especially from the porch. The Holbrook House offers a far more restrained (and more authentic) approach to Victorian interior design than the Cleftstone Manor (*see below*). The downstairs public rooms include a lovely, formal sitting room with bright, summery chintz on chairs and windows and a Duncan Phyfe sofa upholstered in white silk damask. A full breakfast is served on china and crystal in the sunny, glassed-in porch. The guest rooms are furnished with lovingly handled family pieces in the same refined taste as the public rooms. Room 6, on the second floor, has a corner location with four big windows, a four-poster bed, and oil paintings. Room 11, though smaller, is the quietest room, and has a snug, country feel with Laura Ashley fabrics. Right in town, Holbrook House is a short walk to the shops and restaurants of Bar Harbor. A stay at the Holbrook House is like a visit with your most proper (but by no means stuffy) relatives, the ones who inherited all the best furniture and have kept it in impeccable condition. *74 Mt. Desert St., Bar Harbor 04609, tel. 207/288–4970. 10 rooms with bath in*

inn, 2 rooms share 1 bath and living room in Lupine Cottage, 2 rooms share 1 bath and living room in Fern Cottage. Facilities: cable TV in library and cottages; croquet. Rates include full breakfast. MC, V. Closed mid-Oct.–May. Very Expensive.

Cleftstone Manor. Attention, lovers of Victoriana! This inn was made in high Victorian heaven expressly for you. Ignore the fact that it is set amid sterile motels just off Route 3, the road along which traffic roars into Bar Harbor. Do not be put off by the unpromising, rambling, green-shuttered exterior. Inside, a deeply plush, mahogany and lace world of Victorian splendor awaits you. The parlor is cool and richly furnished with red velvet and brocade trimmed sofas with white doilies, grandfather and mantel clocks, and oil paintings hanging on powder-blue walls. In the imposingly formal dining room, Joseph Pulitzer's library table extends for seemingly miles beneath a crystal chandelier. Of the guest rooms, the prize chamber (especially for honeymooners) is the immense Romeo and Juliet, once a section of the ballroom, which now has a pillow-decked sofa; blue velvet Victorian chairs; a lace-canopy bed; and a massive, ornately carved Irish buffet that takes up most of one wall. *Rte. 3, Eden St., 04609, tel. 207/288–4951 or 800/962–9762. 14 rooms with bath, 2 suites. Facilities: 6 rooms with fireplaces. Rates include full breakfast. D, MC, V. Closed Nov.–Apr. Expensive–Very Expensive.*

Mira Monte. Built as a summer home in 1864, the Mira Monte bespeaks Victorian leisure, with columned verandas, latticed bay windows, and landscaped grounds for strolling and sunning; and the inn is set back far enough from the road to assure quiet and seclusion. The guest rooms have brass or four-poster beds, white wicker, hooked rugs, lace curtains, and oil paintings in gilt frames. The quieter, rear-facing rooms offer sunny garden views. Some rooms have porches, fireplaces, and separate entrances. *69 Mt. Desert St., 04609, tel. 207/288–4263 or 800/553–5109. 11 rooms with bath. AE, MC, V. Closed Nov.–Apr. Expensive–Very Expensive.*

Wonder View Motor Lodge. While the rooms are standard motel accommodations, with two double beds and nondescript furniture, this establishment is distinguished by its extensive grounds, the view of Frenchman Bay, and a location opposite the Bluenose ferry terminal. The woods muffle the sounds of traffic on Route 3. Pets are accepted, and the dining room has picture windows. *Rte. 3, Box 25, 04609, tel. 207/288–3358 or 800/427–3358. 80 rooms with bath. Facilities: dining room, outdoor pool. AE, MC, V. Closed late Oct.–mid-May. Inexpensive–Expensive.*

Hancock
Dining
★

Le Domaine. On a rural stretch of Route 1, 9 miles east of Ellsworth, a French chef prepares *lapin pruneaux* (rabbit in a rich brown sauce); sweetbreads with lemon and capers; and coquilles St. Jacques. The elegant but not intimidating dining room has polished wood floors, copper pots hanging from the mantel, and silver, crystal, and linen on the tables. *Rte. 1, tel. 207/422–3395 or 422–3916. Reservations advised. Dress: neat but casual. AE, D, MC, V. Dinner only. Closed Nov.–Apr. Expensive.*

Lodging

Le Domaine. The seven smallish rooms in the inn are done in French country style, with chintz and wicker, simple desks, and sofas near the windows. Four rooms have balconies or porches over the gardens. The 100-acre property offers paths for walking and badminton on the lawn. *Box 496, 04640, tel. 207/422–3395* or *207/422–3916. 7 rooms with bath. Facilities: restaurant. AE, D, MC, V. Closed Nov.–Apr. Rates are MAP. Very Expensive.*

Hulls Cove **Inn at Canoe Point.** Seclusion and privacy are bywords of this
Lodging snug, 100-year-old Tudor-style house on the water at Hulls Cove, 2 miles from Bar Harbor. The Master Suite, a large room with a fireplace, is a favorite for its size and the French doors opening onto a waterside deck. The inn's large living room has huge windows on the water, a fieldstone fireplace, and, just outside, a deck that hangs over the water. *Box 216, Rte. 3, 04609, tel. 207/288–9511. 3 rooms with bath, 2 suites. No credit cards. Very Expensive.*

Northeast Harbor **Asticou Inn.** At night guests of the inn trade topsiders and polo
Dining shirts for jackets and ties to dine in the stately formal dining room, which is open to the public for a prix-fixe dinner by reservation only. A recent menu featured swordfish with orange mustard glaze; lobster; seared catfish; and chicken in a lemon cream and mushroom sauce. *Tel. 207/276–3344. Reservations required. Jacket and tie required. Closed mid-Sept.–mid-June. Expensive.*

Lodging **Asticou Inn.** This grand turn-of-the-century inn at the head of exclusive Northeast Harbor serves a loyal clientele. Guest rooms in the main building have a country feel, with bright fabrics, white lace curtains, and white painted furniture. The more modern cottages scattered around the grounds afford greater privacy; among them, the decks and picture windows make the Topsider Cottages particularly attractive. A stay at the inn includes breakfast and dinner, but the cottages and the Victorian-style Cranberry Lodge across the street operate on a bed-and-breakfast policy from mid-May to mid-June and from mid-September to January 1. *Northeast Harbor 04662, tel. 207/276–3344. 27 rooms with bath, 23 suites, 6 cottages. Facilities: clay tennis court, heated pool. MC, V. Inn closed mid-Sept.– mid-June; cottages, lodge closed Jan.–Mar. Rates are MAP in summer. Very Expensive (lodge, Moderate–Expensive).*

Southwest Harbor **Claremont Hotel.** The large, airy dining room of the inn, open
Dining to the public for dinner only, is awash in light streaming through the picture windows. The atmosphere is on the formal side, with crystal, silver, and china service. Rack of lamb, baked stuffed shrimp, coquilles St. Jacques, and tournedos au poivre are specialties. *Tel. 207/244–5036. Reservations required. Jacket required. No credit cards. Closed mid-Sept.–mid-June. Closed for lunch Sept.–June. Moderate.*

Lodging **Claremont Hotel.** Built in 1884 and operated continuously as an inn, the Claremont calls up memories of long, leisurely vacations of days gone by. The yellow-clapboard structure commands a view of Somes Sound, croquet is played on the lawn, and cocktails are served at the boathouse from mid-July to the end of August. Guest rooms are bright, white, and quite plain; cottages and two guest houses on the grounds are homier and woodsier. Modified American Plan is in effect from mid-June to mid-September. *Box 137, 04679, tel. 207/244–5036. 22 rooms, 20 with bath; 3 suites, 12 cottages, 2 guest houses. Facilities: clay tennis court, croquet, bicycles, private dock and moorings. No credit cards. Hotel closed mid-Sept.–mid-June. Cottages closed Nov.–mid-May. Rates are MAP. Expensive–Very Expensive.*

The Arts

Music **Arcady Music Festival** (tel. 207/288–3151) schedules concerts around Mount Desert Island from mid-July through August.

Bar Harbor Festival (59 Cottage St., Bar Harbor, tel. 207/288–5744; 120 W. 45th St., 7th floor, New York, NY 10036, tel. 212/222–1026) programs recitals, jazz, chamber music, and pops concerts by up-and-coming young professionals from mid-July to mid-August.**Domaine School** (Hancock, tel. 207/422–6251) presents public concerts by faculty and students at Monteux Memorial Hall.

Theater **Acadia Repertory Company** (Masonic Hall, Rte. 102, Somesville, tel. 207/244–7260) mounts plays in July and August.

Nightlife

Acadia has little nighttime activity. The lounge at the **Moorings Restaurant** (Manset, tel. 207/244–7070), accessible by boat and car, is open until midnight from May through October, and the company is a lively boating crowd.

4 New Brunswick

American Express offers Travelers Cheques built for two.

American Express® Cheques *for Two*. The first Travelers Cheques that allow either of you to use them because both of you have signed them. And only one of you needs to be present to purchase them.

Cheques *for Two* are accepted anywhere regular American Express Travelers Cheques are, which is just about everywhere. So stop by your bank, AAA* or any American Express Travel Service Office and ask for Cheques *for Two*.

*By Colleen
Whitney
Thompson*

*Updated by Ana
Watts*

New Brunswick is where the great Canadian forest, sliced by sweeping river valleys and modern highways, meets the sea. It's an old place in New World terms, and the remains of a turbulent past are still in evidence in some of its quiet nooks. Near Moncton, for instance, bees gather nectar and wild strawberries perfume the air of the grassy slopes of Fort Beausejour, where, in 1755, one of the last battles for possession of Acadia took place—the English finally overcoming the French. The dual heritage of New Brunswick (35% of its population is Acadian French) provides added spice. If you decide to stay in both Acadian and Loyalist regions, a trip to New Brunswick can seem like two vacations in one.

More than half the province is surrounded by coastline—the rest nestles into Québec and Maine, creating slightly schizophrenic attitudes in border towns. The dramatic Bay of Fundy, which has the highest tides in the world, sweeps up the coast of Maine, around the enchanting Fundy Isles at the southern tip of New Brunswick and on up the province's rough and intriguing south coast. To the north and east, the gentle, warm Gulf Stream washes quiet beaches.

New Brunswick is still largely unsettled—85 percent of the province is forested lands. Inhabitants have chosen the easily accessible area around rivers, ocean, and lakes, leaving most of the interior to the pulp companies. For years this Cinderella province has been virtually ignored by tourists who whiz through to better-known Atlantic destinations. New Brunswick's residents can't seem to decide whether this makes them unhappy or not. Money is important in the economically depressed maritime area, where younger generations have traditionally left home for higher-paying jobs in Ontario and "The West." But no one wishes to lose the special characteristics of this still unspoiled province by the sea.

This attitude is a blessing in disguise to motorists who leave major highways to explore 2,240 kilometers (1,400 miles) of spectacular seacoast, pure inland streams, pretty towns, and historical cities. The custom of hospitality is so much a part of New Brunswick nature that tourists are perceived more as welcome visitors than paying guests. Even cities often retain a bit of naiveté. It makes for a charming vacation, but don't be deceived by ingenuous attitudes. Most residents are products of excellent school and university systems, generally travel widely, live in modern cities, and are well versed in world affairs.

Essential Information

Important Addresses and Numbers

Tourist
Information

Department of Economic Development and Tourism (Box 6000, Fredericton E3B 5H1, tel. 506/453–2170 or 800/561–0123) can provide information on the seven provincial tourist bureaus. Also helpful are information services of the cities of: **Bathurst** (tel. 506/548–0400), **Campbellton** (tel. 506/753–7767), **Fredericton** (tel. 506/452–9500), **Moncton** (tel. 506/853–3333), and **Saint John** (tel. 506/658–2990).

Emergencies

Dial 911 for medical emergencies and police in New Brunswick cities and their surrounding areas. For other areas find emergency numbers inside the front cover of the local telephone directory.

Hospitals **Dr. Everett Chalmers Hospital** (Priestman St., Fredericton, tel. 506/452–5400); **Moncton City Hospital** (135 MacBeath Ave., Moncton, tel. 506/857–5111); **Dr. Georges Dumont Hospital** (330 Archibald St., Moncton, tel. 506/858–3232); **Saint John Regional Hospital** (Tucker Park Rd., Saint John, tel. 506/648–6000); **Chaleur Regional Hospital** (1750 Sunset Dr., Bathurst, tel. 506/548–8961); **Campbellton Regional Hospital** (189 Lilly Lake Rd., Campbellton, tel. 506/789–5000); **Edmundston Regional Hospital** (275 Hébert Blvd., tel. 507/739–2200); **Hôtel Dieu** (53 Lobban Ave., Chatham, tel. 506/773–4401).

Arriving and Departing by Plane

Canadian Airlines International through **Air Atlantic** (tel. 800/665–1177) operates in Saint John, Fredericton, Moncton, Charlo, and Chatham and serves the Atlantic provinces, Montréal, Ottawa, and Boston. **Air Canada** and its regional carrier **Air Nova** (tel. 800/776–3000) serve the Atlantic provinces, Montréal, Toronto, and Boston.

Arriving and Departing

By Car Ferry There are car ferries from Prince Edward Island and Nova Scotia. **Marine Atlantic** (tel. 902/794–7203) has a car-and-passenger ferry from Digby, Nova Scotia, which takes 2½ hours. For reservations in the United States (except Maine), call 800/341–7981; in Maine, tel. 800/432–7344.

By Train **Via Rail** offers passenger services three times a week from Moncton to Montréal and Halifax. The southern route connects Montréal with Halifax by way of Fredericton Junction, Saint John, and Moncton. The northern route goes through Campbellton and on to Moncton and Halifax. Bus connections are available to Prince Edward Island and Newfoundland.

By Bus **SMT** (tel. 506/859–5100) within the province connects with most major bus lines.

Getting Around

By Car New Brunswick has an excellent highway system with numerous facilities. The only map you'll need is the free one given out at the tourist information centers listed above. Major entry points are at St. Stephen, Houlton, Edmundston, and Cape Tormentine from Prince Edward Island, and Aulac from Nova Scotia.

Guided Tours

Boat Tours Harbor tours are offered in Saint John by **Partridge Island Tours** (tel. 506/693–2598) and **DMK Marine Tours** (tel. 506/635–5100).

City Tours **Heritage Tour Guide Service** (856 George St., Fredericton, tel. 506/459–5950) provides step-on guides for bus tours of Fredericton.

The **Calithumpians** theater company offers guides dressed in 18th-century costumes for free historical walks from City Hall (Queen St., tel. 506/457–1975).

In Saint John free guided walking tours begin in Market Square at Barbours General Store. For information call the Saint John Tourist and Convention Center (tel. 506/658–2990).

Special-interest More than 240 species of seabirds nest on Grand Manan Island, and the island is a paradise for painters, nature photographers, and hikers, not to mention whale-watchers. Any of these activities can be arranged by calling **Tourism New Brunswick** at 800/561–0123. **Covered Bridge Bicycle Tours** (Box 693, Dept. K, Main Post Office, Saint John E2L 4B3, tel. 506/849–9028) offers bike tours. **East Coast Expeditions** (Box 6713, Station A, Saint John, E2L 4S2, tel. 506/658–1906) offers guided hiking in the Fundy area.

Exploring New Brunswick

Our exploration of New Brunswick is broken down into four areas: a tour of the city of Fredericton, a tour of the Saint John Valley ending at the city of Saint John, a tour of the Fundy Coast, and a jog north to the sunny Acadian Peninsula.

Highlights for First-time Visitors

Acadian Historical Village, Grand Anse, Tour 4: Moncton and the Acadian Peninsula
Beaverbrook Art Gallery, Tour 1: Fredericton
Campobello Island, Tour 3: The Fundy Coast
Fundy National Park, Tour 3: The Fundy Coast
Kings Landing, Prince William, Tour 1: Fredericton
Kouchibouguac National Park, Acadian Peninsula, Tour 4: The Acadian Peninsula
Market Square and Market Slip, Saint John, Tour 2: Saint John River Valley
Moncton's Tidal Bore and Magnetic Hill, Tour 4: Moncton and the Acadian Peninsula

Tour 1: Fredericton

Numbers in the margin correspond to points of interest on the New Brunswick and Fredericton maps.

The small inland city of **Fredericton** spreads itself on a broad point of land jutting into the Saint John River. Its predecessor, the early French settlement of Ste-Anne's Point, was established in 1642, during the reign of the French governor, Villebon, who made his headquarters at the junction of the Nashwaak and the Saint John rivers. Settled by Loyalists and named for Frederick, second son of George III, the city serves as the seat of government for New Brunswick's 728,500 residents. From the first town plan, the wealthy and scholarly Loyalists set out to create a gracious and beautiful place, and thus even before the establishment of the University of New Brunswick, in 1785, the town served as a center for "liberal arts and sciences."

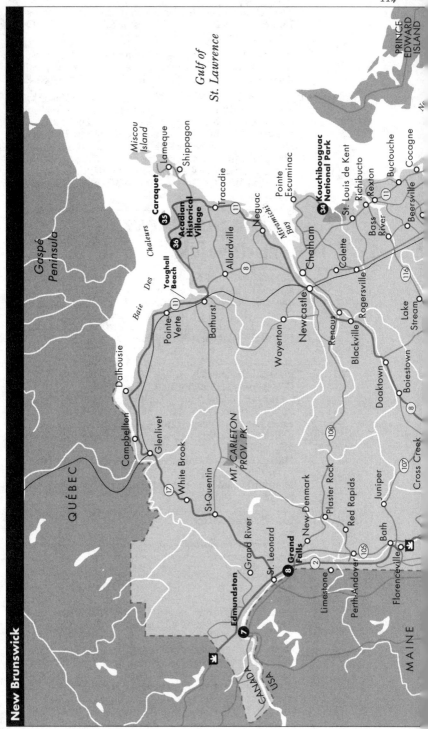

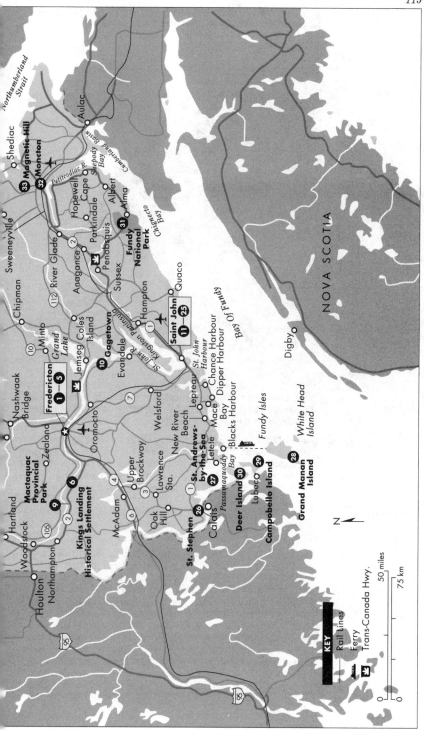

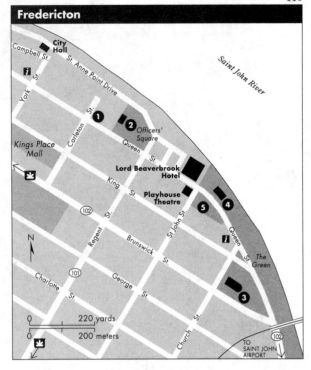

Fredericton's streets are shaded by leafy plumes of ancient elms. Downtown Queen Street runs parallel with the river, and its blocks enclose historic sites and attractions. Most major sites are within walking distance.

1 The **Military Compound** (including Officer's Quarters, parade grounds, Guard House, and Soldiers' Barracks) extends two blocks along Queen Street. The buildings have been restored and are partly open to the public. Redcoats stand guard and act as guides; in summer a changing-of-the-guard ceremony takes place at 11 and 7. *Queen St. at Carleton St., tel. 506/453–3747. Admission free. Open June 15–Labor Day, Sat.–Thurs. 10–5, Fri. 10–9. Closed Labor Day–June 14.*

Within the Military Compound, on the corner of Queen and Carleton streets, stands the John Thurston Clark Building—an outstanding example of Second Empire architecture. On the main floor is the **National Exhibition Centre.** You'll have fun with the scintillating displays of works by local and regional artists and artisans. Upstairs you'll find the Sports Hall of Fame, which celebrates the surprising array of locals who have made sports history, most notably, Ron Turcotte, who won horse racing's Triple Crown on the immortal Secretariat. The Hall of Fame's collection of original charcoal portraits of honored members is the largest of its kind in Canada. *503 Queen St., tel. 506/453–3747. Admission free. Both attractions open May 1–Labor Day, Sat.–Thurs. 10–5, Fri. 10–9; after Labor Day–Apr. 30, Tues.–Fri. noon–4:30, Sat. 10–5, Sun. 1–5.*

② Officer's Quarters houses the **York-Sunbury Museum,** a living picture of the community from the time when only natives inhabited the area, through the pioneer days, to the immediate past. It also contains the shellacked remains of one of Fredericton's legends, the puzzling Coleman Frog. This giant frog, allegedly discovered in nearby Killarney Lake by late hotelier Fred Coleman, supposedly weighed 42 pounds soaking wet at the time of its death (by a dynamite charge set by unorthodox fishermen). Coleman had the frog stuffed and displayed it for years in the lobby of his hotel. Take a look and judge for yourself—the frog just keeps on smiling. *Officer's Sq., Queen St., tel. 506/455–6041. Admission: $1 adults, 50¢ senior citizens and students, $2.50 families. Open May 1–Labor Day, Mon.–Sat. 10–6 (July and Aug., Tues. and Thurs. 10–9 and Sun. noon–6); Labor Day–mid-Oct., weekdays 9–5, Sat. noon–4; mid-Oct.–Apr., Mon., Wed., Fri. 11–3 or by appointment.*

Just a block or so east along the same street, at the intersection where Queen Street becomes Waterloo Row, you'll come to the **③ Christ Church Cathedral,** one of Fredericton's prides. Completed in 1853, the gray stone building is an excellent example of decorated Gothic architecture and the first new cathedral foundation built on British soil since the Norman Conquest. Inside you'll see a clock known as "Big Ben's little brother," the test-run for London's famous timepiece, designed by Lord Grimthorpe.

The late Lord Beaverbrook, former New Brunswick resident and multimillionaire British peer and newspaper magnate, showered gifts upon his native province. Near the cathedral **④** you'll find the **Beaverbrook Art Gallery,** displaying works by many of New Brunswick's noted artists. Salvador Dali's gigantic canvas *Santiago el Grande* is worth more than a passing glance. There are also canvases by Reynolds, Turner, Hogarth, Gainsborough, the Canadian Group of Seven, and even Andy Warhol. The gallery has the largest collection in any institution of the works of Cornelius Krieghoff, famed Canadian landscape painter of the early 1800s. *703 Queen St., tel. 506/458–8545. Admission: $3 adults, $2 senior citizens, $1 students. Open July–Aug., Sun. and Mon. noon–8, Tues. and Wed. 10–8, Thurs.–Sat. 10–5; in fall and winter, Tues.–Sat. 10–5, Sun.–Mon. noon–5.*

Beside the gallery sits **The Playhouse** (686 Queen St., tel. 506/458–8344), a gift of the Beaverbrook and Dunn Foundation to the city and province. It is the home of the professional **Theatre New Brunswick,** whose major season runs from September through May.

⑤ Directly across the street from the gallery is the 1880 **Provincial Legislature.** In its library, past the freestanding spiral staircase, is a rare copy of the Domesday Book, the Western world's first census, commissioned by William the Conqueror in 1085. You must ask to see the piece, however. Also to be found here is a four-volume 1834 set of the priceless king-size Audubon bird books, more than 3 feet high, containing 435 hand-colored pictures. *Queen St., tel. 506/453–2527. Admission free. Legislature tours: mid-June–Labor Day, daily 9–9; early Sept.–mid-June, weekdays 9–4. Library open 8:15–4:30 in summer, 8:15–5 Sept.–June.*

Continue east on Waterloo Row (Rte. 102), turn south at University Avenue to the **University of New Brunswick** campus. Be prepared to climb—the buildings are scattered over a fairly steep hill. The college was established in 1785—ancient by Canadian standards—and was originally called the College of New Brunswick, and later Kings College. Its Old Arts Building is the oldest university structure still in use in the country.

Tour 2: The Saint John River Valley to Saint John

To understand New Brunswick's background and history, visit **❻ Kings Landing Historical Settlement,** located about 30 kilometers (23 miles) west of Fredericton on the Trans-Canada Highway. This reconstructed village—more than 60 buildings, including homes, inn, forge, store, church, school, working farms, and sawmill—illustrates life in the central Saint John River valley between 1790 and 1900. Winding country lanes, creaking wagons, old houses, and freshly baked bread pull you back a century or more. The costumed staff is friendly and informative. The Tap Room of Kings Head Inn is a congenial spot to try a draft of cold beer or a mug of frosty cider; the restaurant upstairs serves tasty, old-fashioned traveler's fare. After a hearty meal of King George III's roast beef or Mrs. Long's chicken vegetable pie, drop by the General Store. It's the heart of the community and the genial storekeeper makes everyone feel welcome. *Box 522, Fredericton, tel. 506/363–5090. Admission: $7.50 adults, $5 senior citizens, $4 students, children under 6 free, $15 families. Other discounts and group rates available. Open June–mid-Oct., daily 10–6.*

The Saint John River forms 120 kilometers (75 miles) of the border with Maine and rolls down to Saint John, New Brunswick's largest, and Canada's oldest, city. Gentle hills of rich farmland and the blue sweep of the water make this a pretty drive. The Trans-Canada Highway (Highway 2) follows the banks of the river for most of its winding, 403-kilometer (250-mile) course.

At the northern end of the valley, near the border with Québec, you will find yourself in the mythical Republic of Madawaska. In the early 1800s the narrow wedge of land was coveted by Québec on one side and New Brunswick on the other; the United States claimed it as well. Seeking to retain it for New Brunswick, Governor Sir Thomas Carleton found it easy to settle with Québec. He rolled dice all night with the governor of British North America at Québec, who happened to be his brother. Sir Thomas won at dawn—by one point. Settling with the Americans was more difficult. The border had always been disputed, and even the lumbermen engaged in combat. Finally, in 1842, the British flag was hoisted over Madawaska county. One old-timer, tired of being asked to which country he belonged, replied, "I am a citizen of the Republic of Madawaska." So began the republic, which exists today with its own flag (an independent eagle on a field of white) and a coat of arms.

❼ Edmundston, the unofficial capital of Madawaska, has always depended on the wealth of the deep forest around it. Even today, Edmundston looks to the Fraser Company pulp mills as the major source of employment. It was in these woods that the legend of Paul Bunyan was born. Tales spread to Maine and even to the West Coast. The Foire Brayonne festival, held annually during the last week of July, is proud to claim the title of the biggest festival outside of Québec's Winter Carnival. It is certainly one of the most lively and vibrant cultural events in New Brunswick, offering prestigious concerts by acclaimed artists as well as local musicians and entertainers who enliven the Arts & Crafts Square. In winter the whole province enjoys skiing on the slopes of Mt. Farlagne.

❽ About 50 kilometers (30 miles) downriver, at **Grand Falls,** the Saint John throws itself over a high cliff, squeezes through a narrow rocky gorge, and emerges as a wider river. The result is a magnificent cascade, whose force has worn strange round wells in the rocky bed—some as much as 16 feet in circumference and 30 feet deep. Take the Gorge Walk ($2 adults, $1 children, $5 families) where you'll see the holes and the magnificent stream up close. According to Indian legend, a young maiden named Malabeam led her Iroquois captors to their deaths over the foaming cataract rather than guide them to her village. Local history is depicted at the **Grand Falls Historical Museum.** *209 Sheriff St., no phone. Admission free. Open July–Aug., Mon.–Sat. 9–5, Sun. 2–5; Sept.–June, by appointment.*

Although Grand Falls is largely French-speaking, English becomes more prevalent as you move down the Saint John River valley. Stop in **Florenceville** for a look at the small but reputable Andrew and Laura McCain Gallery, which has launched the career of many a New Brunswick artist.

The Trans-Canada Highway is intriguingly scenic, but if you're looking for less crowded highways and typical small communities, cross the river to Route 105 at Hartland, via the **longest covered bridge** in the world—1,282 feet in length.

If you prefer, stay on the Trans-Canada Highway until you reach the quiet hamlet of **Woodstock** (population 4,911). The town was named for a novel by Sir Walter Scott, and is most lively during its Old Home Week celebrations, in July. The **Old Courthouse** (built in 1833)—once a coaching stop, a social hall, a political meeting place, and the seat of justice for the area—has been carefully restored.

Time Out	Between Woodstock and Meductic, look for good German food at **Heino's Restaurant,** in the John Gyles Motel (junction Route 2 and Trans-Canada Highway).

❾ Within the **Mactaquac Provincial Park** is Mactaquac pond, whose existence is attributed to the building of the hydroelectric dam, which has caused the upper Saint John River to flood as far up as Woodstock. Although there are several privately owned campgrounds in the area, cars line up sometimes all night to claim an empty site in the morning. *Hwy. 105 and Mactaquac Dam, tel. 506/363–3011. 300 campsites, supervised recreation, 2 beaches, 2 marinas, 18-hole golf course, and lodge with dining room. Admission: $3.50 per vehicle summer, free in off-season. Open May 15–Sept. 2, 24 hrs; early Sept.–Nov., 8–6; Dec.–mid-May, 8–11.*

From Fredericton to Saint John you have a choice of two routes. Route 7 cuts away from the river to run straight south for its fast 109 kilometers (68 miles). Route 102 leads along the Saint John River through engaging communities. You make your decision at **Oromocto,** the site of the Canadian Armed Forces Base, **Camp Gagetown** (not to be confused with the pretty town of Gagetown farther down river), the largest military base in Canada (Prince Charles completed his helicopter training here). An interesting military museum within the base is open to the public. *Tel. 506/422–2630. Admission free. Open June–Aug., weekdays 9–5, weekends 12–5; Sept.–May, weekdays 9–4, closed weekends.*

⑩ Gagetown, one of New Brunswick's pleasant historic communities, bustles with artisans' studios and the summer sailors who tie up at the marina. The gingerbread-trimmed **Tilley House** takes you back to Canada's beginnings. Once the home of Sir Leonard Tilley, one of the Fathers of Confederation, it is now home of the Queens County Museum. *Front St., tel. 506/488–2966. Admission: $1 adults, 25¢ students. Open June–Sept. 15, daily 10–5.*

From Gagetown you can ferry to Jemseg and continue to **Grand Lake Provincial Park** (tel. 506/385–2919), which offers freshwater swimming off sandy beaches. At Evandale you can ferry to Belleisle Bay and the beautiful **Kingston Peninsula,** with its mossy Loyalist graveyards and pretty churches.

As you travel south you'll begin to get a feeling for how old New **⑪** Brunswick really is, and nowhere more so than in **Saint John.** It was the first incorporated city in Canada and has that weather–beaten quality common to so many antique seaport communities. Although sometimes termed a blue-collar town because so many of its residents work for Irving Oil, its genteel Loyalist heritage lingers; you sense it in its grand old buildings, the ladies' teas at the old Union Club, and the beautifully restored downtown harbor district.

The city has spawned many of the province's major artists— Jack Humphrey, Millar Brittain, Fred Ross—along with such Hollywood notables as Louis B. Mayer, Donald Sutherland, and Walter Pidgeon. There's also a large Irish population that emerges in a jubilant Irish Festival every March. In July costumed residents re-enact the landing of the Loyalists during Saint John's Loyalist Days.

In 1604 two Frenchmen, Samuel de Champlain and Sieur de Monts, landed here on St. John the Baptist Day to trade with the natives. Nearly two centuries later, in May of 1785, 3,000 Loyalists escaping from the Revolutionary War poured off a ship to found a city amid the rocks and forests. From those beginnings Saint John has emerged as a thriving industrial port.

Up until a few years ago the buildings around Saint John's waterfront huddled together in forlorn dilapidation, their facades crumbling and blurred by a century of grime. A recent surge of civic pride sparked a major renovation project that reclaimed old warehouses as part of an enchanting waterfront development.

Numbers in the margin correspond to points of interest on the Downtown Saint John and Greater Saint John maps.

You can easily explore Saint John's town center and harbor **⑫** area on foot. Get your bearings on **King Street,** the town's old main street, whose sidewalks are paved with red brick and lit

⑬ with old-fashioned lamps. King Street connects **Market Slip** on the waterfront with King Square at the center of town.

⑭ At Market Slip, where the Loyalists landed in 1783, and the adjoining **Market Square** you can while away a morning among the shops, historic displays, and cafés (some with outdoor dining in summer). Market Slip is the site of **Barbour's General Store** (tel. 506/658–2939), a fully stocked 19th-century shop redolent of the past: Inside, the scents of tobacco, pickles, smoked fish, and peppermint sticks mingle with the tangy, unforgettable aroma of dulse, the edible seaweed. Beside the store is a 19th-century red schoolhouse, now a tourist information center. Skywalks and underground passages lead from Market Square to City Hall, the new Delta Hotel, and Brunswick Square, an adjoining shopping mall.

⑮ Stroll up King Street to Germain Street, turn left, and walk up to the block-long **Old City Market,** built in 1876, which offers a variety of temptations, including red fresh-cooked lobster, great cheeses, dulse, and other inexpensive snacking along with much friendly chatter.

⑯ The imposing **Old Loyalist House,** built in 1810 by Daniel David Merritt, a wealthy Loyalist merchant, is distinguished by its authentic period furniture and eight fireplaces. *120 Union St., tel. 506/652–3590. Admission: $2 adults, 25¢ children. Open Mon.–Sat. 10–5, Sun. 2–5, or by appointment.*

⑰
⑱ Follow Union Street away from the harbor to Sydney Street and turn right to visit the **Old Loyalist Burial Grounds.** At one corner, in adjacent **King Square,** you'll find a strange mass of metal on the ground. It is actually a great lump of melted stock from a neighboring hardware store that was demolished in Saint John's Great Fire of 1877, in which 115 buildings were destroyed.

⑲ At the corner of King and Sydney streets is the **Old Courthouse.** Its spiral staircase, built of tons of unsupported stone, ascends seemingly by miracle for three stories.

⑳ Walk around the south side of King Square to visit **Trinity Church** (115 Charlotte St., tel. 506/693–8558), which dates from 1877, when it was rebuilt after the great fire. Inside, over the west door, note the coat of arms—a symbol of the monarchy—rescued from the council chamber of the colony at Massachusetts Bay. The coat of arms was deemed a worthy refugee and given a place of honor in the church.

㉑ If you have a car, drive north from downtown on Prince William Street to Main Street; in a park on your right you'll find **Fort Howe** (Rockland Road and Magazine Street). The reconstructed fortress sits atop a cliff overlooking the harbor and affords fine views from its walls. It is believed to be near the site of Fort LaTour, a French stronghold resolutely defended by Madame La Tour from her absent husband's fur-trading rival. Finally surrendering on the condition that the lives of her men would be spared, the unfortunate woman was betrayed and forced to watch them all put to death. She died shortly after, of a broken heart it is said—a romantic fate befitting her former profession as star of the Paris stage.

㉒ Main Street soon crosses Douglas Avenue; turn left to reach two of the city's most notable attractions. First is the **New**

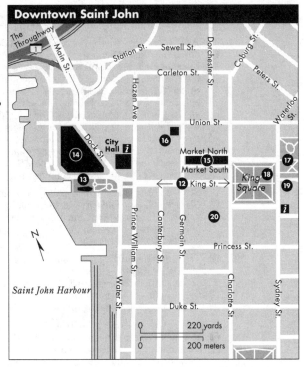

Downtown Saint John

Brunswick Museum, the first museum to be built in Canada, and still recognized as one of the best of its size. Behind its neoclassical facade, supported by Corinthian columns, are exhibits reflecting the history, culture, and spirit of New Brunswick. It displays its own fine arts, natural science, marine history, and immense collection of historical artifacts. Also, many traveling exhibits of universal historic and cultural scope are presented here. *277 Douglas Ave., tel. 506/658–1842. Admission: $2 adults, 50¢ students, senior citizens and children under 6 free, families $4. Group tours can be arranged. Open daily 10–5. Closed only on Good Friday and Christmas Day.*

㉓ Continue west on Douglas Avenue to reach the **Reversing Falls Rapids,** touted by all tourist brochures as a sight no one should miss. Actually, you *should* see it, though less for its beauty than its interest: It's a series of rapids and whirlpools at which, twice a day, the strong Fundy Tides attempt to push the river water back upstream. When the tide ebbs, the river once again pours over the rock ledges and the rapids appear to reverse themselves. A pulp mill on the bank is less scenic, and the stench it occasionally sends out is one of the less-than-charming parts of a visit. To learn more about the phenomenon, see the excellent free film shown in the tourist information center on the site.

㉔ **Cherry Brook Zoo,** at the very northern tip of Rockwood Park, houses Siberian tigers, wildebeest, and other exotic species. *Tel. 506/634–1440. Open daily 10–dusk. $3.25 adults, $2.25 senior citizens and students, $1.40 pre-schoolers, children under 2 free. Tour rates available.*

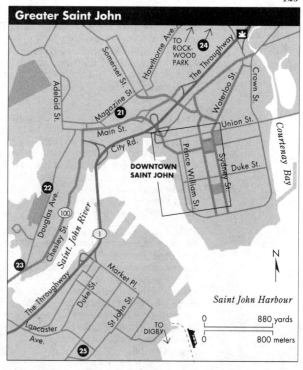

Greater Saint John

Cross the river on Bridge Road to **West Saint John.** Make a right on Lancaster Avenue and proceed to Charlotte Street, where you can't miss the **Carleton Martello Tower.** Like Fort Howe, this is a great place to survey the harbor. The tower was built in 1810 as a precaution against American attack. Costumed guides point out 8-foot-thick walls and pose for photographs. *Charlotte Ext. W, tel. 506/636–4011. Admission free. Open June 1–mid-Oct., daily 9–5.*

Tour 3: The Fundy Coast

Numbers in the margin correspond to points of interest on the New Brunswick map.

Bordering the chilly and powerful tidal Bay of Fundy is some of New Brunswick's loveliest coastline. A tour of the region will take you from the border town of St. Stephen, through tiny fishing villages and past rocky coves, to Fundy National Park, where the world's most extreme tides rise and fall twice daily. **St. Stephen,** on the Maine border, is a mecca for chocoholics, who converge on the small town during the Chocolate Festival held the first week in August. Choctails and chocolate puddings, cakes, and complete meals should come as no surprise when you realize that it was here that the chocolate bar was invented. Sample Ganong's famed hand-dipped chocolates at the factory store, **The Ganong Chocolatier.** *73 Milltown Blvd., tel. 506/465–5611. Open July–Aug., weekdays 9–8, Sat. 9–5, Sun. noon–5; Sept.–Dec., daily 9–5; Jan.–mid-May, Mon.–Sat. 9–5. Closed Dec. 25, Jan. 1.*

A small side trip along Ledge Road will take you to **Crocker Hill Studios,** on the banks of the St. Croix River. Walk down the garden path to the artist's studio with its paintings and carved decoys. It is surrounded by a fragrant, tranquil herb garden. Relax in one of the comfortable garden benches and watch the golfers across the river in the state of Maine. *Tel. 506/466–4251. Admission: $3 adults. Open June–Sept., daily 10–5; Oct.–June by appointment.*

㉗ Take Route 127 off Route 1 to **St. Andrews-by-the-Sea,** one of North America's prettiest and least-spoiled resort towns. Long the summer place of the affluent (mansions ring the town), St. Andrews retains its year-round population of fishermen, and little has changed in the past two centuries. Of the town's 550 buildings 280 were erected before 1880; 14 have survived from the 1700s. Some Loyalists brought their homes with them piece by piece from Castine, Maine, across the bay, when the war didn't go their way.

Pick up a walking-tour map at the tourist information center on Water Street and follow it through the pleasant streets. Particular gems are the **Court House** and **Greenock Church.** The church owes its existence to a remark someone made at an 1822 dinner party about the "poor" Presbyterians not having a church of their own. Captain Christopher Scott, who took exception to the slur, spared no expense on the building, which is decorated with a carving of a green oak tree in honor of Scott's birthplace, Greenock, Scotland. Also along Water Street are numerous antiques shops and artists' studios. The porch of the **Shiretown Inn** (218 Water St., tel. 506/529–8877) is a perfect place for a snack and a view.

The **Ross Memorial Museum** features a fine antiques collection. *188 Montague St., tel. 506/529–3906. Admission free. Open late May–early Oct., Mon.–Sat. 10–4:30, Sun. (July–Sept.) 1:30–4:30.*

A drive up Joe's Point Road takes you to the **Huntsman Aquarium and Museum,** which houses marine life and displays. *Brandy Cove Rd., tel. 506/529–8895. Admission: $4 adults, $3.50 senior citizens, $2.75 children under 18, children under 4 free; families $10.70. Open May–June, daily 10–4:30; July–Aug., daily 10–6; Sept.–mid-Oct., daily 10–4:30. Closed mid-Oct–Apr.*

Back on Route 1 is **St. George,** a pretty town with some excellent bed-and-breakfasts, one of the oldest Protestant graveyards in Canada, and a fish ladder running up the side of a dam.

The Fundy Isles—Grand Manan, Deer Island, and Campobello—are havens of peace that have lured harried mainlanders for generations. **Grand Manan Island,** largest of the three, is also farthest away (about two hours by car-ferry from Black's Harbour); you might see spouting whales, sunning seals, or a rare puffin on the way. Circular herring weirs dot the coastal water, and fish sheds and smokehouses lie beside long wharfs that reach out to bobbing fishing boats. Place names are romantic—Swallowtail, Southern Head, Seven Days Work, and Dark Harbour. It's easy to get around—only about 32 kilometers (20 miles) of road lead from the lighthouse at Southern Head to the one at Northern Head. A living encyclopedia of birds, Grand Manan attracted John James Audubon in 1831. The puffin is the island's symbol. Whale-watching expeditions can be booked at the Marathon Hotel and the Compass Rose, and scuba diving to old wrecks is popular.

㉙ Connected to Lubec, Maine, by an international bridge, **Campobello Island** may be approached from the other side by toll ferry from Deer Island. Neatly manicured, preening itself in the bay, Campobello Island has always had a special appeal to the wealthy and the famous. It was here that the Roosevelt family spent their summers. The home of Franklin Delano Roosevelt, former president of the United States, is now maintained as a lovely museum in his honor. Located in the center of Roosevelt International Park, a joint project of the Canadian and American governments, **President Roosevelt's home** was the setting for the movie *Sunrise at Campobello. Roosevelt Park Rd., tel. 506/752–2922. Admission free. House open late May–mid-Oct., daily 10–6; grounds open year-round.*

The island's **Herring Cove Provincial Park** has camping facilities and a nine-hole golf course.

An easy, 20-minute, free ferry ride from Letete near St. George

㉚ brings you to the relaxing **Deer Island.** You'll enjoy exploring the fishing wharves such as those at **Chocolate Cove.** The world's largest lobster pound is at **Northern Harbour,** and you can walk through a small nature park at **Deer Point** while waiting for the toll ferry to nearby Campobello. If you listen carefully, you may be able to hear the sighing and snorting of "the Old Sow," the second largest whirlpool in the world. If you can't hear it, you'll be able to see it, just a few feet off-shore. Exploring the island takes only a few hours; it's 12 kilometers (7½ miles) long, varying in width from almost 5 kilometers (3 miles) to a few hundred feet at some points.

After returning from the Fundy Isles to the mainland, proceed east along coastal Route 1. If you have the time, dip down to the peaceful, hidden fishing villages of **Maces Bay, Dipper,** and **Chance Harbour,** all much the same as they have been for centuries. At Dipper Harbour, you can rent sea kayaks and canoes, arrange for whale watching and deep-sea fishing (Eastern Outdoors Marine, tel. 506/634–1530), or buy a lobster roll to munch on while strolling the long sun-warmed wharf.

Drive east through Saint John along a scenic stretch of Route 1 to Route 114, which angles south to the 129-square-kilometer

㉛ (80-square-mile) **Fundy National Park.** Stand on a sandstone ledge above a dark-sand beach and watch the bay's phenomenal tide rise or fall. *Box 40, Alma E0A 1B0, tel. 506/887–2000. Admission: $5 per car in summer; free rest of the year.*

Alma is the small seaside town that services the national park. Here you'll find great lobster and the local specialty, sticky buns. Past Alma, the coast road to Moncton winds by covered bridges and along rocky coasts, past photogenic spots such as the wild driftwood-cluttered beach at **Cape Enragé** and **Hopewell Cape,** home of the famous giant flowerpots, rock formations carved by the Fundy Tides.

Tour 4: Moncton and the Acadian Peninsula

A friendly town, often called the Gateway to Acadia because of its mix of English and French and its proximity to the Acadian

㉜ shore, **Moncton** has a pretty downtown where wisely placed malls do a booming business.

This city has long touted two natural attractions, the Tidal Bore and the Magnetic Hill. You may be disappointed if you've read too much tourist hype. In days gone by, before the harbor mouth filled with silt, the **Tidal Bore** was indeed an incredible sight, a high wall of water that surged in through the narrow opening of the river to fill red-mud banks to the brim. It still moves up the river, and the moving wave is worth waiting for, but it's nowhere near as lofty as it used to be, except sometimes in the spring when the tides are very high. Bore Park on Main Street is the best vantage point; viewing times are posted there.

33 **Magnetic Hill,** north of town just off the Trans-Canada Highway, creates a bizarre optical illusion. If you park your car in neutral at the designated spot, you'll seem to be coasting up hill without power. An excellent family water-theme park, **Magic Mountain,** is adjacent to the hill. *On Magnetic Hill, tel. 506/857–9283. Admission: $17.25 adults/$10.50 afternoon; $11.75 children under 12 and senior citizens/$9.50 afternoon; $53.25 for a family of 4 for a full day. Open mid-June–July and mid-Aug.–Labor Day, daily 10–6; July–mid-Aug. 10–8.*

Among Moncton's notable man-made attractions is the **Acadian Museum,** at the University of Moncton, whose remarkable collection of artifacts reflects 300 years of Acadian life in New Brunswick. *Clement Cormier Bldg., University of Moncton, tel. 506/858–4088. Admission free. Open June–Sept., weekdays 10–5, weekends 1–5; Oct.–May, Tues.–Fri. 1–4:30, weekends 1–4. Closed Mon., holidays.*

Turn northeast along the coast from Moncton to the salty shores of unique Acadian communities such as **Shediac, Cocagne, Buctouche,** and **Rexton,** where you'll find long warm sand dunes, lobster feeds, lighthouses, weathered wharves, and sea-stained churches. The friendliness of the Acadians makes this trip a joy, and the white, dune-edged beaches of
34 **Kouchibouguac National Park** are among the finest on the continent. *Kent County, tel. 506/876–2443. Admission: $5 per vehicle, senior citizen $4. Day and annual passes available. Open year-round.*

Route 11 continues north to the Miramichi River and the fabled **Miramichi region** of lumberjacks, fishermen, and "come all ye's." Celebrated for its salmon rivers and the ebullient nature of its residents (Scottish, English, Irish, and a smattering of French and Indian), this is a land of stories, folklore, and lumber kings. Pleasant towns and villages of sturdy wood homes dot the banks of Miramichi Bay at **Chatham** and **Newcastle** (where the politician and British media mogul Lord Beaverbrook grew up and is buried). At **Doaktown** (south of Newcastle on Route 8), the **Miramichi Salmon Museum** (tel. 506/365–7787) provides a look at the endangered Atlantic salmon and at life in noted fishing camps along the rivers.

The **Woodmen's Museum** of Boiestown (in the exact center of the province), with artifacts that date from the 1700s to the present, is housed in what looks like two giant logs set on more than 60 acres of land. The museum portrays a lumberman's life through its displays, but its tranquil grounds are excuse enough to visit. Picnic facilities and camping sites are also available. *Rte 8, Boiestown, tel. 506/369–7214. Admission: $5 adults,*

$4 senior citizens, $2 children, $12 families. Open June–mid-Sept., daily 10–5:30.

㉟ Return to Newcastle and swing north and east on Route 11 to **Caraquet,** on the Acadian Peninsula. The town is perched along the Baie des Chaleurs, with Québec's Gaspé Peninsula beckoning across the inlet.

㊱ The *pièce de résistance* of the Acadian Peninsula is, without doubt, the **Acadian Historical Village,** 10 kilometers (6 miles) west of Caraquet on Route 11, near Grand Anse. As Kings Landing depicts the early English settlement, this village recreates an early Acadian community between 1780 and 1890. Summer days are wonderfully peaceful. A chapel bell tolls, ducks waddle and quack under a footbridge, wagons creak, and the smell of hearty cooking wafts from cottage doors. Costumed staff act as guides, and a restaurant serves old-Acadian dishes. *Tel. 506/727–3467. Admission: $7.50 adults, $4.25 children under 18, $15 families. Open June–Aug., daily 10–6; Sept., daily 10–5.*

Shopping

New Brunswick is famous for its crafts, and the *Directory of New Brunswick Craftsmen & Craft Shops* provides comprehensive listings of potters, weavers, glassblowers, jewelers, and carvers throughout the province. Get a copy from Tourism New Brunswick (Box 6000, Fredericton, E3B 5H1, tel. 800/561–0123).

Fredericton Mammoth crafts markets are held occasionally in town and every Labor Day weekend in Mactaquac Park. **Aitkens Pewter** (81 Regent St.) offers beautiful pewter hollowware, goblets, belt buckles, and jewelry. **Shades of Light Studio and Gift Shop** (28 Regent St.) features stained glass and other local crafts. **Mulhouse Country Classics,** about 2 kilometers (1 mile) from downtown in Lower St. Marys across the river on the north side, is a gem for crafts and handmade furniture.

Excellent men's shoes can be bought at **Hartt's Shoe Factory** (York St.); **The Linen Closet** (King St.) sells laces, exquisite bedding, and Victorian nightgowns.

Gagetown **Flo Grieg's** on Front Street carries superior pottery. **Claremont House B&B,** on Tilley Road, displays unusual batik items and copper engravings. **Loomcrofters,** just off Main Street, is a good choice for handwoven items.

Moncton Five spacious malls and numerous pockets of shops in downtown Moncton make it one of the best places to shop in New Brunswick. Among the crafts to look for are the yarn portraits of La Sagouine, "the old sage" of Buctouche. The sayings of the old Acadian woman as she does her daily chores were made famous in Antonine Maillet's novel *La Sagouine.*

St-Andrews-by-the-Sea This "veddy British" town has many places to buy English and New Brunswick woolens, English bone china, and marvelous wool yarn, among them **The Sea Captain's Loft** (Water St.) and **Cottage Craft** (Town Sq.). Antiques and rare and out-of-print books are sold at the **Pansy Patch** (Carleton St.), a stunning old home across from the Algonquin Hotel. On Water Street, the main shopping strip, head to **Tom Smith's Studio** (Water St.) for highly regarded oriental Raku pottery.

Saint John The little antiques stores and crafts shops sprinkled around the downtown area provide the best shopping in Saint John. **Prince William Street** has interesting browsing in antiques shops and crafts boutiques; **House of Tara** (72 Prince William St.) is wonderful for fine Irish linens and woolens. Airy **Brunswick Square** and **Market Square** in the new harborfront have many top-quality boutiques. **Old City Market,** between Charlotte and Germain streets, bustles six days a week and always stocks delicious local specialties, such as maple syrup and lobster.

St. Leonard A visit to the studio and store of the **Madawaska Weavers** (Main St.), whose handwoven items are known the world over, is a must. Handsome skirts, stoles, and ties are some of the items on sale.

Sports and Fitness

Bicycling Byroads, lanes, and rolling secondary highways run through small towns, along the ocean, and into the forest. Set out on your own; or try a guided adventure with a specialist tour operator such as **Covered Bridge Bicycle Tours** (Dept. F, Box 693, Main Post Office, Saint John, E2L 4B3, tel. 506/849–9028). Bed-and-breakfasts frequently have bicycles for hire and the Department of Economic Development and Tourism has listings and free cycling maps (*See* Important Addresses and Numbers in Essential Information, *above*). Information on competitive cycling and races is available from **Velo New Brunswick** (457 Chartersville Rd., Dieppe, NB, E1A 5H1).

Fishing Dotted with freshwater lakes, crisscrossed with fish-laden rivers, and bordered by 1,129 kilometers (700 miles) of seacoast, this province is one of Canada's natural treasures. Sportspeople are drawn by the excellent bass fishing and the world-famous salmon rivers such as the Miramichi, the Restigouche, and the Nashwaak. Commercial fishermen often take visitors line fishing for ground fish. An annual freshwater fishing license for out-of-province visitors costs $25 for three days; $50 for seven days; $100 for the season (plus GST). For more information, call New Brunswick Fish and Wildlife (tel. 506/453–2440).

Golf There are 36 excellent golf courses in New Brunswick—many, such as the **Algonquin Golf Club** (tel. 506/529–3062) in St. Andrews and the **Gowan Brae Golf and Country Club** (tel. 506/546–2707) in Bathurst, with sparkling views of the sea. The **Fundy National Park Golf Club** (tel. 506/887–2970) at Alma is nestled near cliffs overlooking the restless Bay of Fundy; deer grazing on the course are one of its hazards. Greens fees run about $20–$25, $15 for some nine-hole courses; and visitors are generally welcome. For a list of golf courses, ask for the free "New Brunswick Travel Guide" from the Department of Economic Development and Tourism (Box 6000, Fredericton, E3B 5H1).

Hiking Rocky coastline and inland highland trails offer hiking opportunities for both experienced and casual trekkers. **East Coast Expeditions** (Box 6713, Station A, Saint John, E2L 4S2, tel. 506/658–1906) and **Miramichi Four Seasons Outfitters** (Box

705, RR 2, Newcastle, E1V 3L9, tel. 506/622–0089) offer guided hiking tours. For trail information, call Eric Hadley, of **New Brunswick Trails Club,** at the Department of Natural Resources and Energy (tel. 506/453–2883).

Skiing A perfect province for cross-country skiing, New Brunswick
Cross-country offers groomed trails at provincial and national parks such as Mactaquac Provincial Park near Fredericton, Fundy National Park in Alma, and Kouchibouguac National Park between Moncton and Bathurst. Many communities and small hotels offer groomed trails, but it's also possible to set off on your own in almost every section of the province.

Downhill New Brunswick downhill ski areas usually operate from mid-December through April. They include **Crabbe Mountain Winter Park** (tel. 506/463–8311) in Lower Hainesville (near Fredericton); **Sugarloaf Provincial Park** (tel. 506/789–2366) in Campbellton, northern New Brunswick; **Mont Farlagne** (tel. 506/735–8401) in St. Jacques, near Edmundston; **Poley Mountain Ski Area** (tel. 506/433–3230) in Sussex; and **Silverwood Winter Park** (tel. 506/450–3380) in Fredericton.

Tennis Courts are available in most city and town parks. Most are free. Many resorts and hotels have courts.

Water Sports Kayaking along the coasts of Fundy and Chaleur has become
Canoeing and very popular. A list of canoe and kayak liveries is available from
Kayaking Department of Economic Development and Tourism (Box 6000, Fredericton, E3B 5H1). For canoes, try **A to Z Rentals** (128 Prospect St., tel. 506/452–9758) in Fredericton and in St. John (535 Rothesay, tel. 506/633–1919). Outfitters such as **Fundy Marine** (Brunswick Square, Saint John, tel. 506/634–1530) offer single and double kayaks, lessons, and tours.

Sailing Sailboats can be chartered in many areas including **Fundy Yacht Sales and Charter** (Dipper Harbour, Rte. 2, Lepreau, E0G 2H0, tel. 506/659–2769). Information on charters is available from **The New Brunswick Sailing Association** (Box 4005, Station B, Saint John, E2M 5E6).

Rowing Shells can be rented at the **Kennebecasis Club** (tel. 506/849–9910) in Rothesay, and at the **Aquatic Center** (tel. 506/458–5513) in Fredericton.

Whale watching One New Brunswick experience that is difficult to forget is the sighting of a huge humpback, right whale, finback, or minke. Whale-watching tours are available from a number of operators such as **Ocean Search** (Marathon Inn, North Head, Grand Manan, tel. 506/662–8488) and **West Isles World** (Lambertville, Deer Island, tel. 506/747–2946). **Cline Marine Tours** (tel. 506/529–2287) in St. Andrews and Deer Island offers whale-watching, as well as scenic, tours. **Chaleur Phantom** (tel. 506/684–4722) in Dalhousie combines scenic tours to observe marine life in the calmer waters around the islands with deep-sea fishing excursions.

Dining and Lodging

Dining

Although there are not a lot of choices for fine dining in New Brunswick, a few good restaurants exist, and families will find plenty of quality food in many outlets. A number of gourmet restaurants have popped up in Saint John in recent years—so there is hope that the dining scene will improve throughout the province.

In the spring, once the ice has left streams and rivers, a provincial delicacy–the fiddlehead fern–is picked from the shores. Eaten as a vegetable (boiled, drenched with lemon, butter, salt, and pepper), fiddleheads have something of an artichoke taste and go well with spring's bony fish, shad, and gaspereaux. Silver salmon, once a spring staple when set nets were allowed, is still available but quite costly. Most salmon served in restaurants is farm reared. Lobster, a favorite maritime dish, is available in most restaurants, but is not always cheap. The custom of the residents is to buy it fresh from the fishermen or shore outlets and devour it in huge quantities. Because of the cool waters, shellfish is especially tasty. Look for oysters, scallops, clams, crab, and mussels. And be sure to try the purple seaweed called dulse that the residents eat like potato chips. To be truly authentic, accompany any New Brunswick–style feast with hearty Moosehead beer, brewed in Saint John and one of the province's well-known exports.

Dress is casual everywhere except at the Expensive and Very Expensive listings, and, unless noted, no reservations are needed.

Highly recommended restaurants in each price category are indicated by a star ★.

Category	Cost*
Very Expensive	over $40
Expensive	$20–$40
Moderate	$10–$19
Inexpensive	under $10

per person, excluding drinks, service, and 11% sales tax

Lodging

New Brunswick has a number of officially designated Heritage Inns—historically significant establishments built in the last century. Many have antique china and furnishings or other charming touches, and their accommodations run the gamut from elegant to homey.

Hotels and motels in and around Saint John and Fredericton are adequate and friendly. Accommodations in Saint John are at a premium in summer, so reserve ahead to ensure a place to stay.

Highly recommended lodgings in each price category are indicated by a star ★.

Category	Cost*
Expensive	over $60
Moderate	$45–$60
Inexpensive	under $40

**All prices are for a standard double room, excluding 10%
service charge.*

Campbellton **Aylesford Inn.** Truly a find, this friendly inn housed in a Victo-
Dining and Lodging rian mansion near the Québec border and Sugarloaf Provincial
★ Park has guest rooms handsomely furnished with Eastlake and
Canadian-pine antiques. Large gardens and verandas offer
views of the Restigouche River. Excellent dinners are served
to guests (quail and frogs' legs are featured entrées), and full
breakfasts are included in the room rate. Nonguests are welcome for afternoon tea. *8 MacMillan Ave., E3N 1E9, tel.
506/759–7672. 7 rooms, 1 with bath. Facilities: dining room, croquet. AE, MC, V. Moderate.*

Campobello Island **Island Club Lodge.** Originally a vacation home built by the Adams
Lodging family (friends of the Roosevelts) around the turn of the century,
these three attractive log buildings set on a bluff overlooking the Bay
of Fundy have been converted into a modern guest lodge. The 12
available rooms occupy two of the cabins; the third houses the dining
room, which specializes in simple but well-prepared local seafood.
*Box 16, Welshpool, E0G 3H0, tel. 506/752–2487. 12 rooms. Fa-
cilities: restaurant. MC, V. Moderate.*

★ **Owen House.** Mellow with history, this 200-year-old home was
built by Admiral Owen, who fancied himself ruler of the island.
Its gracious old rooms have hosted such luminaries as actress
Greer Garson, who stayed here (in a room with a fireplace in
the bathroom) when filming *Sunrise at Campobello.* Breakfasts
are wonderful—pancakes come topped with local berries.
Welshpool, E0G 3H0, tel. 506/752–2977. 9 rooms. V. Moderate.

Caraquet **Hotel Paulin.** The word *quaint* really fits this property. There
Dining and Lodging are pretty rooms, a bathroom down the hall, and an excellent
small dining room specializing in fresh fish cooked perfectly.
*143 Blvd. St. Pierre, tel. 506/727–9981. 10 rooms with shared
bath. Facilities: restaurant. MC, V. Inexpensive.*

Deer Island **45th Parallel Motel and Restaurant.** Deer Island has only one
Dining and Lodging motel, and it's clean and comfortable. A full breakfast is complimentary, and everything from lobster to pizza is available at
the informal restaurant. Pets are welcome. *Fairhaven, E0G
1R0, tel. 506/747–2231. 10 rooms, 3 with kitchenette. Facilities:
restaurant. AE, MC, V. Moderate.*

West Isles World B&B. This white frame house overlooks the
cove and offers three snug rooms with an informal country feel;
the big upstairs bedroom has a water view. The owners will
arrange whale-watching cruises for you. A full breakfast is included in the room rate, and other meals are served on request.
*Lord's Cove, E0G 2J0, tel. 506/747–2946. 3 rooms, 1 with bath. No
credit cards. Moderate.*

Fredericton **Luna Steakhouse.** Specialties include huge Caesar salad, garlic
Dining bread, escargots, brochettes, and Italian food. In fine weather
you can dine on an outdoor terrace. *168 Dundonald St., tel.
506/455–4020. AE, DC, MC, V. Moderate.*

Bar B Q Barn. Special children's menus and barbecued ribs and
chicken are the standards; the blackboard lists plenty of other
daily dinner specials, such as salmon, scallops, and chili. This
is a popular, attractive spot, great for winding down, and the
bar serves fine martinis. *540 Queen St., tel. 506/455–2742. AE,
MC, V. Inexpensive–Moderate.*

Pink Pearl. This restaurant features tasty Cantonese food,
with exceptional wontons and weekend buffets. *343 Queen St.,
tel. 506/450–8997. MC, V. Inexpensive.*

Lodging **Howard Johnson Motor Lodge.** This HoJo's, located on the
north side of the river and at the north end of the Princess
Margaret Bridge, has a terrace bar in a pleasant interior courtyard overlooked by balconies from many of the rooms. Guest-
room decor is standard for the chain. *Trans-Canada Highway,
Box 1414, E3B 5E3, tel. 506/472–0480. 116 rooms. Facilities: restaurant, bar, indoor pool, fitness center, indoor tennis courts.
AE, DC, MC, V. Expensive.*

Sheraton Inn Fredericton. Brand-new and within walking
distance of downtown, this big hotel offers modern rooms with
sunset views over the river. *225 Woodstock Rd. Fredericton,
E3B 2H8, tel. 506/457–7000. 223 rooms, all with minibars. Facilities: restaurant with outdoor terrace, bar, indoor and outdoor pools. AE, DC, MC, V. Expensive.*

Lord Beaverbrook Hotel. A central location is this modern,
seven-story hotel's main attraction, although 1991 renovations
spruced things up a bit. Some rooms have Jacuzzis or minibars.
The food in the main dining room is forgettable. There is a
lively bar downstairs. *659 Queen St., E3B 5A6, tel. 506/455–3371.
163 rooms. Facilities: 1 restaurant, bar, indoor pool, nonsmok-
ing rooms. AE, D, DC, MC, V. Moderate–Expensive.*

Auberge Wandlyn Inn. Just off the Trans-Canada Highway, this
hotel is away from the downtown area but close to three shopping malls, many restaurants, and theaters. The guest rooms
are no-frills, but the family-oriented dining room is pretty, and
there's a cozy bar. *58 Prospect St. W, Box 214, E3B 4Y9, tel.
506/452–8937. 116 rooms. Facilities: restaurant, bar, indoor and
outdoor pools, sauna, hot tub. AE, DC, MC, V. Moderate.*

Carriage House Bed and Breakfast. This heritage mansion has
lovely bedrooms. Homemade breakfast is served in the solar-
ium. *230 University Ave., E3B 4H7, tel. 506/452–9924. 7 rooms,
3 with bath. MC, V. Moderate.*

Happy Apple Acres Bed and Breakfast. This B&B offers
friendly atmosphere in a country setting. A full breakfast is
included in the room rate, and the cooking is excellent. *Highway 105 (4.3 km/7 mi north of Fredericton), R.R. 4, Fredericton,
E3B 4X5, tel. 506/458–1819. 3 rooms with bath, whirlpool and
sauna. MC, V. Moderate.*

Grand Manan **Compass Rose.** Lovely guest rooms are available in the two old
Island houses that have been combined into this small inn. It's con-
Lodging veniently near the ferry landing, and whale-watching tours can
be arranged. Breakfast is included in the room rate. *North
Head, E0G 3K0, tel. 506/662–8570. V. Moderate.*

The Marathon Inn. Perched on a hill overlooking the harbor,
this gracious mansion built by a sea captain offers guest rooms

furnished with antiques. The active bar is noisy, so book a room farthest from the fray. Whale- and bird-watching cruises can be arranged for those wishing to explore. *Box 129, North Head, E0G 2M0, tel. 506/662–8488. 28 rooms, 15 with bath. Facilities: restaurant, bar, pool, tennis. MC, V. Moderate–Expensive.*

Ludlow **Pond's Chalet Resort.** You'll get a traditional fishing-camp ex-
Lodging perience here, in a lodge and chalets set among trees overlooking a salmon river. *Ludlow (near Boiestown), E0C 1N0, tel.
506/369–2612. 10 rooms in lodge, 8 camps. Facilities: dining
room. AE, DC, MC, V. Moderate.*

Moncton **Cy's Seafood Restaurant.** This favorite for seafood, decorated
Dining in dark wood and brass, has been serving generous portions
★ for decades. Though renowned for its seafood casserole, the
restaurant also offers reliable scallop, shrimp, and lobster
dishes. You can see the Tidal Bore from the windows. *170 Main
St., tel. 506/857–0032. AE, DC, MC, V. Moderate.*

Fisherman's Paradise. In spite of the enormous dining area,
which seats more than 350 people, this restaurant serves
memorable à la carte seafood dishes in an atmosphere of candlelight and wood furnishings. The children's menu and down-
home specials such as lobster-bake make this a good spot for
families. *375 Dieppe Blvd., tel. 506/859–4388. AE, DC, MC, V.
Moderate.*

Lodging **Hotel Beausejour.** Moncton's finest hotel is decorated in
★ Acadian style. The downtown location is convenient. Besides the standard guest rooms, there are some luxury
suites. Staff in 18th-century costume lend a pleasant ambience to the main dining room, L'Auberge; the other restaurant is more formal. *750 Main St., tel. 506/854–4344. 317
rooms. Facilities: 2 restaurants, bar, outdoor pool, access
to health club. AE, MC, V. Expensive.*

The Crystal Palace. Moncton's newest hotel is unique: There
are theme rooms (want to be Ali Baba for a night?) and, for
families, an indoor pool and a miniature wonderland of rides,
midway stalls, and coin games. Champlain Mall is across the
street. *499 Paul St., tel. 506/858–8584. 115 rooms. Facilities: restaurant, indoor pool. AE, DC, MC, V. Moderate–Expensive.*

Newcastle **Wharf Inn.** Here in Miramichi country, the staff is friendly and
Lodging the restaurant serves excellent salmon dinners. This low-rise
modern building has two wings; guest rooms in the executive
wing have extra amenities. *Jane St., tel. 506/622–0302. 70 rooms.
Facilities: restaurant, patio lounge, indoor pool. AE, MC, V.
Moderate–Expensive.*

Sackville **Marshlands Inn.** In this white clapboard inn, a welcoming dou-
Lodging ble living room with fireplace sets the informal, country atmos-
★ phere. Bedrooms are furnished with sleigh beds or
four-posters, but they also have modern touches such as air-
conditioning and in-room telephones. *Box 1440, E0A 3C0, tel.
506/536–0170. 21 rooms, 14 with bath. Facilities: restaurant. AE,
DC, MC, V. Moderate–Expensive.*

St. Andrews **Algonquin Hotel.** The wraparound veranda of this grand old
Lodging hotel overlooks wide lawns. Bellmen wear kilts. The dining
room is noted for its buffets, and meals can be pleasant here if
the staff is in the mood. *Rte. 127, E0G 2X0, tel. 506/529–8823. 243
rooms. Facilities: 3 restaurants (dining room, coffee shop, and
veranda), 2 bars, pool, 2 golf courses, tennis. AE, MC, V. Closed
winter. Expensive.*

L'Europe. You may be amused by the cheerful decor in this intimate restaurant, in particular the whimsical objets d'art reflecting the tastes of the German owners. The food is European—some French, Swiss, German dishes, and so on, with particular attention given to seafood. All meals are served with delicious homemade Black Forest bread and pâté. *48 King St., E0G 2X0, tel. 506/529–3818. Reservations advised. Open Mother's Day–Sept. Dinner, 6–midnight; closed Mon. V. Expensive.*

★ **Pansy Patch B & B.** Across the street from the Algonquin Hotel is this Norman-style farmhouse, built in 1912, distinguished by a turret and steep roofs. The guest rooms are appointed with antiques and have views of the water. The owners also operate an antiques shop and bookshop on the property. Full breakfast is included in the room rate. *59 Carleton St., E0G 2X0, tel. 506/529–3834. 4 rooms with shared bath. AE, MC, V. Closed mid-Oct.–mid-May. Expensive.*

St. George **Granite Town Hotel.** Although this hotel was just built in 1991,
Lodging it nevertheless has an old-country-inn feeling to it. The decor is subtle, with pine and washed-birch woodwork prominent. Light blues and pinks dominate in the rooms. A restaurant is in the works that should be open for the 1994 season. The scenery is pleasant: one side of the building overlooking an apple orchard, the other just atop the bank of the Maguadavic River. A Continental breakfast is served but is not included in the room rate. *15 Main St., E0G 2Y0, tel. 506/755–6415. 32 rooms, 2 with Jacuzzi. AE, D, DC, MC, V. Moderate–Expensive.*

Saint John **La Belle Vie.** At one of the province's best restaurants, you'll
Dining dine in the drawing rooms of a lovely Second Empire–style
★ mansion, where 19th-century examples of trompe l'oeil adorn the ceilings and fine art graces the walls. The cooking is traditional French; try the lobster bisque. *325 Lancaster Ave., tel. 506/635–1155. Reservations advised. AE, DC, MC, V. Expensive.*
Turn of the Tide. Overlooking the harbor, this large hotel dining room is decorated with antiques. Although the dining is pleasant at all times, the best meal of the week is the Sunday buffet, with a long table full of dishes from the exotic to the tried-and-true. Fill your own crepes for dessert. *Hilton Hotel, Market Sq., tel. 506/693–8484. Reservations advised. AE, DC, MC, V. No lunch Sat. Expensive.*
Mexicali Rosa's. For a franchise, this restaurant has a lot of character. The decor is essentially Santa Fe–style with adobe arches and so forth. The specialty is "Cali-Mex" food, which is heavy on sauces, as opposed to "Tex-Mex," which concentrates more on meats. Guests waiting to be seated can order one of the fine margaritas in the large lounge. The fried chimichangas are with good reason the most popular dish. *88 Prince William St., tel. 506/652–5252. AE, DC, MC, V. Moderate.*
Grannan's. Seafood is featured in this nautically decorated restaurant, and the desserts here are memorable. Dining spills over onto the sidewalk in summer, and there are three lively bars connected to the restaurant. *Market Sq., tel. 506/634–1555. AE, DC, MC, V. No lunch Sun. Inexpensive–Moderate.*
Incredible Edibles. Here you can enjoy down-to-earth food—biscuits, garlic-laden hummus, salads, pastas, and desserts—in cozy rooms or, in summer, on the outdoor terrace. The menu has recently been expanded to include beef, chicken, and crab dishes. You'll get a good cup of coffee here, too. *42 Princess St.,*

tel. *506/633–7554. AE, DC, MC, V. Closed Sun. Inexpensive–Moderate.*

Reggie's. This popular spot near Brunswick Square begins serving breakfast at 6 AM. Later in the day specialties include chowders, bagel burgers, and lobster rolls. The restaurant closes at 6 or 7 PM, so come early if you want dinner. *26 Germain St., tel. 506/657–6270. MC, V. Inexpensive.*

Lodging **Saint John Hilton.** Part of the Market Square complex, the smallest Hilton in the world is furnished in Loyalist decor; guest rooms overlook the harbor or the town. Mellow antiques furnish corners of the dining room and the medieval-style Great Hall, which hosts banquets. Adjoining the 12-story property are shops, restaurants, bars, and a library. *1 Market Sq., E2L 4Z6, tel. 506/693–8484 or 800/361–6140. 197 rooms. Facilities: restaurant, bar, pool. AE, DC, MC, V. Expensive.*

★ **Shadow Lawn Country Inn.** This charming village inn is located in an affluent suburb with tree-lined streets and palatial houses, 10 minutes from Saint John. Tennis, golf, horseback riding, and a yacht club are nearby. The inn has eight old-fashioned bedrooms, some with fireplaces. Besides being open during breakfast (for guests, but not included in the room rate) and Sunday brunch served at 11, the dining room is open to the public for a set-menu dinner by reservation only; specialties include beef Wellington and seafood brioches. Pre-dinner sherry is served in the mahogany-paneled bar. *Box 41, Rothesay Rd., E0G 2W0, tel. 506/847–7539. 8 rooms with bath. DC, MC, V. Moderate–Expensive.*

Shediac **Chez Françoise.** This lovely old mansion with a wraparound
Dining and Lodging veranda has been decorated in Victorian style, with hardwood
★ floors and antiques; an annex across the street contains several guest rooms as well. Front rooms have water views. The dining room, open to the public for lunch and dinner, serves excellent traditional French cuisine with an emphasis on seafood. *93 Main St., tel. 506/532–4233. 10 rooms in main house, 6 with bath; 10 rooms in annex, 4 with bath. Facilities: restaurant. AE, MC, V. Closed Jan. 1–Easter. Inexpensive–Moderate.*

The Arts and Nightlife

The Arts

Theatre New Brunswick performs in the Playhouse in Fredericton (686 Queen St., tel. 506/458–8344) and tours the province. Top musical groups, noted professional singers, and other performers usually appear at the **Aitken Center** on the University of New Brunswick campus, at **Colosseum** in Moncton, and at the **Hilton Trade Center** in Saint John.

Beaverbrook Art Gallery in Fredericton is the province's major gallery, but art exhibitions are also held at the **Aitken Bicentennial Exhibition Center** (ABEC) in Saint John, at **Moncton City Hall,** and at the University of Moncton's **Acadian Museum.**

Nightlife

Fredericton The **Cosmopolitan Club** (King St.) sometimes presents great jazz and also has a back room where a younger crowd hangs out. The **Chestnut Inn,** on York Street, has dining and live country or folk music. Jazz and blues bands occasionally play at **Rye's Deli** (415 King St.), which also features hot-wings and popular Montréal smoked-meat sandwiches.

Saint John Taverns and lounges, usually with music of some kind, provide a lively nightlife. For quiet conversation with a "Play it again, Sam" background, try the **Brigantine,** in the Hilton.

5 Prince Edward Island

Prince Edward Island seems too good to be true, with its crisply painted farmhouses, manicured green fields rolling down to sandy beaches, the warmest ocean water north of Florida, lobster boats in trim little harbors, a vest-pocket capital city packed with architectural heritage.

When you experience PEI, you'll understand instantly that it was no accident that Lucy Maud Montgomery's novel of youth and innocence, *Anne of Green Gables*, was framed against this land. What may have been unexpected, however, was how the story burst on the world in 1908 and is still selling untold thousands of copies every year. After potatoes and lobsters, Anne is the island's most important product, particularly since the advent of the internationally aired television series *Anne of Green Gables* and its successor, *The Road to Avonlea.*

Anne is everywhere on the island: At the Confederation Centre of the Arts in Charlottetown you can peruse Montgomery's original handwritten manuscript; even on cars throughout the province you'll see the freckled redhead, as the government recently stamped her face on the province's license plates. But Anne's fame stretches beyond PEI and Cavendish—fondly referred to as Anne country. She attracts international attention, especially from the Japanese, with whom she is hugely popular.

Those visitors who have come because of Anne usually leave having fallen in love with her island. Outside of the tourist mecca of Cavendish, the island seems like an oasis of peace in a world of turmoil. Here you'll find fishing ports, crossroads villages, small family farms. You can choose full-service resorts and gourmet restaurants, or you can sample the lobster suppers, farm vacations, deep-sea fishing cruises, and bed-and-breakfasts, where you can experience for the first time what life is like on a working farm or fishing harbor.

Visitors often tour the island in a loop: They take the ferry from New Brunswick to Charlottetown, see Anne country and then PEI National Park, and depart by ferry to Nova Scotia. This is a good strategy; but, to more deeply experience the island's character, stray to the wooded hills of the east—to compact, bustling Montague, straddling its river; or to the estuarine maze of Murray Harbour. Or go west to the Acadian parishes of Egmont Bay and Tignish and the silver fox country around Summerside. Even if you're in a rush, it won't take long to get off the beaten path: In most places you can cross the island, north to south, in half an hour or so.

PEI is ringed by beaches, and few of them are heavily used. Ask a dozen islanders to recommend their favorites. Bothwell Beach, near Souris, says one—miles of singing sands, utterly deserted. Drop your clothes on the way in and pick them up on the way out. West Point, says a second—life guards, restaurant nearby, showers at the provincial park. Greenwich, near St. Peter's Bay, another suggests—a half-hour walk through magnificent wandering dunes brings you to an endless empty beach.

When you're back in Charlottetown see the musical "Anne of Green Gables." Have dinner first, though—there's a great little place two blocks from the theater. Let's go.

Essential Information

Important Addresses and Numbers

Tourist
Information

For prices and information before your trip, contact the **Prince Edward Island Department of Tourism and Parks,** Visitor Service Division (Box 940, Charlottetown, PEI C1A 7M5, tel. 902/368–5555 or 800/463–4PEI). The department publishes an excellent annual "Visitor's Guide," and maintains eight Visitor Information Centres (VICs) on the island. The main VIC, open year-round, is in Charlottetown (Oak Tree Pl., University Ave., tel. 902/368–4444), and is open mid-May–October, daily; November—mid-May, weekdays.

Emergencies **Police** and **fire,** dial 0.

Hospitals **Queen Elizabeth Hospital,** Charlottetown, tel. 902/566–6200.

Arriving and Departing by Plane

Charlottetown Airport is 5 kilometers (3 miles) north of town. **Air Canada** (tel. 800/776–3000) and **Canadian Airlines International** (902/892–4581) offer daily service to major cities in eastern Canada and the United States.

Arriving and Departing by Ferry

Two car-ferry services serve Prince Edward Island. **Marine Atlantic** (tel. 902/794–5700 or 902/855–2030) sails between Cape Tormentine, New Brunswick, and Borden, year-round, crossing daily between 6:30 AM and 1 AM. The crossing takes about 45 minutes and costs $17.50 per car round-trip and $6.75 per adult. The second service, **Northumberland Ferries** (tel. 902/566–3838; in the Maritimes, 800/565–0201), sails between Caribou, Nova Scotia, and Wood Islands, from May to mid-December. The crossing takes about 75 minutes, and the round-trip costs $25.75 per automobile and $7.90 per person (reduced price for senior citizens and children). No fares are collected inbound; you pay only on leaving the island. Neither service takes reservations.

Getting Around

By Car

There are more than 3,700 kilometers (2,294 miles) of paved road in the province, including the three scenic coastal drives called Lady Slipper Drive, Blue Heron Drive, and Kings Byway.

Guided Tours

The island offers about 20 sightseeing tours, including double-decker bus tours, cycling tours, harbor cruises, and walking tours. Most tour companies are located in Charlottetown and offer excursions around the city and to the beaches.

Exploring Prince Edward Island

The tours here divide Prince Edward Island into central Queens County, Kings County in the east, and Prince County at the western end of the island. Tour 1 is primarily a walking tour, while tours 2, 3, and 4 follow the major scenic highways—Blue Heron Drive, Kings Byway, and Lady Slipper Drive. There are plenty of chances to get out of the car, go fishing, hit the beach, collect wildflowers, or just watch the sea roll in.

Highlights for First-time Visitors

Anne of Green Gables farmhouse, Tour 2: Blue Heron Drive
North Cape, Tour 4: Lady Slipper Drive
Orwell Corner Pioneer Village, Tour 3: Kings Byway
Province House, Tour 1: Charlottetown
Seascapes and July's wild lupins near Souris, Tour 3: Kings Byway

Tour 1: Charlottetown

Sheltered on an arm of the Northumberland Strait, Prince Edward Island's only city is named for the stylish consort of King George III. Charlottetown, the largest community on the island, is a small city (population 15,800) with generous, gingerbread-clad Victorian houses and tree-shaded squares. It is often called "the Cradle of Confederation," a reference to the 1864 conference held here that led to the union of Nova Scotia, New Brunswick, Ontario, and Québec in 1867.

Charlottetown's main activities center on government, tourism, and private commerce. While new suburbs were springing up around it, the core of Charlottetown remained unchanged and the waterfront was restored to recapture the flavor of earlier eras. Today the waterfront includes the Prince Edward Hotel and Convention Centre, several informal restaurants, and handcraft and retail shops. You can easily explore the downtown by foot in a couple of hours. Irene Rogers's *Charlottetown: The Life in Its Buildings* gives much detail about the architecture and history of downtown Charlottetown.

Numbers in the margin correspond to points of interest on the Prince Edward Island and Charlottetown maps.

❶❷ **Charlottetown's** historic redbrick core is the setting for the modern concrete **Confederation Centre of the Arts,** opened in 1964 as a tribute to the Fathers of Confederation. The Confederation Centre houses a 1,100-seat theater, an art gallery, a library, a children's theater, a memorial hall, and a gift shop with an assortment of Canadian crafts. From June to September the center's **Charlottetown Festival** offers excellent professional theater, including the annual musical adaptation of *Anne of Green Gables. Queen St., bet. Grafton and Richmond Sts., tel. 902/628–1864; box office 902/566–1267. Open July–Sept., daily 9–8; Oct.–June, Mon.–Sat. 9–6, Sun. 2–5.*

❸ Next door, on Richmond Street, is the Georgian-style **Province House,** the meeting place of the provincial legislature. The

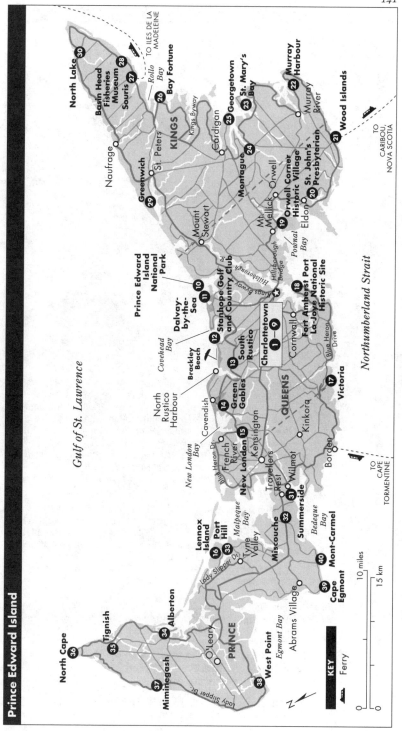

Prince Edward Island

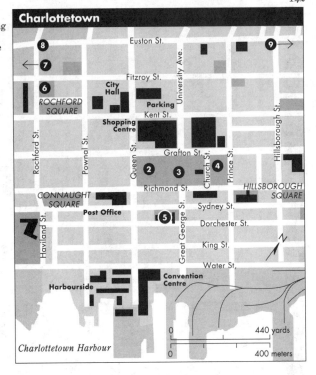

three-story sandstone building, completed in 1847, contains the Confederation Chamber, where representatives of the 19th-century provinces met to discuss creating a union. The room, restored to its 1864 condition, and the legislative chamber are open to the public. Displays and a slide presentation portray the historic meeting. *Richmond St., tel. 902/566–7626. Admission free. Open July and Aug.–Labor Day, daily 9–8; June and Labor Day–mid-Oct., daily 9–5; mid-Oct.–May, weekdays 9–5. Note: When the legislature is in session, certain rooms are closed to the public.*

❹ Two churches near Province House are noteworthy. **St. Paul's Anglican Church** (east of Province House) was erected in 1747,
❺ making it the oldest Protestant church on the island. **St. Dunstan's Basilica,** south of Province House on Great George Street, is the seat of the Roman Catholic diocese on the island. Known for its twin Gothic spires and fine Italian carvings, it is one of Canada's largest churches.

Time Out The **Gainsford** (104 Water St., tel. 903/368–3840), located in a Victorian home near the waterfront, is a cozy spot for a light lunch, a late-afternoon tea, or a full meal. *MC, V.*

❻ A few blocks northeast of Province House, on Rochford Square, is **St. Peter's Cathedral.** All Saints Chapel contains murals by Robert Harris, the famous Canadian portrait painter. The chapel was designed in 1888 by his brother W. C. "Willy" Harris, the most celebrated of the island's architects, and the designer of many historic homes and buildings.

❼ At the southern tip of the city is the beautiful 40-acre **Victoria Park,** overlooking the Charlottetown Harbour. Next to the park, on a hill between groves of white birches, is the white colonial Government House, built in 1835 as the official residence of the province's lieutenant-governors. Near the park **❽** entrance, **Beaconsfield,** a gracious Harris-designed Victorian mansion, contains the offices of the PEI Museum and Heritage Foundation and a bookstore with publications about the island. *Park open year-round, daily sunrise–sunset.*

❾ At the eastern end of the city is the **Charlottetown Driving Park** on Kensington Road, home of a sport that is dear to the hearts of islanders—harness racing. Standardbred horses are raised on farms throughout the island, and harness racing on the ice and on country tracks has been popular for generations. In fact, there are more horses per capita on the island than in any other province of Canada. *Kensington Rd., tel. 902/892–6823. Admission: $2 adults, 50¢ children. Races are held year-round twice a week Jan.–May; three nights a week in June, July, and most of Aug.; and twice daily (except Sun.) during Old Home Week in mid-Aug.*

Tour 2: Blue Heron Drive

Circling the island's center segment and roughly outlining Queens County, Blue Heron Drive is 190 kilometers (114 miles) long. It takes its name from the great blue heron, a stately water bird that migrates to Prince Edward Island every spring to nest in the shallow bays and marshes. You are likely to see several herons along the route. The highway marker is a white square with a blue border and a blue heron in the center.

From Charlottetown, Blue Heron Drive follows Route 15 north to the north shore, then winds along Route 6 through the north-shore fishing villages, the spectacular white sand beaches of Prince Edward Island National Park and Cabot Provincial Park, through the Anne of Green Gables country, and finally along the south shore with its red sandstone seascapes and historic sites. This drive circles some of the island's most beautiful landscapes and best beaches, but its north shore, around picturesque Cavendish and the Green Gables farmhouse, is also cluttered with tourist traps. If you're looking for unspoiled beauty, you'll have to look beyond the fried chicken joints, the tacky gift shops, King Tut's Tomb, and Ripley's Believe It Or Not, and try to keep in your mind's eye the island's simpler days.

❿ **Prince Edward Island National Park** stretches for about 40 kilometers (25 miles) along the north shore of the island on the Gulf of St. Lawrence. Follow the shore road for views of the beaches and bluffs—especially Orby Head, with red sandstone cliffs up to 30 meters (33 yards) high. At Brackley Beach, you can see sand dunes 18 meters (19 1/2 yards) high. The park has several hiking trails; the longest, about 8 kilometers (5 miles), starts near the Cavendish Campground. Among more than 200 species of birds are the northern phalarope, Swainson's thrush, and the protected piping plover. The park **Visitor Centre** in Cavendish provides a slide presentation and exhibit. The 56-acre campground has toilets, showers, electrical hookups, and a laundromat. *24 km (15 mi) north of Charlottetown, tel.*

902/672–6350. Park open daily; Visitor Centre open June–Oct., daily 9–8.

⓫ At the eastern end of the park is **Dalvay-by-the-Sea,** built in the 1890s as a summer home by an oil magnate. The park now operates the hotel as a resort lodge (*see* Lodging, *below*).

Time Out The dining room of **Dalvay-by-the-Sea** (tel. 902/672–2048) specializes in fresh seafood and homegrown vegetables, and is known for a traditional dessert called blueberry grunt.

⓬ A few kilometers west of Dalvay, off Route 6, along beautiful Covehead Bay, is the **Stanhope Golf and Country Club.** The course is among the island's longest, most challenging, and most scenic.

⓭ Moving west, you pass Brackley Beach and then come to **South Rustico,** on Route 243. Rustico is an Acadian French district, one of several on the Island. South Rustico sits on a peninsula on Rustico Bay, with a collection of Victorian houses gathered around a dainty church. One of Canada's first cooperative banks—a precursor of the credit-union movement—was founded here; it is now a National Historic Site and museum.

⓮ Continue along the shore road and follow the signs to **Green Gables,** the green-and-white farmhouse that is the setting for Lucy Maud Montgomery's first and most famous novel, *Anne of Green Gables.* The book was published in 1908, and it became one of the most popular children's books ever written. It's about a young orphan girl adopted by a strict but kindly brother and sister who live on a Prince Edward Island farm. The story has so caught the imagination of readers that thousands from around the world visit Green Gables every summer. The house, once owned by Montgomery's cousins, is organized to reflect the story. *Near Cavendish, in Prince Edward Island National Park, tel. 902/673-6350. Open mid-May–late June, daily 9–5, late June–Aug., daily 9–7; Sept.–Oct., daily 9–5.*

⓯ In **New London,** east of Cavendish on Route 6, is the modest white house where Lucy Maud Montgomery was born in 1874. Among memorabilia on display are the author's wedding dress and personal scrapbooks. *In New London, on Rte. 6, tel. 902/886–2596. Admission: $1 adults, 50¢ children. Open June and early Sept.–mid-Sept., daily 9–5; July–Aug., daily 9–7; mid-Sept.–mid-Oct., daily 9–5.*

⓰ The Blue Heron Drive follows the coastline south to the other side of the island through rolling farmland by the shores of Malpeque Bay, almost into Summerside. Across Malpeque Bay is **Lennox Island,** the largest Micmac Indian reserve in the province. The head of Malpeque Bay almost meets Bedeque Bay, nearly cutting the island in two. At Carleton, Blue Heron Drive intersects with Route 1, the main highway between Charlottetown and Borden and the terminus for the New Brunswick ferries.

⓱ Paralleling the coast, the drive continues past a fine Harris church at Crapaud to **Victoria,** a picturesque fishing village with antiques, art galleries, handcraft shops, and live summer theater in the historic **Victoria Playhouse** (tel. 902/658–2025 for ticket information and reservations).

⓲ The drive winds on through Argyle Shore to **Fort Amherst Port-La-Joye National Historic Site,** at the mouth of Charlottetown Harbour. This pretty spot, with its lighthouses, is the location of the first settlement on the island, established in 1720 during French rule. You can picnic on the site while watching boats and cruise ships sail into the harbor. *32 km (20 mi) south of Charlottetown on Rte. 19 at Rocky Point, tel. 902/675–2220. Open June–Labor Day, daily 10–6.*

Tour 3: Kings Byway

The Kings Byway follows the coastline of Kings County for 375 kilometers (225 miles) on the eastern end of the island. The route passes woodlots, patchwork-quilt farms, fishing villages, and historic sites in this green and tranquil section of the province. Starting at Charlottetown, take Route 1 east and follow Kings Byway counter-clockwise.

⓳ **The Orwell Corner Historic Village** re-creates a 19th-century rural settlement in the form of a living farm museum. Farming is done by methods used by Scottish settlers in the 19th century, including the use of handsome draft horses. The village contains a beautifully restored store and post office, school, church, farmhouse, and barns. Musical evenings (ceilidhs) in the village feature traditional Scottish music by local musicians. *Tel. 902/651–2013. Admission: $3 adults, children under 12 free. Open late June–Labor Day, daily 9–5; mid-May–late June and Labor Day–late Oct., weekdays 10–3.*

⓴ One of the island's most historic churches, **St. John's Presbyterian,** in Belfast, is just off Route 1 on Route 207. This pretty white church, on a hill against a backdrop of trees, was built by settlers from the Isle of Skye who were brought to the island in 1803 by Lord Selkirk.

㉑ Route 1 passes **Wood Islands,** the terminus for the Northumberland Ferries service to Nova Scotia, which operates while Northumberland Strait is free of ice, generally from May **㉒** through December. The island-dotted waters of **Murray Harbour** drain five rivers, and empty through the narrow gut between Poverty Beach and Beach Point. This favorite refuge for island yachtsmen supports a large fishing fleet.

Time Out **Brehaut's Restaurant** (tel. 902/962–3141) in Murray Harbour village, right by the fishermen's wharf, has a take-out and café downstairs and a pleasant dining room upstairs. Tasty, wholesome food in a rustic ambience, with very pleasant service, is what you'll get here.

The eastern coastline is dotted with fishing villages and long uncrowded beaches. Seal-watching and bird-watching boat **㉓** tours are available at Murray River and Montague; **St. Mary's Bay,** inside Panmure Island, offers excellent windsurfing behind a long protective beach. Three rivers enter into Cardigan **㉔** Bay. Seductive **Montague,** on the Montague River, is the busi- **㉕** ness hub of eastern PEI, while **Georgetown,** on a point between the Cardigan and Brudenell rivers, is a shipbuilding town with **㉖** a lively summer theater. **Bay Fortune,** a little-known scenic spot, has been a secret refuge of well-heeled Americans for two generations.

In early summer, you can see whole fields of blue, white, pink, and purple wild lupins sloping down to red cliffs and blue sea.

㉗ The view from the hill overlooking the town of **Souris,** on the northeastern coast, is especially lovely. At Souris, a car-ferry links PEI with the Québec-owned Magdalen Islands. The Souris area is noted for its fine traditional musicians. An outdoor Scottish concert at Rollo Bay in July, featuring fiddling and step-dancing, attracts thousands every year.

Time Out   The **Uptown Restaurant** (tel. 902/687–4123), on the main street in Souris, is a Chinese restaurant with a difference. Ask about the silver aliwana fish—a Chinese species—in an aquarium on the wall, and try the "bumbleberry" pie.

㉘ North of Souris, the **Basin Head Fisheries Museum** is located on a bluff overlooking the Atlantic Ocean. Displays include a boat shed, an aquarium, a smokehouse, a fish-box factory, and fishermen's sheds. On the grounds is a fine beach. *Box 248, Souris, tel. 902/357–2966. Admission: $3 adults, children under 12 free. Open mid-June–Labor Day, daily 9–5; Labor Day–Sept., weekdays 9–5.*

Walk over the cast-iron bridge by the museum. The exquisite, silvery beach stretches northeast for miles, backed by high, grassy dunes. Scuff your feet in the sand: it will squeak, squawk and purr at you. These are known locally as the "singing sands," a phenomenon found in only a few favored locations worldwide.

For even more extensive dune scenery, follow Route 2 to St.

㉙ Peter's Bay, and Route 313 to **Greenwich.** The road ends among sandhills, but from here you can take a half-hour walk through beige dunes to reach the superb beach. These dunes are moving, gradually burying the nearby woods; here and there the bleached skeletons of trees thrust up through the sand like wooden ghosts. Along the eastern and northern coasts of the island you can charter deep-sea fishing boats that will outfit you for angling the world-record bluefin tuna that thrive in

㉚ these waters. An especially good spot is **North Lake,** several kilometers (a few miles) from Basin Head.

Tour 4: Lady Slipper Drive

This drive—named for the delicate lady slipper orchid, the province's official flower—winds along the coast of the narrow indented western end of the island through very old and very small villages, which still adhere to a traditional way of life. Many of these hamlets are inhabited by Acadians, descendants of the original French settlers. The area is known for its oysters and Irish moss, but most famously for its potato farms: The province is a major exporter of seed potatoes worldwide, and half the crop is grown here.

㉛ From Charlottetown, take Route 2 to **Summerside,** the second-largest community on the island. A self-guided walking tour of Summerside, arranged by the Summerside Tourism Office, is a pleasant excursion through the leafy streets, with their spacious houses. Some of these homes are known as "fox houses"; silver foxes were first bred in captivity in western PEI, and for several decades Summerside was the headquarters of a virtual gold rush based on fox ranching. For more history and walking-tour brochures, stop in at the **International Fox Museum and Hall of Fame.** *286 Fitzroy St., tel. 902/436–2400 or 902/436–1589. Admission free; $1 donation accepted. Open May–Sept., Mon.–Sat. 9–6.*

The eight-day **Summerside Lobster Carnival,** held every July, includes livestock exhibitions, harness racing, fiddling contests, and lobster suppers. In early August, **Grand Prix hydroplane races** take place in the harbor. The boats are powered by 1,500-horse power engines and attain speeds of 150 miles (240 kilometers) per hour.

Take Route 1A from Summerside to St. Eleanors, then turn west on Route 2 to the **Acadian Museum of Prince Edward Island,** on your way to **Miscouche.** The museum's artifacts predate the 19th century and include household and farm implements. *Rte. 2, 23 Main Dr. E, tel. 902/436–6237. Admission: $2 adults, $1 children 6–17. Open early Sept.–mid-June, weekdays 9:30–4; mid-June–early Sept., weekdays 9:30–4, Sun. 1–5.*

Relatively few visitors travel west of Summerside, which is unfortunate for them and fortunate for you. Route 2 travels straight as an arrow through the drab plain of the Miscouche Swamp. Avoid this route by following the Lady Slipper signs from Miscouche to **Port Hill,** about 35 kilometers (22 miles) north and west of Summerside. The **Green Park Shipbuilding Museum and Historic House** was originally the home of shipbuilder James Yeo, Jr. This 19th-century mansion, restored and open to visitors, is topped by a cupola, from which Yeo observed his nearby shipyard through a spyglass. The modern museum building on the site details the history of the shipbuilder's craft. *Rte. 12, Port Hill, tel. 902/831–2206. Admission: $2.50 adults, children under 12 free. Open mid-June–Labor Day, daily 9–5.*

Lady Slipper Drive continues around Foxley Bay and Cascumpec Bay to **Alberton,** where Jacques Cartier made his first landing on the island. Oulton Island, just offshore, was the first place foxes were bred successfully in captivity and claims to be the world's first fur ranch.

Follow the shore north to **Tignish,** another Acadian community. Everything in Tignish seems to be co-operative, including the supermarket, insurance company, fishplant, service station, and credit union. The imposing **parish church of St. Simon and St. Jude Parish House** (315 School St. tel. 902/882–2049), across from Dalton Square, has a superb Tracker pipe organ, one of the finest such instruments in eastern Canada, and is often used for recitals by world-renowned musicians.

The **Dalton Centre,** on Church Street, was built by the first fox-breeder, Sir Charles Dalton, a Tignish native; it now includes a museum. *Church St., tel. 902/882–2488. Admission: $1.50 adults, 75¢ children. Open mid-June–Aug., Sun.–Fri. 10– 5.*

Drive on to **North Cape,** where the island fades to a narrow north-pointing arrow of land with an imposing lighthouse. The curious structures nearby are wind turbines at the **Atlantic Wind Test Site,** set up on this breezy promontory to evaluate the feasibility of electrical generation by wind power. *Tel. 902/882–2746. Admission free. Open July–late Aug., daily 10–8.*

Time Out **Wind & Reef** (tel. 902/882–3535) is a full-service seasonal restaurant that offers superb views from its location near the North Cape lighthouse. Not surprisingly, the specialty is seafood, but note that meals can get pricey here.

From the cape, Lady Slipper Drive turns almost due south along the island's western shore. You may have seen draft horses around North Cape: Those were "moss horses," used in harvesting a versatile and valuable sea plant known as Irish

❸⓭ moss. At **Miminegash,** visit the **Irish Moss Interpretive Centre,** and find out how much Irish moss was in your last ice-cream cone. *On Rte. 152 off Rte. 2, tel. 902/882–2920. Admission free. Open late June–Aug., weekdays 9–5.*

❸⓮ At the southern tip of the western shore is **West Point,** with a tiny man-made fishing harbor, provincial campsite, supervised beach, and what one recent visitor called an "insanely friendly" community. Above all, there is the **West Point Lighthouse,** 115 years old and the tallest on the island. When the lighthouse was automated, the community took over the building and converted it into a miniature inn and museum, with a gift shop and an excellent, moderately priced restaurant attached. *Rte. 14, tel. 902/859–3605. Admission: $1.65 adults, $1.40 senior citizens, 85¢ children. Open mid-May–mid-Oct., daily 8–9:30.*

Lady Slipper Drive meanders back to Summerside through Région Evangeline, the main Acadian district of the island. At

❸⓯ **Cape Egmont,** stop for a look at the **Bottle Houses,** two tiny houses and a chapel built by a retired carpenter entirely out of

❹⓪ glass bottles mortared together like bricks. In **Mont-Carmel,** an adjoining community, is a magnificent brick church overlooking Northumberland Strait, and an **Acadian Pioneer Village** with a church, school, blacksmith shop, store and dwellings. *Rte. 11, tel. 902/854–2227. Admission to village: $2 adults, 75¢ students, children 50¢. Open mid-June–mid-Sept, daily 8–9.*

Shopping

Prince Edward Islanders have been making beautiful homemade items since colonial days, when crafts were necessities of life. Island craftspeople excel at quilting, rug-hooking, weaving, knitting, and pottery, to name a few of the crafts. Full information on outlets and types of crafts is provided by the **PEI Crafts Council** (156 Richmond St., Charlottetown, PEI C1A 1H9, tel. 902/892–5152). There are more than 100 crafts outlets throughout the island.

The **Island Craft Shop** has a wide selection of weaving, pottery, woodwork and other items. *156 Richmond St., Charlottetown. Open July–Aug., Mon.–Sat. 9–8, Sun. 11–4; Sept.–June, Mon.–Sat. 10–5:30.*

The **Wood Islands Handcraft Co-op Association Ltd.,** in southeastern Kings County, sells a large number of knitted and crocheted items and other crafts. *Murray River, Kings County, tel. 902/962–3539. Open daily 9–5; July–Aug., 9–6.*

Along Lady Slipper Drive look for hand-turned bird's-eye maple products at the **Leavitts' Wood Craft** in Alberton. *Alberton, tel. 902/853–2504. Open Mon.–Sat. 8–5.*

Shoreline Sweaters, sometimes known as Tyne Valley Studios, in Tyne Valley, is where Lesley Dubey sells handmade sweaters and local crafts. *Lady Slipper Dr., Tyne Valley, tel. 902/831–2950. Open mid-May–Sept., daily 9:30–5:30.*

You can buy fresh, canned, or frozen lobster and other seafood at numerous processing plants and retail stores throughout the island. Some, such as **Crabby's Seafood** in Wood Islands, will pack for travel. *Wood Islands, next to ferry, tel. 902/962–3228. Open daily 7–7.*

Sports and Outdoor Activities

Bicycling Prince Edward Island is popular with bike-touring companies for its moderately hilly and always stunning scenery. Most of the island offers level areas, especially east of Charlottetown to Montague and along the north shore. However, the shoulderless, narrow roads and summer's car traffic can be dismal for cyclists. An 8.7-kilometer (5.4-mile) path near Cavendish campground loops around marsh, woodland, and farmland. Cycling trips are organized throughout the province, and the Department of Tourism and Parks can recommend tour operators (*see* Important Addresses and Numbers in Essential Information, *above*). Also, bicycles can be rented in Charlottetown and Cavendish.

Fishing PEI offers some of the best brook-trout fishing in eastern Canada, as well as excellent deep-sea fishing off the island's northeast coast. Charter boats leave from the fishing ports of Cove Head, North Lake, and North Rustico, daily in summer for very elusive tuna and rich mackerel fishing, and there are more than 20 boat charters to choose from.

Clam digging is possible in many less-populated coastal areas around the island.

Golf Golf isn't a popular pastime of islanders, but it is with tourists. **Stanhope Golf Course** (*see* Tour 2) is one of the more challenging courses on the island. In the western end, **Mill River Provincial Golf Course** (tel. 902/859–2238) in Mill River Provincial Park, 57 kilometers (35 miles) west of Summerside, is among the most scenic and challenging courses in eastern Canada. **Brudenell River Provincial Golf Course** (tel. 902652–2332) at the east end of the island has hosted four national championships and three CPGAs. The latter two courses are within major resort complexes.

Dining

On Prince Edward Island, plain, wholesome, home-cooked fare is a matter of course. The service is friendly—though a little pokey at times—and the setting is informal everywhere but in a few restaurants in Charlottetown. Seafood is generally good anywhere on the island, with top honors being given to lobster and any dish using local produce. Unless noted, there is no need to wear a jacket and tie.

Look for lobster suppers, offered both commercially and by church and civic groups. These meals feature lobster, rolls, salad, and mountains of sweet, home-baked goodies, and are usually presented at New London, New Glasgow, St. Ann's Church in Hope River, and Fisherman's Wharf in North Rustico. Check the local papers or the bulletin boards at local grocery stores.

Highly recommended restaurants in each price category are indicated by a star ★.

Category	Cost*
Very Expensive	over $35
Expensive	$25–$35
Moderate	$15–$24
Inexpensive	under $15

per person, excluding drinks, service, 10% sales tax, and 7% GST.

Brackley Beach
Very Expensive
★

Shaw's Hotel and Cottages. This family-oriented hotel dating from the 1860s offers fine home cooking in an elegant, country setting. Lobster is served twice weekly, and the grand Sunday-night buffets draw people from near and far to sample fresh salmon, seafood casserole, home-baked breads, and a variety of popular desserts, such as cheesecake and fresh berries in season. Lunch is not served. *Rte. 15, tel. 902/672–2022. Reservations advised. AE, MC, V. Closed Oct.–May.*

Cavendish
Inexpensive

Fiddles 'n Vittles. Lively, friendly, and decorated in rustic marine, with fishnets hanging in the dining room, the restaurant is true to its theme: House specialties are fresh and fried seafood. *Bay Vista Motor Inn, R.R.1, Breadalbane, tel. 902/963–3003. AE, DC, MC, V. Closed mid-Sept.–mid-June.*

Charlottetown
Moderate–Expensive
★

Claddagh Room Restaurant. You'll find some of the best seafood in Charlottetown here. The "Galway Bay Delight," one of the Irish owner's specialties, is a savory combination of fresh scallops and shrimp sautéed with onions and mushrooms, flambéed in Irish Mist, and doused with fresh cream. A pub upstairs features live Irish entertainment every night in summer and on weekends in winter. *131 Sydney St., tel. 902/892–9661. AE, DC, MC, V.*

★ **The Griffin Room.** This cozy dining room of the Dundee Arms Motel and Inn has a working fireplace and is filled with antiques, copper, and brass. The French Continental cuisine prepared here uses no artificial preservatives or additives, only fresh natural ingredients. Fresh seafood is served year-round, and salmon, scallops, and crab are available all winter. Specialties include rack of lamb, chateaubriand, and poached or grilled fillet of salmon in a light lime-dill sauce. *Dundee Arms Motel and Inn, 200 Pownal St., tel. 902/892–2496. MC, V.*

Moderate

Off Broadway. Popular with Charlottetown's young professional set is this attractive, cozy spot located near the Confederation Centre of the Arts. It began modestly as a crêpe-and-soup joint, and indeed, you can still make a meal of the lobster or chicken crêpe and the spinach or Caesar salad that's served with it. But the restaurant also has a fairly inventive menu of Continental entrées such as the hearty mussel chowder, fillets, and salmon. The old-fashioned private booths won't reveal your indiscretions—including your penchant for one of the many desserts. *125 Sydney St., tel. 902/566-4620. AE, MC, V.*

Inexpensive **Captain Scott's.** The fish-and-chips served at this spot in the Confederation Court Mall rival any found in England. *Cor. of Grafton and Queen Sts., tel. 902/628-1674. No credit cards. Closed Sun.*

Cornwall **Bonnie Brae.** What you'll find here is a welcoming and comfort-
Expensive able modern restaurant that offers well-prepared fresh sea-food and steaks, as well as Swiss specialties created by the Swiss owner-chef. Summer's nightly all-you-can-eat lobster buffet is guaranteed to satisfy any appetite, but leave room for desserts such as Black Forest cake and raspberry cheesecake. *Trans-Canada Hwy., tel. 902/566-2241. AE, DC, MC, V.*

Grand Tracadie **Dalvay-by-the-Sea.** Choose a table by the stone fireplace or dine
Very Expensive with a lake view on the enclosed terrace. The menu at this elegant Victorian dining room includes island lobster, curried scallops, poached halibut, peppercorn steak, and filet mignon—all served with fresh vegetables. Desserts are baked on the premises by the restaurant's pastry chef; blueberry grunt, a sweet dumpling with blueberry sauce, is the Dalvay's own traditional specialty dessert. *Rte. 6, near Dalvay Beach, tel. 902/672-2048. Reservations advised. AE, MC, V.*

★ **Shady Lady Restaurant.** This restaurant is located in a log house built by the chef-owners—twin sisters—who financed the project by working as cooks in the Yukon. It's a warm and charming place decorated in Victorian style, and each table setting is different, with linens and fine china collected by the owners. The cuisine is basically French, with an emphasis on steaks and seafood. All desserts are made on the premises, including the unforgettable Hawaiian tropical fruit-almond cake, made with fruit soaked in brandy for 30 days. *Rte. 6, tel. 902/672-2003. MC, V. Open daily mid-May–Oct., weekends the rest of the year.*

Lodging

Prince Edward Island offers a variety of accommodations at a variety of prices, from full-service resorts and luxury hotels to moderately priced motels, cottages, and lodges, to farms that take guests. Lodgings on the north coast in summer should be booked early, especially if you're planning a long stay.

Highly recommended lodgings in each price category are indicated by a star ★.

Category	Cost*
Very Expensive	over $75
Expensive	$55–$75
Moderate	$40–$54
Inexpensive	under $40

All prices are for a standard double room, excluding 10% provincial sales tax and 7% GST.

Brackley Beach **Shaw's Hotel and Cottages.** Each room is unique in this 1860s
Very Expensive hotel, with antique furnishings, floral-print wallpapers, and
★ hardwood floors. Half the cottages have fireplaces. This country elegance doesn't come cheap, as Shaw's is one of the most
expensive hotels on the island. Guests can choose to include in
their room rate a home-cooked breakfast and dinner in the
Shaw's dining room (*see* Dining, *above*). *Rte. 15, C0A 2H0, tel.
902/672-2022. 40 units, including 18 cottages and 2 suites. Facilities: cocktail bar, sailboats, windsurfing, beach nearby. AE,
MC, V. Closed late-Sept.–May.*

Cavendish **Bay Vista Inn.** This clean, friendly motel caters to families. Par-
Expensive ents can sit on the outdoor deck and admire the New London
Bay panorama while keeping an eye on their children in the
motel's large playground. Almost all of the rooms have views
of the bay. Fiddles 'n Vittles (*see* Dining, *above*) is a great place
to eat with the family. *R.R.1, Breadalbane, C0A 1E0; in winter,
R.R.1, North Wiltshire, C0A 1Y0, tel. 902/963-2225. 30 units, including 2 motel efficiencies. Facilities: restaurant, outdoor
heated pool, playground, boating, deep-sea fishing, golf nearby.
AE, MC, V. Closed late Sept.–mid-June.*

Charlottetown **Best Western MacLauchlan's Motel.** This is one of the many
Very Expensive good motels in the Best Western chain. Two convenient apartment suites have a bedroom, living room, kitchen, and bathroom. *238 Grafton St., C1A 1L5, tel. 902/892-2461. 149 units,
including 2 suites. Facilities: dining room, lounge, indoor pool,
sauna, Jacuzzi, laundry facilities. AE, DC, MC, V.*

★ **The Charlottetown.** This classic five-story, redbrick hotel
with white pillars and a circular driveway is just two blocks
from the center of Charlottetown. The rooms and public areas
offer the latest amenities but retain the hotel's old-fashioned
flavor, with well-detailed, antique-reproduction furnishings.
*Kent and Pownal Sts., Box 159, C1A 7K4, tel. 902/894-7371.
109 rooms, including 2 suites. Facilities: dining room, lounge
with entertainment, indoor pool, sauna, whirlpool, parking.
AE, DC, MC, V.*

Dundee Arms Motel and Inn. Depending on your mood, you can
choose to stay in either a 1960s motel or a 1904 inn. The motel
is simple, modern, and neat; the inn is homey and furnished
with brass and antiques. The Griffin Room (*see* Dining, *above*),
the inn's dining room, serves fine French cuisine. Continental
breakfast is included in motel and inn rates. *200 Pownal St.,
C1A 3W8, tel. 902/892-2496. 18 rooms, including 2 suites. Facilities: restaurant, pub. MC, V.*

★ **Prince Edward Hotel and Convention Centre.** Two-thirds of the
rooms in this 10-story hotel overlook the developed Charlottetown waterfront. A member of the Canadian Pacific chain of
hotels and resorts, the Prince Edward has all the comforts and
luxuries of its first-rate counterparts—from Jacuzzis in some
suites to a grand ballroom and conference center. Guest rooms
are modern and decorated in warm pastels. The lobby is a
bright, open, two-story atrium complete with a waterfall above
the front desk. *18 Queen St., Box 2170, C1A 8B9, tel. 902/566-
2222 or 800/828-7447. 211 rooms, including 33 suites. Facilities:
3 restaurants, lounge with nightly entertainment, heated indoor
pool, whirlpool, sauna, Nautilus equipment. AE, DC, MC, V.*

Moderate **Duchess of Kent Inn.** This turreted Victorian bed-and-breakfast is packed with antiques, even in the bedrooms. It's within
walking distance of Charlottetown's major sites, including the

Confederation Centre. *218 Kent St., C1A 1P2, tel. 902/566–5826. 8 rooms share 5 baths. Facilities: guest kitchen, bicycle storage. MC, V. Closed Dec.–May.*

Inexpensive **Court Bed and Breakfast.** In a residential area 2 kilometers (1.2 miles) from downtown, this two-story bed-and-breakfast with a welcoming red door offers large, simple, comfortable rooms and a full, hearty breakfast, including ham, eggs, bacon, muffins, and fresh fruits in season. *68 Hutchinson Ct., C1A 8H7, tel. 902/894–5871. 2 rooms with shared bath. No credit cards. Closed early Sept.–Apr.*

Sherwood Motel. This is a small, clean, family-oriented motel about 5 kilometers (3.1 mi) north of downtown Charlottetown on Route. 15. The friendly owners offer help in reserving tickets for events and planning day trips. Don't be daunted by the Sherwood's proximity to the airport—the motel sees very little traffic. *R.R.1, Winsloe C0A 2H0, tel. 902/892–2622. 30 rooms with bath; pets permitted. Facilities: kitchenettes (22 rooms), cable TV. MC, V.*

Cornwall **Blue Heron Hideaways.** The MacAndrews, the owners, are a
Very Expensive film producer and a journalist who run these executive-style cottages, a luxury beach-house, and a honeymoon cottage located just a few minutes from downtown. The safe, private beach offers access to sand dunes and much wildlife and it's a great place for windsurfing. An outboard motorboat and gas barbecues are available for guest use. Weekly rentals only early June through mid-October. *R.R.2, Blooming Point, C0A 1H0, tel. 902/566–2427. One 2-bedroom cottage, 2 3-bedroom cottages, 1 waterfront cottage with bunkhouse. No credit cards.*

Grand Tracadie **Dalvay-by-the-Sea.** Just within the borders of the Prince Ed-
Very Expensive ward Island National Park is this Victorian house, built in 1896
★ as a private summer home. Now a popular inn and restaurant, Dalvay-by-the-Sea offers elegant but homey rooms furnished with original antiques and reproductions. Guests can sip drinks or tea on the porch while admiring the inn's gardens, Dalvay Lake, or the nearby beach. Breakfasts and dinners in the dining room, included in the room rates, are exceptional (*see* Dining, *above*). *Rte. 6, near Dalvay Beach. Box 8, York, C0A 1P0, tel. 902/672–2048, or 902/672–2546 in winter. 31 rooms in main house and 2 cottages. Facilities: restaurant, lounge, 2 tennis courts, driving range, canoes, rowboats, windsurfing. AE, MC, V. Closed mid-Sept.–mid-June.*

Montague **Lobster Shanty North.** Roses growing outside the windows of
Moderate its weathered-wood facade, and old fishnets draped around the barn-board walls of the dining room, contribute to the truly charming style of this motel. All rooms have picture windows and open onto a deck that overlooks the Montague River. *Main St., Box 158, C0A 1R0, tel. 902/838–2463. 11 rooms. Facilities: restaurant, lounge, golf, clam-digging, swimming nearby. AE, MC, V.*

O'Leary **Rodd's Mill River Resort and Conference Centre.** With activi-
Very Expensive ties ranging from night skiing and tobogganing to golfing, this is truly an all-season resort. Ask about family-package weekends, offered year-round. *Box 399, C0B 1V0, tel. 902/859–3555 or 800/565–RODD. 90 rooms including 3 suites. Facilities: dining room, 2 bars, 2 heated indoor pools, golf course, pro shop, tennis court, 2 squash courts, fitness center with whirlpool and sauna, games room, gift shop, canoeing, windsurfing, bike rent-*

al, ice-skating rink, toboggan run, cross-country skiing. AE,
MC, V. Closed Nov.–early Dec., Apr.

Summerside **Quality Inn Garden of the Gulf.** Close to downtown Summer-
Moderate– side, this clean motel is a convenient place to stay. The nine-hole
Expensive golf course on the property slopes to Bedeque Bay. *618 Water
St. E, C1N 2V5, tel. 902/436–2295. 83 rooms, including 6 suites.
Facilities: restaurant, coffee shop, lounge, heated outdoor pool,
9-hole golf course. AE, DC, MC, V.*

Moderate **Glade Motor Inn and Cottages.** Conveniently located 10
minutes from the Borden Ferry Terminal, this property has
comfortable if generic motel rooms as well as one- and two-bed-
room cottages and one four-bedroom "house" that can accommodate up to eight people. What's different about the place is
that it is set on a 300-acre farm, with horseback riding and
nature trails. Kids get free rides in the corral. *Box 1387, C1N
4K2, tel. 902/436–5564. 33 units. Facilities: restaurant, lounge,
heated outdoor pool, horseback riding, nature trails. AE, MC, V.
Closed late-Sept.–mid-June.*

West Point **West Point Lighthouse.** This unique property is still a function-
Expensive ing lighthouse (though automated), situated within a provincial
park. Nearby are nature trails and opportunities to clam-dig,
fish, and bike. Within the lighthouse is a museum and licensed
dining room and patio; outside is the beach. Two rooms have a
whirlpool tub. Complimentary breakfast is served on your first
morning. *R.R.2, O'Leary, C0B 1V0, tel. 902/859–3605. 9 rooms.
MC, V. Open mid-May–late Sept. 27.*

The Arts

The highlights of the island's theater season are the productions of the **Charlottetown Festival,** which take place from June
through October at the Confederation Centre of the Arts.

Special art exhibitions are offered in the Confederation Centre
Gallery, one of Canada's premier museums. The permanent
collection features the country's largest assemblage of paintings by Robert Harris (1848–1919), Canada's foremost portrait
artist. For information and tickets to the festival, contact the
Confederation Centre of the Arts (Box 848, Charlottetown, PEI
C1A 7L9, tel. 902/628–1864; box office, 902/566–1267).

The **King's Playhouse** (tel. 902/652–2053) in Georgetown, 50
kilometers (30 miles) east of Charlottetown, offers varied entertainment from June through early September. The **Victoria
Playhouse** (tel. 902/658–2025) in Victoria, a half-hour's drive
west of Charlottetown, features professional repertory
theater.

Concerts and musical festivals abound on the island, especially
in summer. Live traditional Celtic music, with fiddling and
step-dancing, can be heard almost any day of the week. Best
bets: the outdoor fiddle festival at Rollo Bay in late July (tel.
902/368–5555); Monday night ceilidhs at the **Benevolent Irish
Hall** (tel. 902/892–2367) in Charlottetown; and the Sunday concerts of classical, sacred, and traditional music at **St. Mary's
Church** (tel. 902/836–3733) in Indian River, between Charlottetown and Summerside.

6 Newfoundland and Labrador

By Margaret M.
Kearney
Updated by Peter
Gard

Peter Gard
is a freelance writer
and food critic
and author of
Trails of the Avalon.
He has lived and
traveled throughout
Newfoundland
for 17
years.

Newfoundland was the first place explorers John Cabot (1497) and Gaspar Corte-Real (1500) touched down in the New World. Exactly where they went no one knows, for neither survived a second voyage. But while he was here, Cabot reported that he saw fish in the water so thick you could dip your line in anywhere and catch what you wanted. Within a decade of the explorers' discovery, St. John's had become a crowded harbor. Fishing boats from France, England, Spain, and Portugal vied for a chance to catch Newfoundland's lucrative cod, which was to subsequently shape the province's history and geography.

At one time there were 700 hard-working settlements or "outports" dotting Newfoundland's coast, each devoted to catching, salting, and drying the world's most prolific and useful fish. Today, only about 600 of these settlements survive. Newfoundland's most famous resource has become so scarce that a fishing moratorium was declared in 1992. While the province waits for the cod to return, some 20,000 fishers and processors are going to school instead of going fishing. Still, the waters are busy with boats fishing for lobster, mackerel, herring, caplin, turbot, scallops, shrimp—and cod, too, on the west and south coasts of the island. Don't be shy to walk down to the wharf and find out what's being landed.

Newfoundland and Labrador became part of Canada in 1949. For almost 400 year previous, however, the government had survived perfectly well on its own, until the Great Depression forced its economy to go belly-up. After 40-some years of Confederation with Canada, the economy of the province has improved considerably, but the people are still of independent mind: Newfoundlanders regard themselves as North America's first separatists and have maintained a unique language and life-style and their own customs.

Visitors to Newfoundland find themselves straddling the centuries. Old accents and customs are common in small towns and outports, yet the major cities of St. John's on the east coast and Corner Brook on the west coast are very much part of the 20th century. Regardless of where you visit—an isolated outport or lively Water Street—you're sure to interact with some of the warmest, wittiest people in North America. Strangers have always been welcome in Newfoundland, since the days when locals brought visitors in from out of the cold, warmed them by the fire, and charmingly interrogated them for news of events outside the province.

Before you can shoot the breeze, though, you'll have to acclimate yourself to the language: It's English all right, but provincial dialects are strong and vary from place to place. Newfoundland is one of two provinces in Canada with its own dictionary; Prince Edward Island is the other, but its book has only 873 entries. *The Newfoundland Dictionary* has more than 5,000 words, mostly having to do with fishery, weather, and scenery. To get started, you can practice with the name of the province—it's *New'fun'l'nd*, with the accent on the "land." However, only "livyers" ever get the pronunciation exactly right.

Depending on the time of year you visit, your experiences will be dramatically different. In spring icebergs float down from the north, and fin, pilot, minke, and humpback whales hunt for food along the coast. Their preferred cuisine? Caplin, a small, smeltlike fish that moves in schools and spawns on Newfoundland's many pebble beaches. During the summer, temperate days turn Newfoundland's stark cliffs, bogs, and meadows into a riot of wildflowers and greenery; and the sea is dotted with boats and buoys marking traps and nets. Fall is a favored season: The weather is usually fine; cliffs and meadows are loaded with berries; and the woods are alive with moose, elk, partridges, and rabbits, to name just a few residents. In the winter, the forest trails hum with the sound of snowmobiles and ATVs hauling wood home or taking the fishermen to their favorite lodges and lakes.

The tourist season runs from June through September, when the province is awash with festivals, fairs, concerts, plays, and crafts shows. A popular vacation plan for locals is to go gravel-pit camping: It's the tradition of parking a trailer in a handy place near a brook or pond and setting up camp. There's usually no view, but free campsites and sociable company make up for most inconveniences. Not only is camping—in a bare site or one with amenities—an inexpensive way for the family to vacation together, but it's a good way to take advantage of Newfoundland's pollution-free environment: Nice days are just that, with bright, intense sunshine, free of smog or haze. The temperature in late June through early September hovers between 75 and 85 degrees, and gently cools off in the evening, providing a good night's sleep.

Essential Information

Important Addresses and Numbers

Tourist Information The Department of Tourism and Culture (Box 8730, St. John's, NF A1B 4K2, tel. 709/729–2830) distributes brochures and maps from its offices in the Confederation Building, West Block, St. John's. The province also maintains a tourism information line (tel. 800/563–6353), which operates year-round, 24 hours a day.

From June until Labor Day, a network of **Visitor Information Centers,** open 9–9, dots the province. These centers carry up-to-date information on events, accommodations, shopping, and crafts stores in their area. There are in-season visitor information booths at the airports in Gander and St. John's. The city of St. John's operates a complete information center in a restored railway carriage next to the harbor.

Emergencies Dial 911 for medical emergencies and police.

Hospitals St. Clare's Mercy Hospital (154 La Marchant Rd., tel. 709/778–3111), Grace Hospital (241 La Marchant Rd., tel. 709/778–6222), and General Hospital (300 Prince Philip Dr., tel. 709/737–6300) in St. John's; George B. Cross Hospital (tel. 709/466–3411) in Clarenville; James Paton (tel. 709/651–2500) in Gander; Western Memorial (tel. 709/637–5000) in Corner Brook; Charles S. Curtis Memorial Hospital (tel. 709/454–3333) in St. Anthony; and Captain William Jackman (410 Booth Ave., tel. 709/944–2632) in Labrador City.

Arriving and Departing by Plane, Car Ferry, and Train

By Plane The major airport for the province for connections from all major North American and European destinations is **St. John's. Canadian Airlines International** (tel. 800/426–7000 from the U.S., 800/665–1177 in Canada) and **Air Canada** (tel. 800/776–3000 in the U.S., 709/726–7880 in Canada) fly into Newfoundland. **Air Nova** (tel. 800/776–3000 from the U.S., 800/563–5151 from Newfoundland), **Provincial Airlines** (tel. 709/576–1666), **Labrador Airways** (tel. 709/896–8113 from the U.S., 800/563–3042 in Newfoundland), and **Air Atlantic** (tel. 800/563–8359 from the U.S., 709/576–0274 in Newfoundland) are regional connectors. Airports in Newfoundland are at Stephenville, Deer Lake, St. Anthony, Gander, and St. John's; airports in Labrador are located in Happy Valley–Goose Bay, Wabush, and Churchill Falls.

By Car Ferry **Marine Atlantic** operates a car ferry from North Sydney, Nova Scotia, to Port-aux-Basques, Newfoundland (crossing time is six hours); and, from June through October, from North Sydney to Argentia, twice a week (crossing time 12–14 hours). In all cases, reservations are required. Contact **Marine Atlantic** (Box 250, North Sydney, NS B2A 3M3, tel. 902/794–5700 or 709/772–7701, fax 902/564–3439; hearing-impaired 902/794–8109 or call TDD operator and request collect call). For information about getting to Labrador, *see* Tour 6, *below.*

By Train Rail service (tel. 514/871–1331) is provided between Sept Isles, Québec, and Labrador City by Iron Ore Canada's Québec North Shore and Labrador Railways. For more information about this train, *see* Exploring, Tour 6, *below.* There is no train on the island.

Getting around Newfoundland

By Bus **CN Roadcruiser** (tel. 709/737–5912) runs a trans-island bus service. Buses leave at 8 AM from St. John's and Port-aux-Basques. Small buses known as outport taxis connect the major centers with surrounding communities.

By Car Newfoundland has an excellent highway system, and all but a handful of secondary roads are paved. The province's roads are generally uncrowded, adding to the pleasure of driving. Traveling time along the Trans-Canada Highway from Port-aux-Basques to St. John's is about 13 hours, with time out for a meal in either Gander or Grand Falls. The trip from Corner Brook to St. Anthony at the northernmost tip of the island is about five hours. The trip from St. John's to Grand Bank on the southern tip of the Burin Peninsula takes about four hours.

In winter some highways may close during and after severe snowstorms. For winter road conditions on the west coast and in Labrador, call the **Department of Works, Services, and Transportation** (in Deer Lake, tel. 709/635–2162; in Grand Falls and Central Newfoundland, tel. 709/292–4300; in Clarenville, tel. 709/466–7953; in St. John's, tel. 709/729–2391).

Getting around Labrador

See Tour 6 in Exploring Newfoundland and Labrador, *below.*

Guided Tours

Boat Tours The number of boat tours has increased in recent years. South of St. John's, in Bay Bulls, **O'Brien's Bird Island Boat Tours** (tel. 709/753–4850 or 709/334–2355) and **Gatherall's Sanctuary Boat Charters** (tel. 709/334–2887) offer a popular two-hour excursion featuring whale watching, cod jigging, and a visit to the impressive Witless Bay Islands bird sanctuary. Both companies offer a hotel pickup service. **Great Island Tours** (tel. 800/563–2355) begins farther south in Cape Broyle and includes the abandoned outport of La Manche in its tour.

On the Trinity–Bonavista Peninsula, **Ocean Contact Limited** (tel. 709/464–3269) is an established specialist in whale watching and whale research. **Ocean Watch Tours** (tel. 709/677–2327) operates near Terra Nova National Park in Burnside and features park-approved field guides and an attractive ecological program. **Island Rendezvous** (tel. 709/747–7253) offers two days of boating and an overnight stay on Woody Island, Placentia Bay. **Island View Boat Tours** (tel. 709/535–2258) promises a mussel and lobster boil-up on the beach and a chance to visit abandoned settlements and Indian sites in the Lewisporte area. **Twillingate Island Boat Tours** (tel. 709/884–2242) specializes in iceberg photography in the iceberg-rich waters around Twillingate.

On the west coast, 2,000-foot-high cliffs and spectacular landlocked fjords are the main attraction. **Bontours** (tel. 709/458–2730) runs the best-known of these trips—up Western Brook Pond in Gros Morne National Park. **Tableland Boat Tours** (tel. 709/451–2101) runs tours up Trout River Pond near the southern boundary of the park. **Seal Island Boat Tours** (tel. 709/898–2525) explores St. Paul's Inlet, an area of the park rich in seals, terns, and other marine and shore life.

Bus Tours **McCarthy's Party** (tel. 709/781–2244) in St. John's offers guided bus tours across Newfoundland (May through October) in addition to a variety of convention and charter services. **Fleetline Motorcoach Tours** (tel. 709/722–2608) in Holyrood and **K.P. Motorcoach Tours** (tel. 709/632–5808) in Corner Brook also offer island-wide tours. Local tours are available for Port-aux-Basques, the Codroy Valley, Corner Brook, the Bay of Islands, Gros Morne National Park, the Great Northern Peninsula, and St. John's.

Adventure Tours Adventure touring in Newfoundland and Labrador is experiencing a period of rapid growth. Local adventure tour operators offer sea-kayaking, ocean-diving, canoeing, wildlife viewing, mountain biking, white-water rafting, heli-hiking, and interpretive walks in the summer. In winter, snowmobiling, heli-skiing, and caribou- and seal-watching expeditions are popular. Before choosing an operator it's advisable to contact the Department of Tourism and Culture just to make sure you're calling a reputable outfit. **Eastern Edge Outfitters** (tel. 709/368–9720 or 709/782–1465) offers east coast sea-kayaking tours, as well as white-water rafting expeditions down Newfoundland's Main River. **Gros Morne Adventure Guides** (tel.

709/458–2722 or 709/686–2241) offers sea-kayaking up the fjords and land-locked ponds of Gros Morne National Park, as well as a variety of hikes and adventures in the area. **Tuckamore Lodge** (tel. 709/865–6361) in Main Brook uses its luxurious lodge on the Great Northern Peninsula as a base for viewing caribou, seabird colonies, and other wildlife. **Labrador Scenic Ltd.** (tel 709/497–8326) in North West River organizes tours through central and northern Labrador with an emphasis on wildlife and Labrador's spectacular coast.

Exploring Newfoundland and Labrador

Tours in this chapter divide the province into the island of Newfoundland, beginning with St. John's and the Avalon Peninsula, and move west. Labrador is considered as a whole, with suggested driving and train excursions.

Highlights for First-Time Visitors

Cape St. Mary's Ecological Reserve, Tour 1: St. John's and the Avalon Peninsula
Cape Spear National Historic Site, Tour 1: St. John's and the Avalon Peninsula
Discovery Trail on the Bonavista Peninsula, Tour 2: Clarenville and the Bonavista and Burin Peninsulas
Gros Morne National Park, Tour 4: Deer Lake and the Great Northern Peninsula to St. Anthony
L'Anse aux Meadows National Historic Park, Tour 4: Deer Lake and the Great Northern Peninsula to St. Anthony
Red Bay, Tour 6: Labrador
St. John's Heritage District, Tour 1: St. John's and the Avalon Peninsula
Signal Hill National Historic Park, Tour 1: St. John's and the Avalon Peninsula
Viking Trail, Tour 4: Deer Lake and the Great Northern Peninsula to St. Anthony

Tour 1: St. John's and the Avalon Peninsula

Numbers in the margin correspond to points of interest on the Newfoundland and Labrador map.

When Sir Humphrey Gilbert sailed into St. John's to establish British colonial rule for Queen Elizabeth in 1583, he found Spanish, French, and Portuguese fishermen actively working the harbor. As early as 1627, the merchants of Water Street, then known as the "Lower Path," were doing a thriving business buying fish, selling goods, and supplying booze to soldiers and sailors. Still today the city encircles the snug, punchbowl harbor that helped establish its reputation.

St. John's

❶

True early birds can begin their tour of the area at daybreak by filling up a thermos of coffee, getting some muffins, and driving on Route 11 to **Cape Spear,** so they can be among the first to watch the sun come up over North America. The "chit chit" of song birds in the dim light of dawn and the whooshing and blowing of whales feeding directly below the cliffs make an unforgettable beginning to a day. **Cape Spear Lighthouse** (tel.

709/722–5367), Newfoundland's oldest such beacon, has been lovingly restored to its original form and furnishings and is open to visitors mid-June–Labor Day.

② Those who are less ambitious may wish to begin exploring **St. John's** a little later in the day, when the Tourist Chalet on the waterfront is open. This is an old converted railway caboose, staffed from May through October. *Harbor Drive, tel. 709/576–8514. Open 9–7 daily, May–Oct.*

Whichever way you look—left or right—you'll see the always-fascinating array of ships that tie up along **Harbour Drive.** Walk the harborfront, a favorite route in St. John's, to **The Battery,** a tiny, still-active fishing village perched precariously on the steep cliffs between hill and harbor. A well-maintained 5-kilometer (3-mile) walking path leads along the cliff edge, through the narrows, and zigzags through **Signal Hill National Historic Park.** Alternatively, you can drive on the road that also leads to the park.

In spite of its height, Signal Hill was difficult to defend: Throughout the 1600s and 1700s it changed hands with every attacking French, English, and Dutch force. A wooden palisade encircles the summit of the hill, indicating the boundaries of the old fortifications. En route to the hill is the **Park Interpretation Centre** (tel. 709/772–5367), with exhibits describing St. John's history.

Gibbet Hill, the rocky knob immediately to the west of the Interpretation Centre, was at one time used by local "authorities" as a place to hang miscreants. These dangling unfortunates were meant to send the message to anyone entering the harbor that misconduct would not be tolerated by the ruling fishing admiral. From the top of the hill it's a 500-foot drop to the narrow harbor entrance below.

Cabot Tower, at the summit of Signal Hill, was constructed in 1897 to commemorate the 400th anniversary of Cabot's discovery of Newfoundland. In 1901, in the shadow of the tower, Guglielmo Marconi received the first transatlantic wireless message from Cornwall, England—the opening salvo in a communication revolution that would change the world. The tower is open to the public and contains a display on communications history. *Tel. 709/772–5367. Admission free. Open year-round 8:30–4:30, 8:30–8 mid June–Labor Day; weekend guides in the summer.*

If you are driving, come down from Signal Hill, make a right turn at Quidi Vidi Road, and continue to the right, down Forest Road, to **Quidi Vidi Village,** an authentic fishing community whose history goes back to the beginning of St. John's. If you are walking, paths lead from the summit and the Interpretation Centre to the village. **Quidi Vidi Battery,** near the entrance to the village harbor, is a small, reconstructed 1762 redoubt, staffed by costumed interpreters who will tell you about the hard, unromantic life lived by a soldier of the empire. *Quidi Vidi Village, tel. 709/729–2460 or 709/729–2977. Admission free. Open 10–5:30 daily July–early Sept., winter by appointment.*

Quidi Vidi Lake, to the west of the village, is encircled by a leisurely path, popular with walkers and joggers, and is the site of the **St. John's Annual Regatta**—the oldest continuing sporting event in North America, it first took place in 1826. Weather

Newfoundland and Labrador

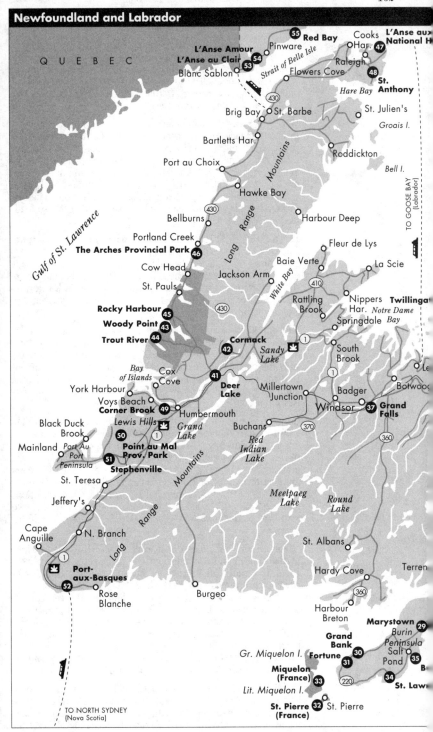

QUEBEC

Gulf of St. Lawrence

Strait of Belle Isle

Red Bay 55
Pinware
Cooks Har.
L'Anse aux National H 47
L'Anse Amour
L'Anse au Clair 54
53
Blanc Sablon
Raleigh
Flowers Cove 48
St. Anthony
Hare Bay

Brig Bay
St. Barbe
St. Julien's
Groais I.

Bartletts Har.
Roddickton
Bell I.

Port au Choix

Hawke Bay
Harbour Deep

Bellburns
Fleur de Lys

Portland Creek
Baie Verte
La Scie

The Arches Provincial Park 46
Cow Head
Jackson Arm

St. Pauls
Rattling Brook
Nippers Har.
Twillinga
Notre Dame Bay

Rocky Harbour 45
Springdale

Woody Point 43
Cormack 42
South Brook

Trout River 44
Sandy Lake

Cox Cove
41
Deer Lake
Millertown Junction
Badger
Botwoo

Bay of Islands
York Harbour
Voys Beach
Corner Brook 49
Humbermouth
Windsor
Grand Falls 37
Le

Black Duck Brook
Lewis Hills
Grand Lake
Buchans

Mainland
50
Point au Mal Prov. Park
Red Indian Lake

Port Au Port Peninsula
51
Stephenville

St. Teresa
Meelpaeg Lake
Round Lake

Jeffery's

Cape Anguille
N. Branch
St. Albans
Terren

Hardy Cove

Burgeo
360

Port-aux-Basques 52
Marystown 29

Rose Blanche
Harbour Breton
Burin Peninsula
Salt Pond 35
B

Grand Bank
Fortune 30
31
34
St. Law

Gr. Miquelon I.
220

Miquelon (France) 33

Lit. Miquelon I.

St. Pierre (France) 32 St. Pierre

TO NORTH SYDNEY (Nova Scotia)

Long Range Mountains

White Bay

TO GOOSE BAY (Labrador)

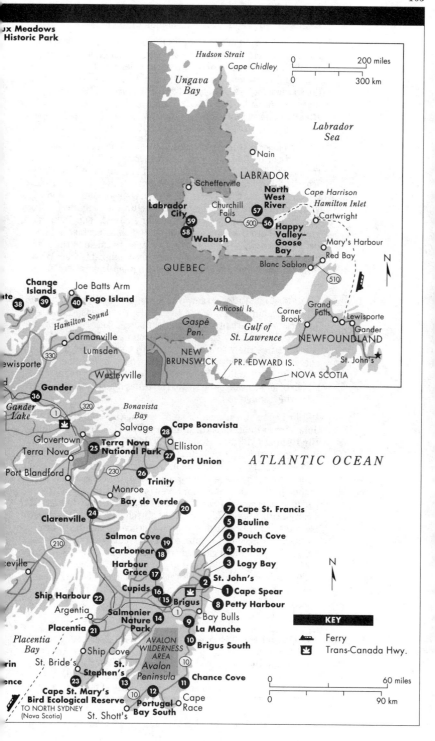

ux Meadows
Historic Park

Hudson Strait
Cape Chidley

Ungava
Bay

Labrador
Sea

Nain

LABRADOR

Scheffervile

Labrador
City

Churchill
Falls

North West River 57

Cape Harrison
Hamilton Inlet
Cartwright

59
58

Wabush

56 **Happy Valley-Goose Bay**

QUEBEC

Mary's Harbour
Red Bay

Blanc Sablon
510

N

Change Islands 38

Joe Batts Arm

te 38

39 40 **Fogo Island**

Hamilton Sound

Carmanville

Lumsden

ewisporte

Wesleyville

Anticosti Is.

Gaspé
Pen.

Gulf of
St. Lawrence

Corner
Brook

Grand
Falls

Lewisporte
Gander

NEWFOUNDLAND

NEW
BRUNSWICK

PR. EDWARD IS.

St. John's

NOVA SCOTIA

d

Gander 36

320

Bonavista
Bay

Salvage

Cape Bonavista

Gander
Lake

1

Glovertown
Terra Nova

25 **Terra Nova National Park**

28

Elliston

27 **Port Union**

Port Blandford

230

26 **Trinity**

ATLANTIC OCEAN

Monroe

Bay de Verde

Clarenville 24

20

210

Salmon Cove 19

Carbonear 18

Harbour Grace 17

eville

7 Cape St. Francis

5 Bauline

6 Pouch Cove

4 Torbay

3 Logy Bay

N

Ship Harbour 22

Argentia

Cupids 16

15 **Brigus**

1

2 St. John's

1 Cape Spear

8 Petty Harbour

Salmonier Nature Park 14

9 **La Manche**

Bay Bulls

Placentia 21

Placentia
Bay

Ship Cove

St. Stephen's 23

13

AVALON WILDERNESS AREA

Avalon
Peninsula

10

10 **Brigus South**

Chance Cove 11

rin

St. Bride's

ence

Cape St. Mary's Bird Ecological Reserve

TO NORTH SYDNEY
(Nova Scotia)

St. Shott's

12 **Portugal Bay South**

Cape
Race

KEY	
⚓	Ferry
⛟	Trans-Canada Hwy.

0 — 60 miles
0 — 90 km

permitting, the regatta begins on the first Wednesday in August: If you're in town you shouldn't miss it.

From the lake follow the **Rennies River Trail** (4 miles) that cuts through the city along a wooded stream and ends at the only public fluvarium in North America, where you can observe spawning trout and char in their natural habitat through underwater windows. *Newfoundland Freshwater Resource Center, Pippy Park, tel. 709/754–3474. Admission: $2.75 adults, $2.25 students and senior citizens, $1.50 children. Open 9–5 June–Aug., 10–4:30 Mon., Wed.–Sat., 12–4:30 Sun. the rest of the year.*

To get back downtown, retrace your steps along the Rennies River Trail by foot, or drive down Prince Phillip's Drive and turn right onto Portugal Cove Road. This runs into New Cove Road—follow this and turn right onto King's Bridge Road which intersects with Water St. As you walk around St. John's, you'll notice the diversity of architectural styles due to two major fires: one in 1846 and another in 1892. The 1892 fire stopped where George and Water streets intersect, at **Yellowbelly Corner.** This junction was so-named because in the 19th century it was a gathering spot for Irish immigrants from Wexford who wore yellow sashes to distinguish themselves from their Waterford rivals.

Look west on Water Street, where the block still resembles a typical Irish market town of the 1840s. To the east, however, Victorian-style architecture predominates, with curved mansard roofs typical of the popular Second Empire style. After the 1892 fire the city's elite moved to **Circular Road,** in the center of the city, out of reach of future fires, and built a string of impressive and highly ornamented Victorian mansions, which bear witness to the sizable fortunes made in the old days from the humble cod.

While you're downtown, take a look at the churches of St. John's, rich in architectural history. The **Basilica of St. John the Baptist** (Military Road, tel. 709/754–2170), with a commanding position above Military Road, overlooks the older section of the city and the harbor. The land was granted to the church by young Queen Victoria, and the edifice was built with stones from both Ireland and Newfoundland. From here you can also see the **Anglican Cathedral of St. John the Baptist** (22 Church Hill, tel. 709/726–5677) on Church Hill, one of the finest examples of Gothic Revival architecture in North America. Both churches conduct summer tours. Nearby is the imposing **Gower Street United Church** (Grower St., tel. 709/753–7286), with its redbrick facade and green turrets. At the bottom of Military Road, adjacent to Hotel Newfoundland, is the **St. Thomas Old Garrison Church** (Military Road, tel. 709/576–6632), where the English soldiers used to worship in the early and mid-1800s.

Time Out The **Commissariat House** (Kings Bridge Rd., tel. 709/729–2460 or 709/729–6730), just around the corner from the Anglican church, has been restored to the way it appeared in the 1830s. Drop in for a bowl of soup or beans, and chat with the interpreters, dressed in period costume, who will show you around.

If you have time, set aside an afternoon to visit the **Memorial University Botanical Gardens,** located at Oxen Pond on Mt. Scio

Road. This 100-acre nature reserve has five attractive trails, an English cottage garden, Newfoundland heritage plants, and heather beds. It is also one of two butterfly farms in North America and home to nesting ospreys. *Oxen Pond, Mt. Scio Rd., Pippy Park, tel. 709/737–8590. Admission free. Open Wed.–Sun. 10–5:30 May–Nov.*

Another beautiful spot in St. John's is **Bowring Park,** on Waterford Bridge Road. The expansive Victorian park was donated to the city by the wealthy Bowring family in 1911, and resembles the famous inner city parks of London, England, after which it was modeled. Dotting the grounds are artfully designed nooks and crannies, ponds, ducks to feed, and rustic bridges; there's also a statue of Peter Pan.

The Avalon Several half-day, full-day, and two-day excursions are possible
Peninsula from St. John's, and in each direction a different personality of the region unfolds. On the southern half of the peninsula are small Irish hamlets separated by large tracts of wilderness. The northern half is more densely populated and still reflects its Dorset and Devon, England, origins. Here, homes are perched on narrow spits of land or tucked into the lee of cliffs.

Coast North of St. You can take a leisurely ¹/₂-day trip to explore the scenic coast-
John's line north of St. John's. Take Route 30 (Logy Bay Road) to Marine Drive, which winds along the coastline, passing
❸ through **Logy Bay** and its remarkable cliffs. Along the way is **Ocean Sciences Centre,** with its outdoor seal tank where you can watch the animals frolic. The seals look happy for good reason: They're participating in experiments to determine their year-round feeding habits. *Marine Lab Road, tel. 709/737–3706. Admission $2.50 adults, $1.50 children and senior citizens, under 6 free. Tours every ¹/₂-hour late June–early Sept., 10–5.*

❹ Follow Route 30 to **Torbay** and turn west onto Route 21 to
❺ **Bauline,** an unspoiled fishing village that overlooks Conception
❻ Bay. Continue on Route 21 to **Pouch Cove,** one of the province's oldest communities, where the adventurous should follow the
❼ unpaved road that leads to **Cape St. Francis.** On the way to the cape, there's a short coastal walk. A local legend centers around the wreck of the *Waterwitch,* which capsized in 1875 in the water at the northern edge of Pouch Cove. Alfred Moores rescued 11 people from the floundering vessel by lowering himself by rope down the cliff. A sign marks the site along the coastal walk, but you can't see the wreck.

Leave Pouch Cove on Route 20 and head straight back, or connect to Route 30, which loops around toward Logy Bay, on your return to St. John's. For one more scenic pleasure en route, take in some views at the village of **Flat Rock,** on Route 20 just past Pouch Cove.

Coast South of St. You can travel part of the peninsula's coast for a one- or two-day
John's excursion, depending on how much time you have. Quaint coastal towns line the road, and the natural sites are beautiful and well-interpreted.

Just south of St. John's pick up Route 10 and follow it along the southern coast toward Trepassey. Locals call this trip "going up the shore," even though it looks like you're traveling down on a map. The wildness of this coast is usually what's most striking to visitors, and La Manche and Chance Cove—both now-abandoned communities turned provincial parks—attest to the bounty of natural resources of the region.

(8) Although a visit to many of the hamlets along the way will fill any void for prettiness, a few favorites are exceptional. **Petty**
(9) (10) **Harbour, La Manche,** and **Brigus South,** have especially attractive settings and strong traditional flavors.

(11) (12) In springtime, between **Chance Cove** and **Portugal Cove South,** in a stretch of land about 36 miles along, hundreds of caribou gather near the road with their calves on the wide barrens. Although the graceful animals are there during other times of the year, their numbers are few and it's difficult to spot them because they blend in so well with the scenery.

Route 10 loops around the peninsula and becomes Route 90,
(13) just past **St. Stephens.**

At the intersection of Routes 90 and 91, in Salmonier, you need to decide whether to continue north toward Salmonier Nature Park and on to Conception Bay, or to head west then south to Route 100 to Cape St. Mary's Ecological Reserve (*see* Route 100: The Cape Shore, *below*). Both options take about three hours.

(14) If you've decided to go north, travel to **Salmonier Nature Park,** 9 miles along, where visitors can see many of the animal species that are indigenous to the province. The park is a 1214 hectare wilderness reserve area and has an enclosed 40.5 hectare exhibit that allows up-close viewing. *Salmonier Line, Rte. 90, tel. 709/729–6974 or 709/229–7888. Admission free. Admission 50¢ adults, 25¢ children, senior citizens free. Open early June–Labor Day, Thurs.–Mon., noon–7.*

Farther along Route 90 the road passes through the scenic Hawkes Hills, before meeting up with the Trans-Canada Highway (Route 1). Turn off at the Holyrood Junction (Route 62)
(15) and follow Route 70, which parallels **Conception Bay,** to **Brigus.** Meander through this beautifully restored village with winding lanes, a tea house, and a museum set in a stone barn, where you can pick up a walking-tour brochure. *Ye Olde Stone Barn Museum, 4 Magistrate's Hill, tel. 709/528–3298. Admission $1 adults, 50¢ children, open noon–5 daily June–Sept.*

Brigus was the home of many sealing captains, including Captain Bob Bartlett, who in 1909 guided Commodore Perry to within 161 kilometers (100 miles) of the North Pole. Perry abandoned Bartlett before going on the last leg so he could claim full honors for himself. The move backfired, however, for without Bartlett's testimony Perry couldn't prove that he actually made the journey.

(16) Continue on Route 70 to **Cupids,** the site of the first permanent colony in Newfoundland, which was founded in 1610 by the Bristol merchant John Guy.

Just beyond Brigus Route 70 passes by Clarke's Beach, where you should turn right and follow Route 72 along a narrow sliver of land to **Port de Grave** and **Hibbs Cove.** The **Port de Grave Fishermen's Museum, Porter House, and Old School House Community Museum** is actually located in Hibbs Cove. Here you can learn about Newfoundland fisherman lifestyles from the 1600s until the present. *Hibbs Cove, off Rte. 72, tel. 709/786–3912 or 709/786–3900. Admission: $1 adults, 50¢ students. Open*

1–5 daily mid–late June, 10–noon and 1–5 Mon.–Sat., Sun. 1–5 July–Labor Day.

⓱ About 10 miles farther on Route 70 is **Harbour Grace,** which once was the headquarters of Peter Easton, a 17th-century pirate. Beginning in 1919, Harbour Grace was the departure point for many attempts to fly the Atlantic. Amelia Earhart left Harbour Grace in 1932 to become the first woman to fly solo across the Atlantic. Several handsome stone churches and buildings remain as evidence of the town's former pride.

⓲ Continue along Route 70 to **Carbonear,** another town with a fascinating history. In 1696 it was burned to the ground by the French, but the inhabitants retreated to a small fortified island in the harbor and successfully defended it against capture. Carbonear Island has been designated a National Historic Site to mark its colorful military past.

⓳ Farther along Route 70 is picturesque **Salmon Cove,** a sheltered bay with a grassy picnic area. The road is narrow and partly unpaved, but you'll be rewarded with the finest views of Conception Bay, especially as you drive up and over Blow Me
⓴ Down Head. If you plan to travel on to **Bay de Verde,** at the northern tip of the peninsula, and down the other side of the peninsula on Route 80 along Trinity Bay, consider turning in for the night at one of the several hotels or bed-and-breakfasts (*see* Lodging, *below*) in the Harbour Grace–Carbonear area. Otherwise turn around and follow the same route back.

Route 100: The Cape Shore If you opted for the Cape Shore route, from Salmonier west on Route 91 and south on Route 100, you're headed to Avalon's Cape St. Mary's Ecological Reserve.

㉑ **Placentia,** at the end of Route 91, was the French capital of Newfoundland in the 1600s. Trust the French to select a beautiful place for a capital! **Castle Hill National Historic Park,** just north of town, is located on what remains of the French fortifications. The visitor's center has a "life at Plaisance" exhibit that shows the life and hardships endured by early English and French settlers. *Off Route 100, tel. 709/227–2401. Admission free. Open 8:30–8 June–Labor Day, 8:30–4:30 rest of year.*

㉒ A worthwhile and nearby diversion from Placentia is **Ship Harbour,** an isolated, edge-of-the-world place that has the curious distinction of being the home of the free world. Off Route 102, amidst the splendor of Placentia Bay, an unpaved road leads to a monument marking the historic Atlantic Charter. It was on a ship in these waters where, in 1941, Roosevelt and Churchill signed the charter and formally announced the "Four Freedoms," which still shape the politics of the world's most successful democracies: freedom of speech, freedom of worship, freedom from want, and freedom from fear.

To continue on the Cape Shore tour, double back to Route 100
㉓ and travel 24 miles to the **Cape St. Mary's Ecological Reserve** (tel. 709/729–2424), where about 5,000 pairs of gannets nest on Bird Rock, and as many again on the nearby cliffs. Additionally, there are thousands of kittiwakes and murres, especially during the nesting season, which is usually between June and August. An interpretation center is on the grounds and on-site nature guides are available during the summer. While walking out to the sanctuary, you'll experience some of the most dramatic coastal scenery in Newfoundland—that's if you hit it

lucky and encounter a rare clear day on the cape. Fog is far more usual. Fortunately, the birds are close-at-hand, so you'll see and hear them no matter what the weather.

Tour 2: Clarenville and the Bonavista and Burin Peninsulas

㉔ Clarenville is about two hours from St. John's via the Trans-Canada Highway (Route 1) and is the departure point for two different excursions: the Discovery Trail and Terra Nova National Park. If you're interested in rugged terrain, golf, fishing, and camping, head 15 miles west along the Trans-Canada
㉕ Highway to **Terra Nova National Park,** on the exposed coastline that adjoins Bonavista Bay. If you are a golfer, you can play on one of the most beautiful courses in Canada, and the only one where a licensed salmon river cuts through the course. Call 709/543–2525, 800/461–0808 in Canada for a reservation. Fees run between $24 and $30 per person, 18 holes, depending on the season. The park also offers attractive campsites, whale-watching tours, and nature walks. *Tel. 709/533–2801 or 709/533–2358, fax 709/533–2706. Open year-round. Vehicle permit required in summer: $5 per day per vehicle, $10 for 4-day pass, $20 for seasonal pass.*

If history and quaint towns interest you, begin the tour in Clarenville, the starting point for Route 230—the "**Discovery Trail.**" The route goes as far as the town of Bonavista, one of John Cabot's reputed landing spots in 1497. On your way visit
㉖ the historic village of **Trinity,** known as one of the jewels of Newfoundland. The village's picturesque views, winding lanes, and snug houses are the main attraction, and several homes have been turned into museums and inns. In the 1700s Trinity competed with St. John's as a center of culture and wealth. Its more contemporary claim to fame, however, is that its intricate harbor was a favorite anchorage for the British navy, and it was here that the smallpox vaccine was introduced to North America, by a local rector.

㉗ Port Union, just north of Trinity on Route 230, was built as a model fishing community a century ago by the pioneer unionist Sir William Coaker. **The Port Union Museum** (contact Linda Clarke, tel. 709/464–3315) in the old railway station follows his career.

㉘ Still farther north along Route 230 is **Cape Bonavista,** a popular destination because of its association with Cabot's landing. The lighthouse on the point has been restored to the 1870 period. While here, visit the Mockbeggar Property to learn about the life of a well-to-do outport merchant in the years immediately before Confederation. *Off Route 230, tel. 709/729–2460 or 709/468–7300. Admission free. Open 10–5:30 late June–early Sept; by appointment in winter.*

Burin Peninsula The journey down to the Burin Peninsula is a three- to four-hour drive from the intersection of Route 230 and Route 1 through the sometimes incredible landscapes along Route 210. The peninsula's history is tied to the rich fishing grounds of the Grand Banks, which established this area as a center for European fishery as early as the 1500s. By the early 1900s, one of the world's largest fishing fleets was based on the Burin Peninsula. Today its inhabitants still operate the fishery in the modern trawlers that harvest the Grand Banks.

㉙ **Marystown** is the largest town on the peninsula and is its major commercial center. The town's name was changed from Mortier to Marystown by a priest during World War I, and to keep the faith a 15-foot statue of the Virgin Mary watches the town and harbor. West from here the road meets with Route 220 and

㉚ passes through **Grand Bank,** an unusually attractive community with a fascinating fishing history. This town is famous in the area as one of the most beautiful communities on the Atlantic Seaboard. For details about the town's past visit the **Southern Newfoundland Seamen's Museum,** housed in a sail-shaped building that was the Yugoslavian Pavilion in Expo '67. *Marine Dr., tel. 709/832–1484. Admission free. Open 9–12, 1–5 Mon.–Fri., 2–5 weekends, closed holidays.*

㉛ Just south of Grand Bank is **Fortune,** where you can catch the ferry to France's only colony in North America—the islands of

㉜ ㉝ **St. Pierre** and **Miquelon.** These islands are the place to go if you have a hankering for a French lunch or a bottle of perfume. Shopping and eating are both popular pastimes, and if you plan to stay overnight, consider the Hotel Robert. The ferry ride takes about two hours, and tourists should carry proof of citizenship. People from outside the U.S. and Canada will have to show valid visas and passports. Two passenger ferry companies provide service: **Lloyd G. Lake Ltd.** (tel. 709/832–2006) leaves Fortune daily at 2:15 PM from mid-June to late Sept. Crossing takes 55 minutes. The ferry leaves St. Pierre at 1:00 PM daily, and the round trip costs $47.95; children under 16 are free. **SPM Tours** (tel. 709/832–0429) leaves Fortune daily at 1:15 PM and leaves St. Pierre at 11 AM daily. Season and fares same as above.

㉞ Back on Route 220, you may wish to stop at **St. Lawrence,** where in 1942 one of the worst disasters befell the U.S. Navy. It was here that warships *Pollux* and *Truxton* went aground during a February storm. Two hundred sailors perished, but the people of the area heroically pulled another 182 over the cliffs to safety. In gratitude the U.S. Navy built a hospital for the community. In the summer of 1992, some survivors of the disaster returned to renew their friendships with the people of St. Lawrence and to unveil the "Echoes of Valour" monument on the cliff overlooking the spot where the ship sank.

㉟ Following Route 220 will take you around the peninsula to the old town of **Burin,** a community amidst intricate cliffs and coves. This was an ideal setting for pirates and privateers who used to lure ships into the rocky, dead-end areas in order to escape. Captain Cook was among those who watched for smugglers from "Cook's Lookout" on a hill that still bears his name. Also in Burin is the Heritage House museum (tel. 709/891–2217, admission free, open 9–5 Mon., Tues., 9–9 Wed.–Sun.), considered one of the best community museums in Newfoundland, which gives you a sense of what life was like in past eras.

Tour 3: Gander, Grand Falls–Windsor, and Notre Dame Bay

The interior of Newfoundland is unpopulated beyond the main roads, with the towns of Gander and Grand Falls–Windsor the

㊱ focal points for the region. **Gander,** a busy center with 12,000 people, is the site of the Gander International Airport. During World War II it was chosen by the Canadian and U.S. Air

Forces as a major strategic air base because of its favorable weather and secure location. After the war, the airport became an international hub, and young islanders would hang around to see the stars come and go, among them Zsa Zsa Gabor and Tyrone Power. Now, like all modern airports, it's tightly secured. Gander has many hotels and still makes a good base for your travels. The **Aviation Exhibition** in the airport's Domestic Passenger's Lounge (tel. 709/729–2460; open daily), traces Newfoundland's role in the history of air travel.

㊲ Grand Falls, 50 minutes west of Gander along the Trans-Canada Highway (Route 1), was a paper-milling town founded by Lord Northcliffe in the early 1900s to supply newsprint for his growing newspaper empire. Within Grand Falls is the **Mary March Regional Museum,** which depicts the lives of the Beothuk Indians before they fell victim to disease and competition from early settlers. The museum is named for 23-year-old Demasduit (also named Mary March, for the month in which she was captured), one of the last Beothuks, who was captured in 1819 during a brutal encounter that resulted in the death of her husband and child. *St. Catherine St., off Rte. 1, tel. 709/489–9331. Admission free. Open weekdays 9–4:45, weekends and holidays, 10–5:45.*

Using either Route 330 from Gander via the Trans-Canada Highway (Route 1) or Route 340 from Grand Falls, wander north through wooded countryside and small villages to **㊳ Twillingate.** The inhabitants of this charming old fishing village make their living from the sea and have been doing so for nearly two centuries. Every year on the last weekend in July, the town hosts the **Fish, Fun and Folk Festival,** where all different kinds of fish are cooked every kind of way. Twillingate is also one of the best places on the island to see icebergs, and is known to the locals as "Iceberg Alley." These majestic and dangerous mountains of ice are awe inspiring to see while they're grounded in early summer.

You might also be interested in taking a ferry ride to either **㊴ ㊵ Change Islands** or **Fogo Island.** Branch off Route 340 to Route 335 which takes you through scenic coastal communities on the way to the ferry to either of the islands, located in Farewell. These islands give one the impression of a place frozen in time. Clapboard homes are precariously perched on rocks or built on small lots surrounded by vegetable gardens. As you walk the roads, watch out for moose and herds of wild Newfoundland ponies who spend their summers grazing and enjoying the warm breeze off the ocean.

Tour 4: Deer Lake and the Great Northern Peninsula to St. Anthony

㊶ Deer Lake was once just another small town on the Trans-Canada Highway, but the opening of Gros Morne National Park in the early '70s and a first-class paved highway passing right through to St. Anthony changed all that. Today, with an airport and car rentals available, Deer Lake is a good starting point for a fly-drive vacation.

Head north out of Deer Lake on Route 430 to Route 422 to **Sir Richard Squires Memorial Park.** This drive will take you **㊷** through **Cormack,** which is one of the best farming regions in the island. The park remains natural and unspoiled, and it contains one of the most interesting salmon fishing areas in New-foundland.

Return to Route 430, and in a short while you'll be on the **Viking Trail** leading into **Gros Morne National Park** (tel. 709/458–2059). Because of its geological uniqueness and immense splendor, this park has been named a UNESCO World Heritage Site. Among the more breathtaking visions are the expanses of wild orchids in springtime. There is an excellent **Interpretation Centre** (tel. 709/458–2066), which has displays and videos about the park. Camping and hiking are popular recreations in the park, and boat tours are available. It takes at least two days to see Gros Morne properly.

Scenic **Bonne Bay,** a deep, mountainous fjord, divides the park in two. You can either drive around the perimeter of the fjord on Route 430 going north, or make a ferry-crossing near its mouth from Route 431.

❸ In the south of the park is **Woody Point,** a charming community of old houses and imported Lombardy poplars. Until it was bypassed by the railway, the community was the commercial capital of the West Coast. Rising behind Woody Point are the **Tablelands,** a unique rock massif that was once an ancient sea-bed. Its rocks are toxic to most plant life, and Ice Age conditions linger in the form of persistent snow and moving rock glaciers.

❹ Follow Route 431 to scenic **Trout River Pond** and the once-isolated and still unusual community of **Trout River.** The **Green Gardens Trail,** a four- to five-hour hike, is along the way and it's one you'll remember for your lifetime, but be prepared to do a bit of climbing on your return journey. The trail passes through the Tablelands barrens and descends sharply down to a fairy tale coastline of eroded cliffs, sea stacks, and lush green meadows.

❺ On the northern side of the park, situated along coastal Route 430, is **Rocky Harbour,** with a wide range of services and a luxurious indoor public pool—the perfect thing to soothe tired limbs after a strenuous day. The most popular attraction on the northern portion of Gros Morne is the boat tour up **Western Brook Pond,** which is reached by a leisurely 45-minute walk from the main highway through an interesting mix of bog and woods. Cliffs rise 2,000 feet on both sides of the gorge and high waterfalls tumble over ancient rocks. If you have strong legs and are in good shape, another decent attraction is the 10-mile hike up **Gros Morne Mountain,** at 2,644 feet the second-highest peak in Newfoundland. Weather permitting, your labor will be rewarded by a unique arctic landscape and spectacular views. The park's coast in the north offers visitors an unusual mix of sand beaches, rock pools, and trails through tangled dwarf forests known locally as "tuckamore." Sunsets, seen from Lobster Point Lighthouse, are spectacular. Keep an eye out for whales and visit the lighthouse museum, devoted to the human history of the area.

❻ Just a short distance north of the park, on Route 430, is **The Arches Provincial Park,** a geological curiosity where the pounding sea has cut a succession of caves through a bed of dolomite.

Continuing north, parallel to the Gulf of St. Lawrence, you'll find yourself refreshingly close to the ocean and the wave-tossed beaches: Stop to breathe the fresh sea air and listen to the breakers. The Long Range Mountains to your right reminded Jacques Cartier, who saw them in 1534, of the long, rectangular-shaped farm buildings of his home village in France. Small villages are interspersed with rivers where salmon and trout get to be "liar-size." The remains of the Maritime Archaic Indians and Dorset Eskimos have been found in abundance along this coast, and there's an interesting Interpretation Centre (tel. 709/623–2601) at Port aux Choix.

Proceed about 130 miles on Route 430, then turn onto Route ❹ 436 to **L'Anse aux Meadows National Historic Site.** This UNESCO World Heritage Site was discovered in 1960 by a Norwegian team, Helge and Anne Stine Ingstad. Most believe the remains of the long sod houses here were built around 1000 as the site of Norseman Lief Erikson's colony in the New World. The Canadian Parks Service has established a marvelous **Interpretation Centre** (tel. 709/623–2601) and has meticulously reconstructed some of the sod huts. With fires burning inside and sheepskins about, one does get a sense of centuries past. *Rte. 436, tel. 709/623–2601 or 709/623–2608. Admission free. Visitor center open mid-June–Labor Day, daily 9–8.*

Return to Route 430 and about 10 miles from the junction with ❹ 430 is **St. Anthony,** a beautiful town settled around a natural harbor, at the tip of the Great Northern Peninsula. Take a trip out to the lighthouse—you may see an iceberg or two floating by.

Here is also the home of the **Grenfell Mission.** The huge hospital attests to the work done by Sir Wilfred Grenfell, a British medical missionary, who established nursing stations and cooperatives and provided medical services to the scattered villages of northern Newfoundland and the south coast of Labrador in the early 1900s. The main foyer of the hospital has a decorative tile mural that's worth a visit. **Grenfell House,** the home of Sir Wilfred and Lady Grenfell, has been restored to period condition and can also be visited. *On the west side of St. Anthony on a hill overlooking the harbor, adjacent to Charles S. Curtis Memorial Hospital, tel. 709/454–3333. Admission: $2 adults, $1 students and senior citizens, children under 5 free. Open daily 10–8 mid-May–mid-Oct., by appointment in winter.*

Don't leave without visiting the **Grenfell Handcraft** store (tel. 709/454–3576). Importing craftspeople to train the villagers to become self-sufficient in a harsh environment was one of Grenfell's aims. A windproof cloth that villagers turned into well-made parkas came to be known as Grenfell cloth. Beautiful clothes fashioned out of Grenfell cloth have quality and style not found anywhere else and they are available for sale here. Return to Deer Lake along Route 430.

Tour 5: Corner Brook and the West Coast

❹ **Corner Brook** is Newfoundland's second-largest city and the hub of the west coast of the island. Mountains fringe three sides of the city and there are beautiful views of the harbor and the Bay of Islands. Corner Brook is also home to one of the largest paper mills in the world. Every July the city hosts the **Hangashore Folk Festival,** where you can go to hear some great traditional Canadian and Newfoundland music.

If you plan to explore the west coast, Corner Brook is a convenient hub and point of departure. It is only three hours from the Port aux Basques ferry and is an attractive and active city. The town enjoys more clearly defined seasons than most of the rest of the island, and in summer there are many pretty gardens to view and enjoy. **The Marble Mountain Ski Resort** (tel. 709/639–8531 on the slopes or 709/634–2160 for the development office), just north of the city, has the highest slopes and snowfall in Eastern North America and is growing rapidly as a ski center.

The north and south shores of the **Bay of Islands** have fine paved roads—Route 440 on the north shore and Route 450 on the south—and both offer a pleasant and scenic half-day drive. On both roads, farming and fishing communities exist side by side. Take a camera with you—the scenery is breathtaking, with farms, mountains, and beautiful pockets of brilliant wildflowers.

On another day, drive farther west on the Trans-Canada Highway and turn off at Route 460. Spend some time on the **Point au Mal Provincial Park** stopping at **Stephenville,** home of the old Harmon Air Force Base and now home to the annual Stephenville Arts Festival (mid-July to early August). The peninsula itself was largely settled by the French who brought their way of life and language to this small corner of Newfoundland.

As you move farther down the Trans-Canada Highway toward **Port aux Basques,** Routes 404, 405, 406, and 407 will bring you into the small Scottish communities of the **Codroy Valley.** Nestled in the valley are some of the finest salmon rivers and most productive farms in the province, all of this against the backdrop of the Long Range Mountains and the Lewis Hills, from which gales strong enough to stop traffic hurl off the plateau and down to the coast.

Tour 6: Labrador

Isolated from the rest of the continent, Labrador has remained one of the world's truly wild places, and yet its two main centers of Labrador City–Wabush and Happy Valley–Goose Bay offer all the amenities available in larger, urban centers. Labrador is steeped in history, a place where the past invades the present and life evolves as it did many years ago, a composite of natural phenomena, wilderness adventure, history, and culture.

Labrador's vast landscape—294,330 square kilometers (113,204 square miles) of land and 8,000 kilometers (5,000 miles) of coastline—is home to a small but richly diverse population with a history that in some cases stretches back thousands of years; in other cases, the mining towns of Labrador West for example, the history goes back less than four decades.

Getting There From the island of Newfoundland, you can fly to Labrador via St. John's, Gander, Deer Lake, or Stephenville. Route 500 was opened in 1992 linking Labrador City with Happy Valley–Goose Bay via Churchill Falls. If you plan on doing any extensive driving in any part of Labrador, you should contact the Department of Tourism and Culture (tel. 709/729–2830 or 800/563–6353) for advice on the best routes and road conditions.

To explore the south coast of Labrador, catch the ferry at St. Barbe on Route 430 in Newfoundland to Blanc Sablon, Québec. From here you can drive to Red Bay along Route 510. Conditions on this 439-kilometer (300-mile) unpaved wilderness road are best between June and October.

In summer, you can travel by car ferry through **Marine Atlantic** (in Lewisporte, Newfoundland, tel. 709/535–6876; in Happy Valley–Goose Bay, Labrador, 709/896–0041; or in the United States, 800/341–7981). The ship travels from Lewisporte in Newfoundland to Cartwright, on the coast of Labrador, and then through the Hamilton inlet to Happy Valley–Goose Bay. Room is limited and reservations can be made only from within the province.

The Straits The trip from Blanc Sablon to Red Bay on Route 510 will take you through the small fishing communities of L'Anse au Clair, **㉝** Forteau, and L'Anse au Loup. In **L'Anse au Clair,** you can walk the "Doctor's Path," where long ago Dr. Marcoux searched out herbs and medicinal plants in the days when hospitals and nursing stations were few and far between. Anglers can try their luck for trout and salmon on the scenic Forteau and Pinware rivers. The Straits were a rich hunting-and-gathering ground for the continent's earliest peoples.

The elaborate Maritime Archaic Indian burial site discovered **㉞** near **L'Anse Amour,** about 12 miles from L'Anse au Clair, is 9,000 years old. A plaque marks the site. The L'Anse Amour lighthouse was constructed in 1857 and is the second-tallest lighthouse in Canada. During the month of August, the annual **Labrador Bakeapple Festival** in **Forteau** draws people from miles around for music, feasting, and celebration. The **Labrador Straits Museum** (Route 510, between Forteau and l'Anse-au-Loup, tel. 709/927–5659. Admission $1.50. Open daily during the summer.) provides an interesting glimpse into the history and life-style of the area.

You must drive to the very end of Route 510 to visit the area's **㉟** main attraction: **Red Bay,** the site of a 16th-century Basque whaling station and the province's newest UNESCO World Heritage Site. Basque whalers began harpooning migrating whales from flimsy boats in frigid waters a few years after Cabot's discovery of the coast in 1497. Between 1550 and 1600 Red Bay was the world's whaling capital. A new visitor center (tel. 709/920–2197, open 8–8 Mon.–Sat., noon–8 Sun., mid-June–early Oct.) interprets the Basque heritage through film and artifact. Between June and October, a boat will take you on a short journey over to the actual site of excavations on Saddle Island.

Coastal Labrador You can tour coastal Labrador aboard Marine Atlantic's car ferry (*see* Arriving and Departing, *above*) from Lewisporte, Newfoundland, which also carries of all types of food and goods for people living along the coast. The trip takes 33 hours one-way, and two regularly scheduled return trips are made weekly. A second ferry travels from Happy Valley–Goose Bay to Nain, Labrador's northernmost settlement. This trip takes two weeks to complete. As both ferries are supply boats, you'll stop at a number of summer fishing stations and coastal communities.

㊱ **Happy Valley–Goose Bay** is the chief service center for coastal Labrador. The town was founded in the 1940s as a top-secret air base used to ferry fleets of North American–manufactured aircraft to Europe. It is still used as a low-level flying training base by the British, Dutch, and German air forces.

③ **North West River** is a pleasant, half-hour drive to the east on Route 520, and on the way you'll pass the **Snow Goose Mountain Ski Club** (tel. 709/896–5923). North West River was founded as a Hudson's Bay trading post and is the former Labrador headquarters of the International Grenfell Association. It retains its frontier charm. Nearby **Sheshatshit** is the home of the Montagnais Innu, natives of Labrador. The spirit in which the Innu (Naskapi-Montagnais) people inhabited the interior for centuries can still be felt the moment you step outside the region's modern mining communities.

Labrador West   Labrador West's subarctic landscape is challenging and unforgettable. The area offers some of the world's best angling and wilderness adventure opportunities.

The best way to see this area is by taking the **Québec North Shore and Labrador Railway** (tel. 709/944–8205), which leaves Sept Isles, Québec, twice weekly. The 10-hour trip takes you through 419 kilometers (260 miles) of virgin forest, spectacular waterfalls, and majestic mountains. The refurbished vintage dome car is ideal for an expanded view of this breathtaking panorama. The train, though, is more than a pleasure ride—it carries iron ore from Wabush and Labrador City (site of the largest open-pit mining operation in the world) to various distribution points in Québec.

③ ③   The modern towns of **Wabush** and **Labrador City** have all the amenities of larger, urban centers, including accommodations, sports and recreational facilities, good shopping, live theater, and some of the finest hospitality you will find anywhere. Nearby are the **Smokey Mountain Alpine Skiing Center** (open mid-November–early May, tel. 709/944–3505) and the **Menihek Nordic Ski Club** (tel. 709/944–6339 or 709/944–2154), with trails and slopes for both beginners and advanced skiers.

Shopping

The main centers of Newfoundland and Labrador—St. John's, Clarenville, Gander, Grand Falls, Corner Brook, Labrador West—all have modern shopping centers. However, the smaller communities often offer interesting crafts and native wares. Wander about—each town and village has its own country store and crafts store or general store. There are even some stores where packages are still being wrapped in brown paper and tied with twine.

NONIA (Newfoundland Outport Nurses Industrial Association), at 286 Water Street in St. John's, was started in 1923 to give Newfoundland women an opportunity to earn extra money. Throughout history, the women of Newfoundland had earned a reputation for turning homespun wool into exquisite clothing. In 1923 Jubilee Guilds supplied these outport women with wool of all kinds and colors, and in this shop on Water Street, even today, you can buy their well-made knitware. Other fine crafts stores in St. John's are the Salt Box, The Cod Jigger, the Devon House Craft Gallery, and the Newfoundland

Weavery. For antiques, Murray's Antiques and Livyers are well worth a visit.

At St. Anthony, on the northern tip of Newfoundland, browse in the Grenfell Handcraft Store (*see* Exploring, *above*).

Most bookstores have a prominent section devoted to local history, fiction, and memoirs. **Word Play** (221 Duckworth St., tel. 709/726–9193 or 800/563–9100) also carries a wide selection of newspapers, magazines, and books of general interest to travelers. **Fred's Records** (198 Duckworth St., tel. 709/753–9191) has the best selection of local tapes and CDs, as well as other music.

Sports and Fitness

Many provincial and all national parks in Newfoundland have hiking and nature trails. The west coast offers opportunities for mountain climbing in the summer and skiing in the winter. There are also ski resorts near Clarenville, Labrador City, and Happy Valley–Goose Bay, and groomed cross-country ski trail systems in St. John's, Clarenville, Terra Nova National Park, Gros Morne National Park, Labrador City, and Happy Valley–Goose Bay, among other places.

Coastal and woods trails radiate from most small communities. However, you can never be sure how far the trail will go unless you ask a local. Be careful: Landmarks are few, the weather is changeable, and it is surprisingly easy to get lost. Many small communities now also have formal walking trails.

Newfoundland has 105 salmon rivers and trout streams. Angling in these unpolluted waters is a fisherman's dream. Seasonal and regulatory information can be obtained from the **Department of Tourism and Culture** (tel. 800/729–2830).

Dining and Lodging

Dining

John Cabot and Sir Humphrey Gilbert raved about "waters teeming with fish." Today Newfoundland's fish are still some of the best in the world and one of the best dining bargains you will find anywhere. In Newfoundland, if you ask for "fish," you will always get cod. In season you will be treated to local delicacies such as panfried, baked, or poached cod, cod tongues, salt cod, fish and brewis (cod of course!). Fresh lobster, halibut, scallops, mussels, and Atlantic salmon are also good choices in season.

Two other foods you shouldn't leave without trying are partridgeberries and bakeapples. Partridgeberries are a small, lush-tasting relative of the cranberry and locally they are used for just about everything—pies, jams, cakes, pancakes, and even as a sauce for turkey and game. Bakeapples in the wild are a low-growing berry that looks like a yellow raspberry— you'll see them ripening in bogs in August throughout Newfoundland and Labrador. Enterprising youngsters sell them by the side of the road in jars. If the ones you buy are hard, wait a few days and they'll ripen into a rich-tasting jam. They're popular on ice cream or spread on fresh homemade bread. In Scandinavia they're known as "cloudberries" and are made into a liqueur.

You may also hear Newfoundlanders talk about the herb they call summer savory. Newfoundlanders are so partial to this peppery herb that they slip it into most stuffings and stews. Growers in the province ship the product all over the world, and Newfoundlanders visiting relatives living outside the province are usually asked to "bring the savory."

Only the large urban centers across the province, especially St. John's and Corner Brook, have gourmet restaurants. Fish is a safe dish to order just about everywhere—even in the lowliest take-out. You'll be agreeably surprised by the quality of the meals along the Trans-Canada Highway: Restaurants in the Irving Gas Station chain, for example, offer thick homemade soups with dumplings, and Sunday dinners that draw in local customers for miles around. Don't be shy about trying some of the excellent meals offered in the province's expanding network of "hospitality homes," where home cooking goes hand in hand with the warm welcome for which Newfoundlanders are famous.

Dress is casual everywhere except at the Very Expensive listings.

Highly recommended restaurants in each price category are indicated by a star ★.

Category	Cost*
Very Expensive	over $50
Expensive	$35–$50
Moderate	$20–$35
Inexpensive	under $20

per person, excluding drinks, service, and 12% sales tax

Lodging

Newfoundland and Labrador offer lodgings that range from modestly priced "hospitality homes" to luxury accommodations. In between, visitors can choose from affordable, basic lodging and mid-priced hotels. In remote areas, visitors should be prepared to find very basic lodgings. However, the lack of urban amenities is usually made up for by the home-cooked meals and the great hospitality that you'll encounter. Life is definitely more relaxed here: If you're expected at a "hospitality home" and you're running late, your host or hostess will leave your room key with a welcome note in the mailbox!

Highly recommended lodgings in each price category are indicated by a star ★.

Category	Cost
Expensive	over $100
Moderate	$60–$90
Inexpensive	under $50

Clarenville
Dining and Lodging

Holiday Inn. There are no surprises at this chain member. Rooms are standard Holiday Inn fare. The daily buffet is plentiful and well worth the drive. *Box 967, Clarenville, A0E 1J0, tel. 709/466–7911, fax 709/466–3854. 64 rooms. AE, MC, V. Moderate.*

Corner Brook
Dining and Lodging
★

The Glynmill Inn. This charming inn has the feel of old England. The inn was once the staff house for the visiting top brass of the mill. Rooms are cozy and the dining room serves basic and well-prepared Newfoundland seafood, soups, and specialty desserts made with Newfoundland partridgeberries. There's also a popular steak house in the basement. *Cobb La., Box 550, Corner Brook, A2H 6E6, tel. 709/634–5106, fax 709/634–5106. 90 rooms. AE, MC, V. Moderate.*

Holiday Inn. Again, there's nothing extraordinary here, aside from the convenience of being located right in town. The rooms were completely remodeled in 1991, so there are none of the '70s-style oranges and browns. The restaurant is average but has good seasonal fish dishes. *48 West St., Corner Brook A2H 2Z2, tel. 709/634–5381. 103 rooms. Facilities: lounge, restaurant, cable TV, minibars in some rooms, heated swimming pool. Pets allowed. AE, D, DC, MC, V. Moderate.*

Journey's End Motel. This is a comfortable, modern motel (built in 1988) with an attractive interior (the dominating colors are dusty rose and blue) and beautiful views of either the city or the Bay of Islands. *Box 1142, Corner Brook A2H 6T2 (on Rte. 1), tel. 709/639–1980. 81 rooms with color TV, pets allowed. AE, MC, DC, V. Moderate.*

★ **Mamateek Inn.** Rooms are more modern than at the Glynmill Inn. The dining room, which serves good Newfoundland home-cooked food, is known for its exquisite view looking out over the whole city. Sunsets, seen from the restaurant are remarkable. *Rte. 1, Box 787, Corner Brook, A2H 6G7, tel. 709/639–8901, fax 709/639–7567. 55 rooms. AE, MC, V. Moderate.*

Deer Lake
Dining and Lodging

Deer Lake Motel. The guest rooms here are clean and comfortable, and the food in the café is basic, home-cooked fare. You'll find the seafood dishes exceptionally well prepared. *Box 820, Deer Lake, A0K 2E0, tel. 709/635–2108, fax 709/635–3842. 54 rooms, 2 suites. AE, MC, V. Moderate.*

Gander
Dining and Lodging
★

Albatross Motel. This newly renovated motel has a deserved reputation as an attractive place to stop off for a meal. Try the cod au gratin—you won't find it this good anywhere else. Rooms are basic and clean. *Box 450, Gander, A1V 1W8, tel. 709/256–3956, fax 709/651–2692. 107 rooms, 4 suites. AE, MC, V. Moderate.*

Grand Falls
Dining and Lodging

Mount Peyton Hotel. The rooms aren't soundproof here, but they are clean and comfortable. And the excellent Newfoundland menu makes this a great place to break your journey across the island. *214 Lincoln Rd., Grand Falls, A2A 1P8, tel. 709/489–2251. 150 rooms. AE, MC, V. Moderate.*

L'Anse aux Meadows
Lodging

Valhalla Lodge Bed & Breakfast. Located adjacent to the Viking site at L'Anse aux Meadows, this is the only game in town, but that doesn't make it any less comfortable and inviting. Note the interesting fossils in the rock fireplace in the dining room. Hot breakfasts are available, and extra meals can be had on request. *Gunner's Cove, Griquet A0K 2X0, tel. 709/623-2018 (summer), 709/896-5476 (winter). 6 rooms. V. Inexpensive.*

Port aux Basques
Dining and Lodging

St. Christopher's Hotel. This clean, comfortable hotel is a new addition in Port aux Basque that offers air-conditioned rooms and good food. Caribou Rd., Box 2049, Port aux Basques, A0M 1C0, tel. 709/695–7034, fax 709/695–9841. 58 rooms. Facilities: banquet room, restaurant (reservations not necessary, dress casual), conference room, satellite TV. AE, MC, V. Moderate.

St. John's
Dining
★

The Cellar. This restaurant situated in a historic building on the waterfront gets rave reviews for its innovative Continental cuisine featuring the best local ingredients. Menu selections include blackened fish dishes and tiramisu for dessert. *Baird's Cove, between Harbour and Water Sts., St. John's, tel. 709/579–8900. Reservations advised. No jeans or sweatshirts. AE, MC, V. Expensive.*

★ **Stone House.** Situated in one of St. John's most historic buildings—an old restored 19th-century stone cottage—this dining room features imported game and Newfoundland specialties. *8 Kennas Hill, St. John's, tel. 709/753–2380. Reservations advised. Dress: casual. AE, MC, V. Expensive.*

Dining and Lodging
★

Hotel Newfoundland. This hotel replaces an old hotel that stood on this site for many years. St. John's residents gather here for many special occasions, and it's noted for its Sunday and evening buffets, its charming rooms that overlook St. John's harbor, its atrium, and the fine cuisine of the Cabot Club. *Box 5637, St. John's A1C 5W8, tel. 709/726–4980, fax 709/726–2025. 288 rooms, 14 suites. AE, MC, V. Expensive.*

★ **Radisson Plaza Hotel.** In this new convention hotel in downtown St. John's, rooms overlook the harbor and the city. It offers two dining rooms: Brazil Square, noted for its breakfast and noon buffets; and Newman's, a secluded dining room serving elaborately presented international dishes and Newfoundland cuisine. *120 New Gower St., St. John's A1C 1J3, tel. 709/739–6404. 276 rooms, 9 suites. AE, MC, V. Expensive.*
Journey's End Motel. This is the newest member of this hotel chain and it overlooks St. John's harbor. Like other Journey's Ends, it offers clean, comfortable rooms at a reasonable price. The hotel's restaurant, Rumplestiltskins, has a splendid view and an unpretentious, attractive menu. *Hill O'Chips, St. John's A1C 6B1, tel. 709/754–7788. 164 rooms. AE, MC, V. Moderate.*

Lodging
★

Compton House Bed & Breakfast. Housed in a charming, restored historic St. John's residence in the west end of the city, this inn is professionally run and beautifully decorated. Twelve-foot ceilings and wide halls give the place a majestic feeling, and rooms done in pastels and chintzes add an air of coziness. The location, within easy walking distance of downtown St. John's, is ideal. *26 Waterford Bridge Rd., St. John's A1E 1C6, tel. 709/739–5789. 4 rooms, 2 suites. AE, MC, V. Moderate.*

★ **Prescott House Bed & Breakfast.** Local art decorates the walls of this house, which has received a Heritage Award. It's the city's most popular bed-and-breakfast, made even better by a modernization that tastefully blended the new and the old. Located downtown, it's central to shopping and attractions. *17–19 Military Rd., St. John's A1C 2C3, tel. 709/753–6036. 10 rooms, 2 suites. MC, V. Moderate.*

The Arts and Nightlife

It has been a long-standing claim (since at least the 1700s) that St. John's has more bars per mile than any other city in North America. Each establishment has its own personality. Irish music, in particular, can be heard at Erin's Pub, Water Street, and the Blarney Stone on George Street. A mix of traditional folk songs and Irish music can be had at Bridgett's, Cookstown Road, St. John's.

George Street, in downtown St. John's, is a street of pubs and restaurants that has been beautifully restored. Open-air concerts can be heard there during the annual George Street Festival and on many other occasions.

Newfoundlanders love a party, and from the cities to the smallest towns they celebrate their history and unique culture throughout a summer of festivals and events. The **Newfoundland and Labrador Folk Arts Festival,** held in St. John's in early August, is the province's best-known traditional music festival. Local folk music festivals occur in every part of the province during the summer. You'll also encounter a host of community celebrations, community dinners, and church teas.

The province has an unusually active arts community, as well. Most major towns have an arts and culture center, which offers live theater presentations, ballet, and concerts by local, national, and international artists. The **Resource Centre for the Arts** (LSPU Hall), on Victoria Street (tel. 709/753–4531), is one of the country's oldest and most innovative experimental theaters. Like the arts and culture centers, it has a busy fall and winter season but is generally inactive during the summer. The **Stephenville Festival** (tel. 709/643–4982) is held throughout July and into August in Stephenville, an hour's drive south of Corner Brook. The festival is the province's major annual summer theatrical event and features a well-produced mix of light musicals and serious drama.

St. John's has a dozen commercial and public art galleries, nearly all of which feature local artists. Newfoundland's unique landscape, portrayed realistically or more experimentally, is a favorite subject. The province's largest public gallery, the **Memorial University Art Gallery** (tel. 709/737–8209) is located in the St. John's Arts and Culture Centre. The **Emma Butler Gallery** (tel. 709/739–7111) on George Street and **Christina Parker Fine Art** (tel. 709/753–0580) on Plank Road, in St. John's, offer the best selection of local fine art for sale. Several galleries specialize in reasonably priced work aimed at the visitor market.

Index

Personal Itinerary

Departure *Date*

Time

Transportation

Arrival *Date*   *Time*

Departure *Date*   *Time*

Transportation

Accommodations

Arrival *Date*   *Time*

Departure *Date*   *Time*

Transportation

Accommodations

Arrival *Date*   *Time*

Departure *Date*   *Time*

Transportation

Accommodations

Personal Itinerary

Arrival *Date*   *Time*

Departure *Date*   *Time*

Transportation

Accommodations

Arrival *Date*   *Time*

Departure *Date*   *Time*

Transportation

Accommodations

Arrival *Date*   *Time*

Departure *Date*   *Time*

Transportation

Accommodations

Arrival *Date*   *Time*

Departure *Date*   *Time*

Transportation

Accommodations

Fodor's Travel Guides

Available at bookstores everywhere, or call 1–800–533–6478, 24 hours a day.

U.S. Guides

Alaska

Arizona

Boston

California

Cape Cod, Martha's Vineyard, Nantucket

The Carolinas & the Georgia Coast

Chicago

Colorado

Florida

Hawaii

Las Vegas, Reno, Tahoe

Los Angeles

Maine, Vermont, New Hampshire

Maui

Miami & the Keys

New England

New Orleans

New York City

Pacific North Coast

Philadelphia & the Pennsylvania Dutch Country

The Rockies

San Diego

San Francisco

Santa Fe, Taos, Albuquerque

Seattle & Vancouver

The South

The U.S. & British Virgin Islands

The Upper Great Lakes Region

USA

Vacations in New York State

Vacations on the Jersey Shore

Virginia & Maryland

Waikiki

Walt Disney World and the Orlando Area

Washington, D.C.

Foreign Guides

Acapulco, Ixtapa, Zihuatanejo

Australia & New Zealand

Austria

The Bahamas

Baja & Mexico's Pacific Coast Resorts

Barbados

Berlin

Bermuda

Brazil

Brittany & Normandy

Budapest

Canada

Cancun, Cozumel, Yucatan Peninsula

Caribbean

China

Costa Rica, Belize, Guatemala

The Czech Republic & Slovakia

Eastern Europe

Egypt

Euro Disney

Europe

Europe's Great Cities

Florence & Tuscany

France

Germany

Great Britain

Greece

The Himalayan Countries

Hong Kong

India

Ireland

Israel

Italy

Japan

Kenya & Tanzania

Korea

London

Madrid & Barcelona

Mexico

Montreal & Quebec City

Morocco

Moscow & St. Petersburg

The Netherlands, Belgium & Luxembourg

New Zealand

Norway

Nova Scotia, Prince Edward Island & New Brunswick

Paris

Portugal

Provence & the Riviera

Rome

Russia & the Baltic Countries

Scandinavia

Scotland

Singapore

South America

Southeast Asia

Spain

Sweden

Switzerland

Thailand

Tokyo

Toronto

Turkey

Vienna & the Danube Valley

Yugoslavia

Special Series

Fodor's Affordables

Caribbean

Europe

Florida

France

Germany

Great Britain

London

Italy

Paris

Fodor's Bed & Breakfast and Country Inns Guides

Canada's Great Country Inns

California

Cottages, B&Bs and Country Inns of England and Wales

Mid-Atlantic Region

New England

The Pacific Northwest

The South

The Southwest

The Upper Great Lakes Region

The West Coast

The Berkeley Guides

California

Central America

Eastern Europe

France

Germany

Great Britain & Ireland

Mexico

Pacific Northwest & Alaska

San Francisco

Fodor's Exploring Guides

Australia

Britain

California

The Caribbean

Florida

France

Germany

Ireland

Italy

London

New York City

Paris

Rome

Singapore & Malaysia

Spain

Thailand

Fodor's Flashmaps

New York

Washington, D.C.

Fodor's Pocket Guides

Bahamas

Barbados

Jamaica

London

New York City

Paris

Puerto Rico

San Francisco

Washington, D.C.

Fodor's Sports

Cycling

Hiking

Running

Sailing

The Insider's Guide to the Best Canadian Skiing

Skiing in the USA & Canada

Fodor's Three-In-Ones (guidebook, language cassette, and phrase book)

France

Germany

Italy

Mexico

Spain

Fodor's Special-Interest Guides

Accessible USA

Cruises and Ports of Call

Euro Disney

Halliday's New England Food Explorer

Healthy Escapes

London Companion

Shadow Traffic's New York Shortcuts and Traffic Tips

Sunday in New York

Walt Disney World and the Orlando Area

Walt Disney World for Adults

Fodor's Touring Guides

Touring Europe

Touring USA: Eastern Edition

Fodor's Vacation Planners

Great American Vacations

National Parks of the East

National Parks of the West

The Wall Street Journal Guides to Business Travel

Europe

International Cities

Pacific Rim

USA & Canada

WHEREVER YOU TRAVEL, *H*ELP IS NEVER FAR AWAY.

From planning your trip to providing travel assistance along the way, American Express® Travel Service Offices* are always there to help.

Nova Scotia

Halifax
American Express Travel Service
City Centre Atlantic
5523 Spring Garden Road
(902) 423-3900

Truro
Atlantic Travel Service, Ltd.
523 Prince Street
(902) 895-5454